T0135722

Bibliografische Information der Deutschen Nationalbibliothek

Die Deutsche Nationalbibliothek verzeichnet diese Publikation in der
Deutschen Nationalbibliografie; detaillierte bibliografische Daten sind
im Internet über http://dnb.d-nb.de abrufbar.

©Copyright Logos Verlag Berlin GmbH 2010
Alle Rechte vorbehalten.

ISBN 978-3-8325-2527-9

Logos Verlag Berlin GmbH
Comeniushof, Gubener Str. 47,
10243 Berlin
Tel.: +49 (0)30 42 85 10 90
Fax: +49 (0)30 42 85 10 92
INTERNET: http://www.logos-verlag.de

Virtual Separation of Concerns: Toward Preprocessors 2.0

Dissertation
zur Erlangung des akademischen Grades
Doktoringenieur (Dr.-Ing.)

angenommen durch die Fakultät für Informatik
der Otto-von-Guericke-Universität Magdeburg

von Dipl.-Wirt.-Inform. Christian Kästner
geb. am 21. September 1982 in Schwedt/Oder

Gutachter:
Prof. Dr. Gunter Saake
Prof. Don Batory, Ph.D.
Prof. Krzysztof Czarnecki, Ph.D.

Promotionskolloquium: Magdeburg, den 31. Mai 2010

Kästner, Christian:
Virtual Separation of Concerns: Toward Preprocessors 2.0
Dissertation, Otto-von-Guericke-Universität Magdeburg, 2010.

Abstract

Conditional compilation with preprocessors such as *cpp* is a simple but effective means to implement variability. By annotating code fragments with *#ifdef* and *#endif* directives, different program variants with or without these annotated fragments can be created, which can be used (among others) to implement software product lines. Although, such annotation-based approaches are frequently used in practice, researchers often criticize them for their negative effect on code quality and maintainability. In contrast to modularized implementations such as components or aspects, annotation-based implementations typically neglect separation of concerns, can entirely obfuscate the source code, and are prone to introduce subtle errors.

Our goal is to rehabilitate annotation-based approaches by showing how tool support can address these problems. With views, we emulate modularity; with a visual representation of annotations, we reduce source code obfuscation and increase program comprehension; and with disciplined annotations and a product-line–aware type system, we prevent or detect syntax and type errors in the entire software product line. At the same time we emphasize unique benefits of annotations, including simplicity, expressiveness, and being language independent. All in all, we provide tool-based separation of concerns without necessarily dividing source code into physically separated modules; we name this approach *virtual separation of concerns*.

We argue that with these improvements over contemporary preprocessors, virtual separation of concerns can compete with modularized implementation mechanisms. Despite our focus on annotation-based approaches, we do intend not give a definite answer on how to implement software product lines. Modular implementations and annotation-based implementations both have their advantages; we even present an integration and migration path between them. Our goal is to rehabilitate preprocessors and show that they are not a lost cause as many researchers think. On the contrary, we argue that – with the presented improvements – annotation-based approaches are a serious alternative for product-line implementation.

Acknowledgments

Finishing this dissertation would have been impossible without the help of many persons. First and foremost, I would like to thank Sven Apel with whom I worked together closely for the last three years. Sven supported me since my Master's thesis and guided my research in many ways. Despite communicating mostly via email and telephone due to different locations, our collaborations were reliable, efficient, and productive, and I highly value his feedback. Sven guided me to interesting research questions, for example, regarding type checking, formalisms, and empirical evaluation. Often, we have addressed the same problem from different perspectives (roughly speaking, he as proponent of compositional approaches, me as proponent of annotative approaches) which repeatedly lead to interesting insights and trade-offs, many of which are discussed in this thesis.

Second, Don Batory has constantly supported and challenged me. When I visited him at the University of Texas at Austin for my Master's thesis and observed several problems in my aspect-oriented decomposition of Berkeley DB, he challenged me to look for better variability mechanisms and consistently encouraged me to pursue my early ideas with colors and annotations in CIDE (which went into quite a different direction from his and my work up to that time). Many ideas discussed in this thesis, including visual representation, views, and type checking, emerged in an early raw form already during my visit in his group. Since then, he provided support and ideas for many research topics. It is always a pleasure to work with Don.

Third, I want to thank Gunter Saake who gave me the opportunity to pursue a PhD in his group. Gunter has provided an excellent environment for research and has guaranteed me entire freedom. His support for our lecture on product-line implementation for graduate students laid the ground for many interesting projects and young scientists with interest in software product lines. His group proved to be an excellent place for academic development and collaboration.

Fourth, I like to express my deepest gratitude to all my colleagues and students with whom I had the pleasure to collaborate and discuss, including Danilo Beuche, Alexander Dreiling, Janet Feigenspan, Armin Größlinger, Sebastian Günther, Florian Heidenreich, Andy Kenner, Martin Kuhlemann, Thomas Leich, Christian Lengauer, Jörg Liebig, Andreas Lübcke, Mario Pukall, Syed Saif ur Rahman, Marko Rosenmüller, Malte Rosenthal, Sandro Schulze, Norbert Siegmund, Friedrich Steimann, Sagar Sunkle, Thomas Thüm, and Salvador Trujillo. Of them, I would specifically like to address a special thanks to Martin, Janet, Thomas T., and Jörg for their great collaboration on significant parts of this thesis; to Marko and Norbert for their support in my ongoing struggle with C and C++; to Armin and Malte for their patient help with Haskell; and to Thomas L. for his continuous support with the capabilities on an industrial partner. Last but not least, I gratefully thank my family and friends for their ongoing support far beyond this thesis.

Contents

List of Figures

List of Tables

List of Abbreviations

AST   Abstract Syntax Tree

CFJ   Colored Featherweight Java

FFJ   Feature Featherweight Java

FJ   Featherweight Java

HTML   Hypertext Markup Language

SAT   Boolean Satisfiability Problem

UML   Unified Modeling Language

XHTML   Extensible Hypertext Markup Language

XML   Extensible Markup Language

1. Introduction

Tailor-made software can provide a significant competitive advantage compared to general-purpose standard software. While standard software – such as broadly used operating systems, database management systems, word processors, and many more – aims at a mass market and provides little diversification, tailor-made individual software is able to focus on a specific use case or scenario. This focus can enable more efficient implementations in terms of smaller binary size and less memory consumption, better performance due to task-specific implementations and optimizations, and fewer security risks caused by unused code. Especially in the growing market of embedded systems, heterogeneity and resource limitations demand tailor-made solutions.

At the same time, tailor-made software poses significant costs and risks. Software development is a complex process that consumes significant time and effort. One way to reduce development costs is to systematically reuse development artifacts. Experience has shown that reuse is most efficient between products in a single domain [e.g., Biggerstaff, 1998].

Software product line engineering (and the related program-family development) is a paradigm of systematic reuse to develop a set of related software systems (which we call *variants*) in a well-defined domain from a common code base [Parnas, 1976; Bass et al., 1998]. Differences between variants are described in terms of *features*; for example, there are variants of embedded database systems with either feature PERSISTENT STORAGE or feature IN-MEMORY STORAGE, with or without a feature TRANSACTIONS, and so on. Variants in a software product line are specified in terms of a feature selection, for example, "the embedded database system with PERSISTENT STORAGE but without TRANSACTIONS".

A software product line is implemented such that different variants can be derived for different feature selections from a common implementation. Since artifacts of features are developed in a coordinated fashion and systematically reused in multiple variants, software product lines promise faster production of tailor-made variants, with lower costs and higher quality. Software product lines offer a new perspective compared to general-purpose standard software, they can efficiently tailor each variant to a specific use case or scenario. Similarly, software product lines allow companies to adapt to changed markets and to move into new markets quickly. For example, in a product line of embedded database systems, we can implement a new feature for a new hardware device and reuse existing features, and we can then offer tailor-made variants for both old and new hardware devices instead of a single system to fit all.

There are many approaches to implement software product lines, ranging from simple ad-hoc mechanisms to sophisticated architectures and to specialized languages. In practice, developers often use simple tools such as the C preprocessor *cpp* to implement variability. In a common implementation, developers annotate code fragments with *#ifdef X* and *#endif* directives or similar constructs – in which X represents a feature. Based on a feature selection provided as configuration file or command line parameters, developers can later include or exclude the annotated code fragments to generate a variant. We refer to such mechanisms more generally as *annotative approaches*, because they annotate and conditionally remove code fragments from a common implementation.

In literature, annotative approaches are heavily criticized as summarized in the claim "#ifdef considered harmful" [Spencer and Collyer, 1992] and in the colloquial term "#ifdef hell" [Lohmann et al., 2006]. Numerous studies discuss the negative effect of preprocessor usage on code quality and maintainability [e.g., Spencer and Collyer, 1992; Krone and Snelting, 1994; Favre, 1995, 1997; Ernst et al., 2002; Pohl et al., 2005; Adams et al., 2008]: The use of *#ifdef* and similar directives breaks with the fundamentally accepted concepts of separation of concerns and modularity, obfuscates the source code, and is prone to introduce errors.

Despite this criticism, practitioners implement many software product lines with preprocessors.[1] For example, HP's product line Owen for printer firmware with over 2000 features implements variability with the C preprocessor [Pearse and Oman, 1997; Refstrup, 2009]; so do many open source programs such as the Linux kernel with over 5000 features [Tartler et al., 2009; She et al., 2010]. Three more examples of industrial product lines presented at the last Software Product Line Conference 2009 that implement variability at least partially with preprocessors are Danfoss' product line of frequency converters [Jepsen and Beuche, 2009], Wikon's product line of remote control systems [Pech et al., 2009], and the product line of flight control systems by the National Aeronautics and Space Administration (NASA) [Ganesan et al., 2009]. Furthermore, both commercial product-line tools *pure::systems* [Beuche et al., 2004] and *Gears* [Krueger, 2002] provide their own preprocessor.

In academia however, annotative approaches have received little attention. Except for some simple analysis and visualization tools [e.g., Krone and Snelting, 1994; Pearse and Oman, 1997; Hu et al., 2000; Vidács and Beszédes, 2003], annotative approaches have hardly advanced in the last 30 years. Instead, academics

---

[1]We are unaware of any statistics or surveys on industrial product-line implementation – actually, most industrial experience reports focus on economic and management issues but exclude descriptions of implementation mechanisms. Nevertheless, our personal communication with tool providers and developers indicates that actually a majority of software product lines were implemented with annotative approaches. Also in open-source software, variability is often implemented with preprocessors.

typically recommend to limit or entirely abandon the use of preprocessors and implement software product lines with "modern" implementation techniques that encapsulate features in some form of modules (such as components [Szyperski, 1997], frameworks [Johnson and Foote, 1988], feature modules [Prehofer, 1997; Batory et al., 2004], aspects [Kiczales et al., 1997], and others) or that use generators or model-driven approaches [e.g., Czarnecki and Eisenecker, 2000; Voelter and Groher, 2007; Trujillo et al., 2007].

Interestingly, this gap between research and practice mirrors a well-known debate in the product-line community published as a discussion between Clements and Krueger [2002]: Clements, representing the academic side, emphasizes the need to plan a software product line ahead as a key to maximize benefits. In contrast, Krueger, a tool provider representing industry, recommends "lightweight technologies" (which include annotative approaches) that are easy to adopt in existing projects and that impose less risk, even at the costs of lower overall benefits in the long run.

In this thesis, we survey different implementation approaches, but we take sides with annotative approaches. Although annotative approaches are mostly considered as ad-hoc or quick-and-dirty solution in literature, we explore how to improve them. We contribute extensions of concepts and tools to avoid many pitfalls of preprocessor usage and we highlight some unique advantages over contemporary modularization techniques in the context of product-line development. With views, we emulate modularity despite scattered implementations, so developers can directly trace a feature to its implementation in a cohesive view. Visual representations of annotations reduce source code obfuscation and improve program comprehension by up to 43 %. With disciplined annotations and a product-line–aware type system, we prevent or detect syntax and type errors for the entire software product lines. Thus, as we demonstrate, our improved annotations are no longer prone to errors; instead, we enforce consistency for all variants during all development activities. At the same time, we keep the benefits of annotative approaches as simplicity, fine granularity, and uniformity. All in all, we provide a tool-based separation of concerns without dividing feature-related code into physically separated modules; we name this approach *virtual separation of concerns*.

Despite our focus on annotative approaches, we do not intend to give a definite answer on how to implement software product lines. Modular implementations and improved annotative approaches both have their advantages; we even present an integration and discuss its benefits. We have excellent experiences with our improved annotative approaches, but others may argue that, in the long term, modular implementation approaches may provide the superior form of product-line implementation. Nevertheless, even with a preference for modular implementations, in the short term and medium term, it is difficult to convince practitioners to adopt "modern" implementation approaches because the adoption barrier is still high and mainstream programming languages embrace variability mechanisms only hesitantly. Thus, for some developers, virtual separation of concerns will provide an adequate solution for practical product-line development; for others, we provide at least an interim solution and a migration path to lower the adoption barrier of "modern" implementation approaches. Still, much empirical evaluation is necessary to make objective recommendations for one or the other approach. Our goal is to show that annotative approaches are not a lost cause. On the contrary, we argue that virtual separation of concerns is a serious alternative for product-line implementation.

1.1. Contribution

First, we analyze problems and benefits of annotative approaches. While problems are discussed at length in literature, benefits become apparent by comparing annotative approaches to alternative implementation mechanisms. Specifically, we group product-line implementation approaches into compositional approaches and annotative approaches and compare them regarding several criteria including modularity, error detection, granularity, uniformity, and adoption.

Second, we propose, implement, discuss, and evaluate five improvements of annotative approaches, which we name – in their combination – as *virtual separation of concerns*. Specifically, we contribute the following five improvements:

1. *Integrating a feature model* enforces consistent annotations. A feature model encapsulates configuration knowledge and documents all features and their relationships. This is a straightforward improvement over contemporary preprocessors, but necessary for the remaining mechanisms as views and type checking. Among others, we prevent that annotations refer to undefined features.

2. *Views* on features and variants emulate modularity. We outline different kinds of views and discuss design decisions and their implications, and implement a solution. Despite scattered feature implementations, our views allow developers to directly trace a feature to its implementation in a cohesive view, similar to modular implementations.

3. A *visual representation* of annotations reduces source code obfuscation. We use background colors instead of textual annotations to represent annotated code fragments. In a controlled experiment, we confirm that a visual representation of annotations can significantly increase program comprehension for some tasks.

4. *Disciplined annotations* prevent syntax errors during generation. We provide a language-independent mechanism to determine disciplined annotations

and demonstrate that disciplined annotations do not restrict expressiveness in practice. By construction, all variants generated from a product-line implementation with disciplined annotations are syntactically correct, thus, we prevent subtle, hard to find syntax errors in the first place.

5. A *product-line–aware type* system on top of disciplined annotations detects type errors in the entire product line. We develop a type system and describe it with the formal CFJ calculus. We formally prove that variants generated from a well-typed product line are always well-typed. This way, we enforce consistency and can guarantee that all variants of a product line will compile without generating each variant in isolation.

We implement all improvements in a prototype called CIDE. We show that, in their combination, these improvements address all discussed problems of annotative approaches, only modularity deficits remain. At the same time, we preserve the benefits of annotative approaches such as fine granularity, uniform applicability independent of the language, and easy adoption.

Third, we provide a perspective on how to integrate compositional and annotative approaches. This integration improves annotative approaches and can be used as a long-term migration path toward modular implementations. Specifically, we discuss automated refactorings between different implementation mechanisms that can be used to gradually refactor an annotation-based implementation into a modular form.

1.2. Outline

In Chapter 2 *(Background)*, we briefly introduce the general concepts of software product lines, domain engineering, variability modeling, and separation of concerns. This way, we establish context and terminology for readers unfamiliar with these concepts.

In Chapter 3 *(Software product line implementation)*, we survey two groups of approaches to implement software product lines and discuss their respective benefits and drawbacks. This survey guides us in our search for better implementation mechanisms for the remainder of the thesis. In the context of other implementation approaches, we explain our focus on annotative approaches – which are common in practice, but dismissed and neglected in academia – and discuss their problems.

In Chapter 4 *(Views and visual representation)* and Chapter 5 *(Error detection)*, we propose, discuss, and evaluate five improvements of annotative approaches. In Chapter 4, we integrate feature models into annotative tools to enforce consistency, we provide views on features and variants to emulate modularity, and we represent annotations visually to reduce obfuscation and support program comprehension. In Chapter 5, we address error detection. We prevent syntax errors by enforcing disciplined annotations and we detect type errors with a product-line–aware type system. Instead of checking all variants in isolation, we lift error detection to check the entire software product line in a single step.

In Chapter 6 *(Comparison and integration)*, we take a step back to look at the big picture. We integrate the proposed improvements as *virtual separation of concerns* and compare them with other implementation approaches. We argue that virtual separation of concerns can address all discussed problems, except modularity, of which we can only emulate some facets. To provide a long-term perspective, we discuss the benefits and technical realization of integrating annotative approaches with other modular forms of product-line implementation.

In Chapter 7 *(Conclusion and future work)*, we summarize our contributions and list suggestions for future work.

2. Background

In this thesis, we discuss different implementation approaches for software product lines and improvements thereof. In this section, for readers unfamiliar with software product lines, we give a brief introduction into the idea of product-line engineering and its main concepts, including domain engineering and variability modeling. Furthermore, we review the seminal concept of separation of concerns, which is a repeating theme in our discussions.

2.1. Software product lines

Traditionally, software engineering has focused on developing individual software systems, one system at a time. A typical development process starts with analyzing the requirements of a customer. After several development steps, typically some process of specification, design, implementation, testing, and deployment, a single software product is the result. In contrast, *software product line engineering* focuses on the development of *multiple* similar software systems in one domain from a common code base [Bass et al., 1998; Pohl et al., 2005]. Although the resulting software products are similar, they are each tailored to the specific needs of different customers or to similar but distinct use cases. We call a software product derived from a software product line a *variant*.

Software product lines establish the idea of *mass customization* known from automobile industry and many other industries (see [Pine II, 1993] for an introduction) for software products. Instead of individually developing each product for each customer from scratch, product line engineering develops related variants in a coordinated fashion, developing commonalities between the products only once. Instead of developing a single one-size-fits-all solution that intends to cover all potential customer needs in a mass market, software product lines provide tailor-made solutions for different customers.

Bass et al. [1998] define a software product line as *"a set of software-intensive systems sharing a common, managed set of features that satisfy the specific needs of a particular market segment or mission and that are developed from a common set of core assets in a prescribed way."* The idea to develop a set of related software products in a coordinated fashion (instead of each starting from scratch or copying and editing from a previous product) can be traced back to concepts of *program families* [Parnas, 1976; Habermann et al., 1976]. The term "software product line" emerged in the mid 1990s with a special focus on business and organizational factors, such as market analysis, institutionalizing a family-oriented development process, assigning responsibilities, managing risks, and many others [Bass et al., 1997]. In this thesis, we take a technical view and use the term "software product line" in a broad sense, which includes all software development efforts that can produce a family of related software products.

Software product lines promise several benefits compared to individual development [Bass et al., 1998; Pohl et al., 2005]: Due to co-development and systematic reuse, software products can be produced faster, with lower costs, and higher quality. A decreased time to market allows companies to adapt to changed markets and to move into new markets quickly. Especially in embedded systems, in which resources are scarce and hardware is heterogeneous, efficient variants can be tailored to a specific device or use case [Beuche et al., 2004; Tešanović et al., 2004; Pohl et al., 2005; Rosenmüller et al., 2009]. There are many companies that report significant benefits from software product lines. For example, Bass et al. [1998] summarize that, with software product lines, Nokia can produce 30 instead of previously 4 phone models per year; Cummins, Inc. reduced development time for a software for a new diesel engine from one year to one week; Motorola observed a 400 % increase in productivity; and so on.

2.2. Domain engineering and application engineering

The process to develop an entire software product line instead of a single application is called *domain engineering*. A software product line must fulfill not only the requirements of a single customer but the requirements of multiple customers in a domain, including both current customers and potential future customers. Hence, in domain engineering, developers analyze the entire domain and its potential requirements. From this analysis, they determine commonalities and differences between potential variants, which are described in terms of *features*. In this context, a feature is a first-class domain abstraction, typically an end-user visible increment in functionality (see [Apel and Kästner, 2009] for a detailed discussion of the term "feature"). Finally, developers design and implement the software product line such that different variants can be constructed from common and variable parts.

Czarnecki and Eisenecker [2000] additionally distinguish between *problem space* and *solution space*. The problem space comprises domain-specific abstractions that describe the requirements on a software system and its intended behavior. Domain analysis takes place in the problem space, and its results are documented in terms of features. The solution space comprises implementation-oriented abstractions, such as code artifacts. Between features in the problem space and artifacts in the solution space, there is a mapping that describes which artifact belongs to which feature. Depending on the implementation approach and the degree of

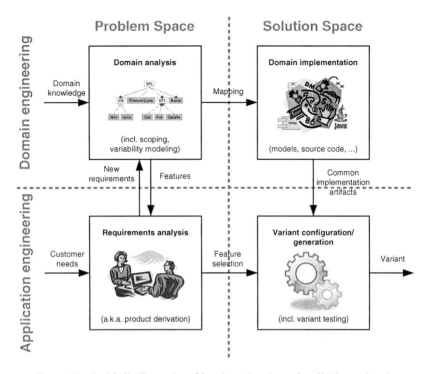

Figure 2.1.: *An (idealized) overview of domain engineering and application engineering.*

automation, this mapping can have different forms and complexity, from simple implicit mappings based on naming conventions to complex machine-processable rules encoded in generators [Czarnecki and Eisenecker, 2000].

Application engineering is the process of deriving a single variant tailored to the requirements of a specific customer from a software product line, based on the results of domain engineering. Ideally, the customer's requirements can be mapped to features identified during domain engineering (problem space), so that the variant can be constructed from existing common and variable parts of the product line's implementation (solution space). In practice, sometimes some custom development is required in application engineering. Depending on the form of implementation, there can be different automation levels of the application engineering process, from manual development with some reusable parts to automated variant configuration and generation (the latter is known as *generative programming* [Czarnecki and Eisenecker, 2000]; see also Chapter 3). In our work, we strive for a form of product line development in which all implementation effort is part of domain engineering so that application engineering can be reduced to requirements analysis and automated code generation.

A software product line always targets a specific domain, such as operating systems for mobile phones, control software for diesel engines, and embedded databases. The *scope* of a software product line describes which variability is offered and which kind of variants the product line can produce. A software product line with a narrow scope is easier to develop, but less flexible (it provides only few very similar variants). The wider the scope is, the higher is the development effort, but the more flexibility a software product line can offer. Selecting the right scope of a product line is a difficult design, business, and strategy decision. In practice, the scope is often iteratively refined; domain engineering and application engineering are not performed strictly separated and in a linear fashion. For example, it is common to implement not all features upfront, but implement features incrementally, when needed. Furthermore, requirements identified in domain engineering may be incomplete, so new requirements arise in application engineering, which developers must either feed back into the domain engineering process or address with custom development during the application engineering of a specific variant. Typically, an iterative process evolves [Czarnecki and Eisenecker, 2000].

Domain engineering and application engineering describe a general process framework as summarized in Figure 2.1. For each step, different approaches, formalisms, and tools can be used. For example, there are different product line scoping approaches [see survey in John and Eisenbarth, 2009], different domain analysis methods [e.g., Kang et al., 1990; Griss et al., 1998; Czarnecki and Eisenecker, 2000; Pohl et al., 2005], different mechanisms to model variability (see Sec. 2.3), different implementation mechanisms (focus of this thesis, see Chapter 3ff), and different approaches to derive a variant based on customer requirements [e.g., Rabiser et al., 2007; Siegmund et al., 2008].

2.3. Variability modeling

During domain analysis, developers determine the scope of the software product line and identify its common and variable features, which they then document in a variability model. We introduce variability models, because they are central not only for documenting variability in the problem space, but also for many implementation approaches, for automated reasoning and error detection, and for automated generation of variants. There are several different variability-modeling approaches (see [Chen et al., 2009] for an overview). Without loss of generality, we focus on FODA-style *feature models* [Kang et al., 1990; Czarnecki and Eisenecker, 2000] in this thesis, because they are well known and broadly used in research and practice; other variability models can be used similarly.

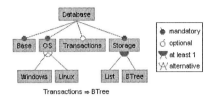

Figure 2.2.: *Feature-diagram example of a small database product line.*

A feature model describes a set of features in a domain and their relationships. It describes which features a product line provides (i.e., its scope), which features are optional, and in which combination features can be selected in order to derive variants. With a selection of features (a subset F of all features), we can specify a variant (e.g., "the database variant for Linux, with transactions, but without a B-Tree"). Not all feature combinations may make sense, for example, two features representing different operating systems might be mutually exclusive. A feature model describes such dependencies. Feature selections that fulfill all constraints are *valid* ("F is valid").

In practice, feature models contain hundreds or thousands of features.[1] Therefore, feature models are often developed with tool support and structured in smaller connected models [Beuche et al., 2004]. The number of potential variants can grow exponentially with the number of features. In theory, a software product line with n independent optional features can produce 2^n variants; already with 33 independent optional features, we could produce a distinct variant for every person on the planet. In practice, many dependencies between features reduce the number of valid feature selections, but nevertheless, most software product lines have millions or billions of valid feature selections.

A typical graphical representation of features and their dependencies is a *feature diagram* [Kang et al., 1990], as shown in Figure 2.2. A feature diagram represents features in hierarchical form and different edges between features describe their relationship. A filled dot, describes that a feature is mandatory and must be selected whenever its parent feature is selected. In contrast, a feature connected with an empty dot is optional. Multiple child features connected with an empty arc are alternative (mutually exclusive), exactly one child feature must be selected when the parent feature is selected. From multiple child features connected with a filled arc, at least one must be selected, but it is also possible to select more than one. Dependencies that cannot (or should not) be expressed with the hier-

---

[1]According to personal communication with D. Beuche most feature models in industry have about 500 features, but also models with several thousand features exist. For example, Bosch's product line of engine control software has over 1000 features [Steger et al., 2004], HP's Owen product line has about 2000 features [Refstrup, 2009] and the Linux kernel has over 5000 features [Tartler et al., 2009; She et al., 2010].

archical structure may be provided as additional cross-tree constraints in form of a propositional formula. In Figure 2.2, we show nine features from the core of a fictional database product line. Each variant must contain features DATABASE, BASE, OS, and STORAGE, but feature TRANSACTIONS is optional, variants may or may not include it; each variant must select exactly one operating system feature, either WINDOWS or LINUX; each variant must contain at least one storage structure; finally, a cross-tree constraint specifies that TRANSACTIONS are only supported if also feature B-TREE is selected. In this example, ten feature selections are valid.

Alternative to the graphical notation, dependencies between features can be expressed by a propositional formula. Each feature corresponds to a Boolean variable, which is assigned *true* when selected and *false* otherwise. The propositional formula evaluates to *true* for all valid feature selections. Feature diagrams can be transformed into propositional formulas by translating all edges into formulas according to Table 2.1 and conjoining them with the root feature and all cross-tree constraints [Batory, 2005] (even the reverse transformation is possible to some degree [Czarnecki and Wąsowski, 2007]). The feature diagram from Figure 2.2 is equivalent to the following propositional formula:

$$\text{DATABASE} \wedge (\text{BASE} \Leftrightarrow \text{DATABASE}) \wedge (\text{OS} \Leftrightarrow \text{DATABASE})$$
$$\wedge (\text{TRANSACTIONS} \Rightarrow \text{DATABASE}) \wedge (\text{STORAGE} \Leftrightarrow \text{DATABASE})$$
$$\wedge (\text{WINDOWS} \vee \text{LINUX} \Leftrightarrow \text{OS}) \wedge \neg (\text{WINDOWS} \wedge \text{LINUX})$$
$$\wedge (\text{LIST} \vee \text{B-TREE} \Leftrightarrow \text{STORAGE}) \wedge (\text{TRANSACTIONS} \Rightarrow \text{B-TREE})$$

Representing feature models as propositional formula has the advantage that we can automatically reason about them, which we use in Section 5.3 to develop a product-line–aware type system. With simple algorithms or with automated reasoning techniques – including Boolean-satisfiability-problem solvers (SAT solvers), constraint-satisfaction-problem solvers, and binary decision diagrams – we can efficiently answer a series of questions, including the following:

- Is a given feature selection valid?

- Has this feature model at least one valid selection (i.e., is the formula satisfiable; see [Benavides, 2007])?

- How many valid feature selections are possible in this model (see [Benavides et al., 2005])?

- Are there dead features that can never be selected (see [Benavides, 2007])?

- Does a change to a feature model change the valid feature selections (see [Thüm et al., 2009])?

- Given a partial selection, which information about the remaining features can be inferred (constraint propagation, see [Batory, 2005])?

Feature diagram edge	Propositional formula
	$f \Leftrightarrow p$
	$f \Rightarrow p$
	$(f_1 \vee \ldots \vee f_n \Leftrightarrow p) \wedge \bigwedge_{i<j} \neg(f_i \wedge f_j)$
	$f_1 \vee \ldots \vee f_n \Leftrightarrow p$

Table 2.1.: *Translating feature diagrams to propositional formulas [adapted from Batory, 2005].*

- Is there a valid feature selection that includes feature X but not feature Y (see [Batory, 2005] and Sec. 5.3)?

Even though some of these algorithms are NP-complete, SAT solvers and other techniques can answer such queries efficiently, even for very large feature models [Mendonça et al., 2008, 2009; Thüm et al., 2009]. For a survey of automated analysis operations and tools see Benavides et al. [2010]

In addition to a list of features and their dependencies, a feature model may include information for each feature such as a description, a rational for its selection, a list of interested stakeholders, a priority, and others [Czarnecki and Eisenecker, 2000]. Furthermore, there are many extensions and dialects of feature diagrams in literature [e.g., Griss et al., 1998; Streitferdt et al., 2003; Beuche et al., 2004; Czarnecki et al., 2005; Schobbens et al., 2007], most of which can be translated to propositional formulas as well [see Thüm, 2008]. In the context of this thesis, a feature model consisting of a list of features and their dependencies described as above is sufficient.

2.4. Separation of concerns

Separation of concerns is a fundamental principle in software engineering, credited to Parnas [1972] and Dijkstra [1976]. We give an overview, because we come back to separation of concerns in several discussions of product-line implementation in this thesis. In a nutshell, separation of concerns is the idea to divide software into smaller manageable pieces, such that each piece corresponds to a semantically coherent issue of the problem domain of interest, called *concern*. Features in a software product line are important concerns in a program (but there can be many more concerns than features) [Apel, 2007].

Dividing software into localized and separated parts makes it easier to understand the system, because developers can focus their attention on one part at a time. In addition, separation of concerns provides a guideline of *how* to divide software and which parts are worth focusing on. Parnas [1972, 1979] suggests dividing programs according to concerns instead of purely technical considerations, because such separation encapsulates design decisions and makes it easier to understand and evolve the code.

A typical means to separate concerns in source code is to *decompose* a program. On a small scale, we can separate different concerns into distinct functions or classes; on a large scale, we can decompose a program into modules [Parnas, 1972]. In this thesis, we explore an alternative virtual separation of concern, more on this later. A decomposed concern is implemented in a cohesive way (e.g., in a function, class, file or directory). *Modularity* is often associated with separation of concerns. Modularity adds information hiding and encapsulation (typically via interfaces) to decouple concerns; it provides advanced opportunities for modular reasoning [Parnas, 1972; Ostermann, 2008], parallel development [Griswold et al., 2006], separate compilation [Bracha and Lindstrom, 1992; Cardelli, 1997], local changes [Sullivan et al., 2001], and reuse [Krueger, 1992]. Most programming languages offer sophisticated language mechanisms for modularity.

However, it has been observed that a modular decomposition is problematic for some concerns, which Kiczales et al. [1997] named *crosscutting concerns*. Although we can distinguish concerns conceptually, in their representations (source code, documentation, and other artifacts) concerns may crosscut each other. For example, the implementation of one concern (e.g., transactions in a database) is intertwined with the implementations of other concerns (e.g., query processing and B-tree).

Traditional programming languages provide hierarchical means of decomposition (e.g., functions, classes, modules), which is sufficient to decompose the representation of many, but not of all concerns. Tarr et al. [1999] describe this limitation as the *tyranny of the dominant decomposition*: With traditional programming languages, we have to impose a hierarchical decomposition (along one dominant dimension) on complex representations of concerns. While some representations align well with the dominant decomposition, others become *scattered* (the representation of one concern is distributed over multiple modules) and *tangled* (the representations of multiple concerns are interspersed in one module) [Kiczales et al., 1997]. A decomposition along multiple dimensions at the same time is not possible with traditional languages (we will discuss an example in Sec. 3.1.5). Mezini and Ostermann [2005] and Ostermann [2008] even argue that a hierarchical decomposition and the related monotonic modular reasoning do not align with multi-dimensional human organization of knowledge in general; hence, it is not surprising that crosscutting concerns have been found in many different concern representations and in many different modularization approaches [e.g., Kiczales et al., 1997; Tarr et al., 1999; Rashid et al., 2002; Apel et al., 2009a].

Crosscutting concerns are important for our discussion, because many features in software product lines are crosscutting concerns, and as such difficult to modularize with traditional programming languages [Apel, 2007; Kästner et al., 2007a]. We come back to different forms of feature implementation and their limitations regarding separation of concerns and modularity in the next chapter.

3. Software product line implementation

This chapter shares material with the ICSE'08 paper "Granularity in Software Product Lines" [Kästner et al., 2008a] and the SPLC'07 paper "A Case Study Implementing Features Using AspectJ" [Kästner et al., 2007a].

There are many different approaches to implement variability in software product lines, ranging from simple textual tools to sophisticated languages and generators. We give an overview of different implementation approaches and discuss benefits and drawbacks that will guide us in the remainder of this thesis in the search for better implementation mechanisms. In contrast to other surveys [e.g., Anastasopoules and Gacek, 2001; Muthig and Patzke, 2002; Mezini and Ostermann, 2004; Svahnberg et al., 2005; Lopez-Herrejon et al., 2005], we do not focus on individual tools or languages, but group them by common characteristics as *compositional approaches*, *annotative approaches*, and others. This helps to abstract from concrete languages or tools and instead discuss more generally advantages and limitations of the common underlying mechanisms.

In *compositional approaches*, features are implemented separately in distinct modules (files, classes, packages, plug-ins, etc.). To generate variants, these modules can be composed in different combinations. Compositional approaches include frameworks, mixin layers, aspects, and many other techniques. They represent a disciplined approach to product-line development and are usually favored in academia; therefore, we discuss them first in Section 3.1. Nevertheless, we will point out some limitations, especially regarding granularity and multidimensional separation of concerns.

In *annotative approaches* code fragments are annotated in a common code base and removed in order to generate variants. The C preprocessor *cpp* is a typical example. Annotative approaches are pragmatic, flexible, and easy to use; they do not share many of the limitations of compositional approaches. Annotative approaches are common in practice, nevertheless, they are often criticized for a number of problems, such as neglecting separation of concerns, being error prone, and obfuscating the source code. In Section 3.2, we discuss benefits and problems of annotative approaches. Especially the discussed problems motivate our search for better annotation mechanisms in Chapters 4 and 5.

Most, but not all, approaches fall into either group. Among others, we exclude generators, version control systems, build systems, and approaches that do not offer a full automation in application engineering (i.e., for each feature selection, some additional implementation effort is needed). In Section 3.3, we briefly give an overview of the remaining implementation mechanisms.

3.1. Compositional approaches

Compositional approaches implement features in distinct modules.[1] To generate a product line member, these approaches *compose* selected modules, usually at compile-time or deploy-time. Variability implemented with compositional approaches is sometimes described as positive variability, because variable parts are added together. There is a variety of different languages and tools that can be used for module composition.

First, frameworks are a common implementation strategy. The framework provides a common platform for all variants and offers extension points (a.k.a. hot spots) that can be extended [Johnson and Foote, 1988]. Often, these extension points employ design patterns, such as *Strategy* or *Observer* [Gamma et al., 1995, pp. 293ff. and 315ff.]. Each feature of the software product line is implemented as extension to the framework (typically as a plug-in), and a variant is composed by compiling the desired extensions (or assembling the selected plug-ins).

Beyond frameworks, in the last decade, researchers have invested immense efforts into developing novel programming language concepts to separate extensions from a common code base. Concepts like step-wise refinement [Wirth, 1971; Parnas, 1976; Batory et al., 2004], subject-oriented programming [Harrison and Ossher, 1993], aspect-oriented programming [Kiczales et al., 1997], feature-oriented programming [Prehofer, 1997; Batory et al., 2004; Apel et al., 2009b], multi-dimensional separation of concerns [Tarr et al., 1999], mixin layers [Smaragdakis and Batory, 2002], virtual classes [Mezini and Ostermann, 2003], open classes [Clifton et al., 2006], classboxes [Bergel et al., 2005], expanders [Warth et al., 2006], traits [Ducasse et al., 2006; Bettini et al., 2010], invasive software composition [Aßmann, 2003], and many more, have been proposed to separate and modularize concerns. Many of these approaches focus on modularizing crosscutting concerns (see Section 2.4), which is beneficial for product-line implementation, since features in product lines often have an inherently crosscutting behavior [Apel, 2007; Apel et al., 2008d; Kästner et al., 2007a]. To derive the final behavior of a program, modules are composed, typically with a specialized com-

---

[1]The term "module" is highly overloaded in literature. In line with Batory et al. [2004], we use the terms "module" and "feature module" in a very loose sense as a container to group code elements. The concrete nature of such module differs significantly between compositional approaches and does not always provide encapsulation, information hiding, or separate compilation as stricter definitions demand [e.g., Parnas, 1972; Wirth, 1979; Cardelli, 1997], it may just be a file or directory [e.g., Batory et al., 2004; Apel et al., 2009b]. In contrast, we use the term "component" in a stricter sense for self-contained, independent, black-box units of composition and deployment, in line with Szyperski [1997]. We discuss components in Section 3.3.

piler. With languages from these concepts, we can implement each feature as an extension in a distinct module; we can generate variants of a software product line by deciding which modules to compose into the program.

In Figure 3.1, we exemplify two compositional implementations of a simple stack example that can be extended by two features LOCKING and LOGGING.

- First, in Figure 3.1a, we use class refinements of the feature-oriented language Jak [Batory et al., 2004]. In Jak, a module can introduce new classes and extend existing classes using the *refines* keyword. In an extended class, it can introduce new methods and fields and extend existing methods with method refinements (by overriding using the *Super* keyword to call the original implementation). In Figure 3.1a, a module representing feature LOCKING contains a new class *Lock* (Line 14) and a class refinement of the existing class *Stack* (Lines 6–13), which introduces a new method *lock* (Line 12) and refines method *push* with additional *lock* and *unlock* calls (Lines 7–11). In a second module, another class refinement (Lines 15–21) introduces an additional method *log* (Line 20) and wraps method *push* again (Lines 16–19).

- Second, in Figure 3.1b, we implement the same features with the aspect-oriented language AspectJ [Kiczales et al., 2001]. AspectJ provides pointcuts to intercept the program execution at certain events (called join points), advice to execute additional behavior at these events, and inter-type declarations to statically modify the program (e.g., to introduce a method). In this case, aspect *Locking* (Lines 6–17) introduces method *lock* (Line 15), introduces a new (static inner) class *Lock* (Line 16), and intercepts the execution of method *push* and executes additional *lock* and *unlock* calls (Lines 7–14); aspect *Logging* similarly extends the behavior of method *push*.

In both languages, a specialized compiler composes these modules.

To provide some insight into the capabilities of compositional approaches, we discuss benefits (indicated by "+") and limitations (indicated by "−"). We conclude with experience from a case study, in which we used a compositional approach to refactor the embedded database engine Berkeley DB into composable feature modules.

3.1.1. Modularity (+/–)

Compositional approaches separate features into distinct modules. Modularity fosters information hiding and modular reasoning to reduce overall complexity. Ideally, developers can understand a feature's implementation in isolation, without reading the code of other features. Ideally, developers can type check and test features independently, and they can work independently on different features (divide and conquer).

Feature BASE

```
1  class Stack {
2    void push(Object o) {
3      elementData[size++] = o;
4    }
5  }
```

Feature LOCKING

```
6  refines class Stack {
7    void push(Object o) {
8      Lock l=lock(o);
9      Super.push(o);
10     l.unlock();
11   }
12   Lock lock(Object o) { /*...*/ }
13 }
14 class Lock { /*...*/ }
```

Feature LOGGING

```
15 refines class Stack {
16   void push(Object o) {
17     Super.push(o);
18     log("added_" + o);
19   }
20   void log(String msg) { /*...*/ }
21 }
```

(a) Implementation with Jak.

Feature BASE

```
1  class Stack {
2    void push(Object o) {
3      elementData[size++] = o;
4    }
5  }
```

Feature LOCKING

```
6  aspect Locking {
7    around(Object o, Stack stack):
8      execution(void Stack.push(..))
9      && args(o) && this(stack)
10   {
11     Lock l = stack.lock(o);
12     proceed(o);
13     l.unlock();
14   }
15   Lock Stack.lock(Object o) { ... }
16   static class Lock { /*...*/ }
17 }
```

Feature LOGGING

```
18 aspect Logging {
19   after(Object o):
20     execution(void Stack.push(..))
21     && args(o)
22   {
23     log("added_" + o);
24   }
25   void log(String msg) { /*...*/ }
26 }
```

(b) Implementation with AspectJ.

Figure 3.1.: *Two compositional implementations of a stack example with three features.*

For example, in Figure 3.1, the entire implementation of the feature LOCKING is modularized. A developer can understand the entire locking mechanism (e.g., class *Lock*, methods *lock* and *unlock* and how they effect the execution of *push*) inside this module, without referring to the base code or to other features. The modules for features LOCKING and LOGGING can be developed and maintained independently.

Although modularity is beneficial, there are restrictions in several contemporary compositional approaches. Strict modularity as discussed in the programming-language community (allowing modular reasoning, local testing, separate compilation, black-box reuse, etc.) can be achieved with some implementations, such as black-box frameworks [Johnson and Foote, 1988] and Jiazzi [McDirmid et al., 2001]. However, when supporting implementation of crosscutting concerns and extensions at a finer granularity, many of the novel language concepts are less strict regarding modularity.

For example, already subclasses impose problems [Szyperski, 1992; Stata and

Guttag, 1995] and languages like Jak or AspectJ can even extend virtually all existing methods and break the interfaces of existing implementations and establish a strong implicit coupling, if misused [Bracha, 1992; Sullivan et al., 2005; Aldrich, 2005; Steimann, 2006; Apel et al., 2009c; Steimann et al., 2010]. A developer can no longer just change internal methods of a class, since a subclass, class refinement, or an aspect may have extended this behavior. For example, in Figure 3.1, a developer who wants to rename method *push* in the base code has to check whether this method was extended in any class refinement or aspect, without additional tool support there is no indication of this extension in the base code and the developer has only limited means to prevent such extension. Compared to strict modularity, these approaches cause challenges for modular reasoning [Szyperski, 1992; Steimann, 2006; Ostermann, 2008], local testing [Elrad et al., 2001; Parizi and Ghani, 2007], and reuse [Elrad et al., 2001; Mezini and Ostermann, 2003].

There are several suggestions, how to enforce a stricter modularity with additional interfaces or annotations [e.g., Sullivan et al., 2005; Aldrich, 2005; Hutchins, 2009; Steimann et al., 2010], but they pay a price of more complex implementation patterns and their effect on program comprehension has still to be evaluated. For example, Steimann et al. [2010] introduce new interfaces toward aspects; an aspect can only extend code elements, when the element is exposed in the interface, all other elements are hidden in the module. For example, with such construct, we could explicitly expose method *push* in an interface in the example from Figure 3.1b; then, method *push* can be extended by aspects, whereas all other methods remain unexposed so that we can reason about them in a modular fashion.

Overall, modularity can be achieved, but only few contemporary compositional approaches enforce it strictly.

3.1.2. Traceability (+)

By mapping features to modules, we gain traceability. A developer can trace a feature from the feature model or some requirements directly to its implementation inside one cohesive module. Ideally, there can be a one-to-one mapping between a feature in the feature model and its implementation in a single module. When enhancing a feature or fixing a bug, a developer can directly look up the corresponding code of a feature in a single module, instead of searching in scattered implementations.

For example, the entire implementation of feature LOCKING is located in a single module in Figure 3.1. When developers want to change the locking mechanism, they can directly look up the implementation of feature LOCKING.

Traceability can also be achieved without modular implementations, often with external mappings or additional documentation. There is an entire research community that analyzes how traceability between different development artifacts (such as requirements, documentation, models, and code) can be detected, documented, and updated [e.g., Gotel and Finkelstein, 1994; Ramesh and Jarke, 2001; Cleland-Huang et al., 2003; Mäder et al., 2008]. A main difficulty is to update traceability links when maintaining or evolving an artifact. However, when a feature is implemented in a cohesive module, traceability is reduced to a trivial mapping between feature and module.

Together, modularity and traceability promises lower development and maintenance costs. Therefore, compositional approaches are generally favored in academia and research is constantly focusing on better languages or techniques to separate concerns.

3.1.3. Language support for variability (+)

As another benefit, compositional approaches make variability explicit in the language or architecture. Instead of ad-hoc tools that operate on plain text, the program is extended in a disciplined way at well-defined explicit extension points or with well-defined language constructs, such as class refinements or advice.

Many explicit language mechanisms allow to instantiate multiple objects or subsystems with different features in the same program [e.g., Mezini and Ostermann, 2003; Czarnecki and Eisenecker, 2000]. If needed, also the composition order can be changed and can have an effect on the program's semantics [e.g., Batory and O'Malley, 1992; Apel et al., 2008b].

This disciplined approach prevents certain errors. Syntax errors can be detected for each feature in isolation. Black-box frameworks [cf. Johnson and Foote, 1988] and several languages [e.g., Ossher and Tarr, 2000a; McDirmid et al., 2001; Huang and Smaragdakis, 2008; Bettini et al., 2010] allow modular type checking. Testing becomes easier when the functionality to be tested is modularized [Beck, 2003]. Also some formal approaches to detect semantic errors, such as specification or model checking, can take advantage of modules [e.g., Fisler and Krishnamurthi, 2001; Fisler and Roberts, 2004; Poppleton, 2007].

Furthermore, we can reason about and optimize the composition process itself. For example, Batory et al. [2000] optimize feature compositions of container data structures for performance; Apel et al. [2008e] show that feature composition à la Jak is associative with a feature algebra; Andrews [2001] proves the correctness of an aspect composition algorithm.

3.1.4. Coarse granularity (−)

Despite these benefits, there are also limitations. One is the coarse granularity of compositional approaches. We distinguish between different granularity levels of extensions that a product-line implementation approach can perform to implement a feature [Kästner et al., 2008a]. This ranges from coarse-grained extensions

```
1  class Stack {
2    void push(Object o, Transaction txn) {
3      if (o == null || txn == null) return;
4      Lock l = txn.lock(o);
5      elementData[size++] = o;
6      l.unlock();
7      fireStackChanged();
8    }
9  }
```

Figure 3.2.: *Example of a fine-grained extensions [Kästner et al., 2008a].*

that add entire files, to fine-grained extensions that introduce statements or extend even individual tokens.

Compositional approaches tend to be rather coarse grained. In frameworks, plug-ins add entire bundles of classes and can extend only the program's behavior at predefined explicit extension points. This is restrictive, but enforces strict modularity.

Many of the language-based compositional approaches, such as aspect-oriented and feature-oriented programming, allow extensions at the granularity of methods; that is, methods can be injected into existing classes and virtually every method in the system can be wrapped with additional behavior (e.g., using around advice, method refinements, or method overriding). Some aspect-oriented languages can extend also certain events during a method's execution, for example, method invocations and field access in AspectJ [Kiczales et al., 2001].

The coarse granularity provided by compositional approaches is sometimes insufficient to implement features. For certain extensions, developers need to change the behavior inside a method, for example, introduce new statements, extend expressions or change even method signatures. Some extensions require access to the local context of a method. With compositional approaches, such fine-grained extensions are usually not possible without workarounds. Several researchers have reported that such fine-grained extensions are quite frequent [e.g., Murphy et al., 2001; Sullivan et al., 2005; Kästner et al., 2007a], especially, when extending a legacy application that was not designed with feature modularity in mind.

We exemplify the three limitations that we observed most frequently by means of the code snippet in Figure 3.2, in which the underlined code belongs to a feature SYNCHRONIZATION and should be implemented in its own module:

- **Statement Extensions.** In most compositional approaches it is not possible to introduce statements in the middle of an existing method in order to extend certain statements or sequences of statements therein.[2] For example,

---

[2]A notable exception is *AspectJ* that enables to extend method calls or field access inside specific methods [Kiczales et al., 2001]. This feature can be used to emulate statement extensions in some, but not in all cases [see Kästner et al., 2007a].

consider how to synchronize only the statement in Line 5. A simple method refinement around the whole method is not sufficient. Instead, we have to introduce the locking statements in Lines 4 and 6 specifically. In some cases, statement extensions might access also local variables. Usually, workarounds introduce artificial extensions points for extension. Typically, a developer would introduce calls to empty hook methods [Murphy et al., 2001] or perform an extract-method refactoring [Fowler, 1999, pp. 110ff.], which would move Line 5 to a dedicated method such that we can implement locking from Lines 4 and 6 as method refinement of this dedicated method. Local variables, if accessed in the extension, are passed as parameters. Either workaround requires explicit or implicit annotations and severely obfuscates the source code [Murphy et al., 2001; Kästner et al., 2007a].

- **Expression Extensions.** Extensions to an individual expression can occur as well. An example is shown in Line 3, in which the condition of the *if* statement is extended. A typical workaround again creates a new method and moves the expression there, so that it can be extended with method refinements.

- **Signature Changes.** To the best of our knowledge, there is no compositional approach that allows introducing an additional parameter into an existing method signature, as the parameter *txn* in Line 2. Instead, method signatures are considered fixed. Typical workarounds store the additional parameters in thread-safe fields, duplicate code, or use complex language mechanisms like the Wormhole Pattern in AspectJ [Laddad, 2003, pp. 256ff.]. However, all of these workarounds introduce different problems and reduce code quality [Rosenmüller et al., 2007; Kästner, 2007]. Note that it is necessary to adapt also all invocations of a method when extending its signature.

In Figure 3.3, we show an implementation of our example with the compositional language Jak. This implementation uses the workarounds discussed above: statements and expression extensions are implemented with the two hook methods *h1* and *h2*; and the parameter is passed with a thread-safe field *pushTxn* and the original *push* method is deactivated by throwing an exception. This (admittedly extreme) example makes obvious how code quality of both base code and extension can suffer when implementing fine-grained extensions with compositional approaches.

The coarse granularity of compositional approaches restricts developers in their expressiveness, or leads to several problems when developers use them to implement fine-grained extensions anyway. Workarounds often obfuscate the source code and are verbose and hard to understand. Many workarounds replicate code or use heavy-weight architectures that induce performance penalties [Murphy et al., 2001; Kästner et al., 2007a; Rosenmüller et al., 2007].

```
1  class Stack {
2    void push(Object o) {
3      if (h1(o)) return;
4      h2(o);
5      fireStackChanged();
6    }
7    boolean h1(Object o) { return o == null; }
8    void h2(Object o) {
9      elementData[size++] = o;
10   }
11 }
```

```
12 refines class Stack {
13   ThreadLocal<Transaction> pushTxn = new ThreadLocal<Transaction>();
14   void push(Object o, Transaction txn) {
15     pushTxn.set(txn);
16     Super.push(o);
17   }
18   void push(Object o) {
19     throw new UnsupportedOperationException(
20         "Call_push(Object,Transaction)_instead");
21   }
22   boolean h1(Object o) {
23     return Super.h1(o) || pushTxn.get() == null;
24   }
25   void h2(Object o) {
26     Lock l = pushTxn.get().lock(o);
27     Super.h2(o);
28     l.unlock();
29   }
30 }
```

Figure 3.3.: *Implementation of fine-grained extensions with Jak.*

Conceptual limitations of granularity. Extending compositional approaches with new language constructs for fine-grained extensions is not trivial, because of several conceptual problems.

First, signatures are used to identify the methods that are to be extended. If changing method signatures for an optional feature was possible, another naming scheme would need to be used to identify methods. Consequently, most languages consider signatures as immutable, and do not account for the possibility of signature changes.

Second, compositional approaches introduce new code fragments only in positions in which the order does not matter. Thus, in Java, it is possible to introduce new classes into the program or new methods into a class, but not new statements at a fixed position inside a method. This target position is not known when implementing the feature and could move if other features introduced statements as well. Therefore, compositional approaches usually offer only wrapping mechanisms (e.g., method refinements, advice) that add statements at the beginning or the end of a method, but not at a finer granularity. Similarly, parameters in method signatures are ordered, which makes parameter introductions difficult.

These limitations are reflected also in the feature algebra of Apel et al. [2008e] and the corresponding composition engine in FeatureHouse [Apel et al., 2009b]. Although, we can chose arbitrary granularity for the structures in this algebra, choices that are too fine grained run into problems regarding stable addresses and ordering and are not usable in practice, see [Apel et al., 2008e] for details.

3.1.5. The optional feature problem (–)

Another limitation of compositional approaches becomes obvious when multiple dimensions or interacting features are involved. Features are not always independent from each other and there is often code that belongs not only to a single feature, but that connects multiple features. In the context of software product lines, this problem is known as *optional-feature problem* [Liu et al., 2006; Kästner et al., 2009c], as *feature interactions* [Calder et al., 2003], or more generally in the context of multi-dimensional separation of concerns as *tyranny of the dominant decomposition* [Tarr et al., 1999].

To illustrate the problem, consider the seminal *expression problem*.[3] We have an evaluator of mathematical expressions and want to be able to add new operations to our expressions (EVALUATE, PRINT, SIMPLIFY, ...). At the same time, we want to be able to add new kinds of expressions (PLUS, POWER, LN, ...). In a software product line, we want to freely mix and match features from both dimensions, operations and kinds of expressions. The implementation of *"evaluate a plus expression"* (e.g., $3 + 1 = 4$) concerns both feature PLUS and feature EVALUATE. If feature EVALUATE is not selected, code to implement *"evaluate a plus expression"* is not needed; if feature PLUS is not selected, this code is not needed either. But how can we modularize code such that we can freely select features from both operations and expressions?

In Figure 3.4a and 3.4b, we illustrate the two standard forms of modularization: We modularize either expressions or operations (the latter typically with the Visitor pattern [Gamma et al., 1995, pp. 331ff.]). Thus, in Figure 3.4a, we can easily remove or add expressions but not operations, and in Figure 3.4b, we can remove and add operations but not expressions. With most compositional approaches (especially those that have been designed to modularize crosscutting concerns), we can extend the code with a new optional feature, independent of what modularization has been used initially [for an overview, see Lopez-Herrejon et al., 2005]. As visualized in Figure 3.4c, we can add a new module SIMPLIFY without changing existing modules, and then add a new module LN, without changing existing

---

[3]The expression problem was named by Phil Wadler in 1998 on the Java-Genericity mailing list but has been known for many years [e.g., Reynolds, 1994; Cook, 1991]; see Torgersen [2004] for a retrospective overview.

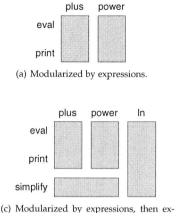

(a) Modularized by expressions.

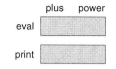

(b) Modularized by operations.

(c) Modularized by expressions, then extended twice.

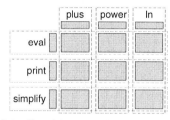

(d) Small modules grouped by data types and operations in the expression problem.

Figure 3.4.: *Modularization of interacting features.*

modules. But still, we cannot mix and match features freely, but we create very specific constraints between features instead.

A solution to this problem – described in different contexts as *lifters* [Prehofer, 1997], as *origami* by Batory et al. [2002], or as *derivatives* by Liu et al. [2006] – is to break down these modules into smaller modules and group them back again. The small modules may belong to multiple features. This is illustrated in Figure 3.4d, in which the code that implements the evaluation of a plus expression is encapsulated in its own module (top-left) and belongs to both features SIMPLIFY and PLUS (indicated by dashed lines). In this figure, the narrow boxes represent modules for those code fragments that belong only to a single feature.

Generally, when we want to be able to compose two interacting features independently, we can refactor their implementation into three modules, one module for each feature, and one additional feature to encapsulate the "interaction code" or "glue code". The additional module belongs to both features and is included if and only if both features are selected. In Figure 3.5, we visualize this concept with two features A and B as overlapping circles, which are modularized into three modules A, B, and $A \backslash B$. When more than two features interact at the same time, this can be solved with more additional modules (described as higher-order derivatives by Liu et al. [2006]).

The expression problem is an academic example with two dimensions, in which every feature from one dimension interacts with every feature from the other dimension, and almost the entire code of the software product line belongs to two

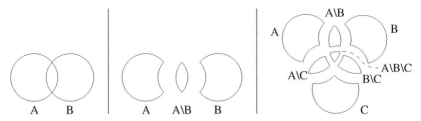

Figure 3.5.: *Additional modules to modularize feature interactions.*

features at the same time. In practice, not every feature interacts with so many other features, but studies have shown that feature interactions are still frequent and hinder modularization [e.g., Hall, 2005; Liu et al., 2006; Kästner et al., 2009c]. For example, in a case study of Berkeley DB Java Edition with 39 features, we found 53 feature interactions that would require an additional module each; in a case study of Berkeley DB C Edition with 24 features, we found 78 feature interactions; in a case study of FAME-DBMS with 14 features, we found 34 feature interactions (for details see [Kästner et al., 2009c] and Section 3.1.7).

Whether modularization with additional modules scales in practice is still under controversial debate. Concerns have been raised after the presentation of Liu et al. [2006] at ICSE'06, and our experience in our case studies shows also that adding additional modules adds significant development effort and lowers comprehensibility [Kästner, 2007; Kästner et al., 2009c]. Splitting a program into too many small modules can be problematic. Although concerns have been separated, the developer who wants to understand a feature in its entirety (e.g., the entire evaluation mechanism in the expression problem or the entire transaction subsystem in a database management system) has to look into many modules and reconstruct the behavior in her mind. Modular reasoning often applies not only to a single module, but the implementation of a feature is scattered over multiple modules. That is, with modular implementations of feature interactions, we reduce the benefits of traceability and modular reasoning, for which we separated concerns into distinct modules in the first place.

3.1.6. Difficult adoption (–)

With the exception of frameworks, developers in industry rarely adopt compositional approaches for product-line implementation, so far. Although several academic case studies have shown applicability of novel composition languages and tools [e.g., Hunleth and Cytron, 2002; Zhang and Jacobsen, 2003; Batory et al., 2004; Tešanović et al., 2004; Apel and Batory, 2006; Kästner et al., 2007a; Figueiredo et al., 2008; Rosenmüller et al., 2009; Bettini et al., 2010; Apel, 2010], they are rarely used in practice. One of the reasons is that most approaches introduce new language concepts and raise complexity. Developers need to learn new languages and to think in new ways. Implementing features modularly is more difficult (and thus more expensive), while there is no immediate benefit of modularity. Modularity is rather a long term investment for maintenance and future extensions [Clements and Krueger, 2002]. All this makes it difficult to convince developers to adopt compositional approaches.

Typically, each compositional approach is designed for one specific language. An extended language must be provided for every language that is used in a software product line (e.g., AspectJ for Java, AspectC for C, Aspect-UML for UML, and AspectXML for XML). AHEAD [Batory et al., 2004] and FeatureHouse [Apel et al., 2009b; Boxleitner et al., 2009] are two notable exceptions that address multiple languages in a uniform way, but they trade off this generality with other benefits; for example, they are less expressive and cannot provide modular type checking and separate compilation.

Many languages are usable only at a large scale with tool support, so developers really depend on tools [Kästner et al., 2007a, 2009d]. Most compositional languages are experimental and do not provide the tool support to which developers have grown accustomed with modern development environments as Visual Studio or Eclipse. The influence on mainstream programming languages has been low so far, with the notable exception of partial types in C# and Visual Basic, which roughly resemble class refinements without method refinements.

3.1.7. Case study: Berkeley DB

In a large-scale case study, we refactored the Java edition of Oracle's Berkeley DB[4] into a software product line (see also Appendix A.1). In this process, we experienced first hand the described limitations of compositional approaches [Kästner et al., 2007a; Kästner, 2007]. We summarize our experience in this section, to illustrate the impact of the discussed problems on practical software product lines. The case study was performed with one specific compositional language, AspectJ, but many of the problems we experienced can be generalized to other compositional approaches as well.

Feature-refactoring Berkeley DB

Berkeley DB is an open-source database engine, which can be included into an application as a library. Due to its performance and transaction safety, Berkeley DB is broadly used in open source and commercial applications. Berkeley DB is available in three editions, Berkeley DB, Berkeley DB Java Edition, and Berkeley DB XML. We focus on Berkeley DB Java Edition, which itself is written entirely in Java. In the domain of embedded database management systems, tailored variants

---

[4]http://oracle.com/technology/products/berkeley-db

promise smaller binary size, lower memory consumption, and better performance. In the Java edition, it is possible to dynamically deactivate some features such as transactions at startup, but it is not possible to create a tailored variant of the database engine during build time that excludes unnecessary code.

By analyzing domain, manual, configuration parameters, and source code, we identified many parts of Berkeley DB that were candidates to be refactored into features, such that we can configure their inclusion at build time. These features were implicit in the legacy code. They varied from small caches, to entire transaction or persistence subsystems. All identified features represent program functionality that a user would select or deselect when customizing a database management system. From these features, we chose 38 features for actual refactoring. See [Kästner et al., 2007a] and [Kästner, 2007] for a feature diagram and a detailed description of how we identified and selected features.

We performed the actual refactoring manually within one month, following various refactorings from object-oriented to aspect-oriented implementations suggested in literature [e.g., Hanenberg et al., 2003; Monteiro and Fernandes, 2005; Cole and Borba, 2005]. Of our 38 refactored features, 16 were small, each with less than 140 lines of code and less than 10 extensions. Four features were large, each with 958–1864 lines of code, with 118–345 extensions, and with 24–30 affected classes. The remaining 18 features have a size in-between. With these 38 features, we refactored about 10 % of the code base of Berkeley DB.

Observations

During the refactoring process, we observed several problems. For our AspectJ-specific experience, with problems such as pointcut fragility or third-person perspective, see [Kästner et al., 2007a]. Here, we report those observations that can be generalized to other compositional approaches.

Granularity. When decomposing Berkeley DB, we encountered fine-grained extensions in almost every feature [Kästner et al., 2008a]. Although most extensions were coarse grained, there was still a significant number of fine-grained extensions, such as feature code in the middle of a method, which required workarounds.

Of overall 1144 extensions used to implement the 38 features, 640 extensions (56 %) introduced new classes, methods, or fields. Further 214 extensions (19 %) were simple method extensions that added method refinements of existing methods. They were well supported by AspectJ and can be implemented with most compositional approaches. However, we needed 261 extensions (23 %) at statement level and 24 (2 %) at expression level, which we implemented with hook methods (or in 121 cases with AspectJ-specific call pointcuts).

We faced also the problem that certain method parameters of the code base belonged to a feature and should be removed when the feature is not selected. This made it very difficult to refactor some features in Berkeley DB, because compositional approaches do not permit method-signature changes. We first noticed the problem in feature TRANSACTIONS, which provides a parameter with transaction context to 59 methods. In variants without feature TRANSACTIONS, these parameters are not needed. We invested significant effort to implement workarounds for these 59 methods [see Kästner et al., 2008a]. Afterward, we did not attempt to refactor any further features that involved a large amount of parameters. Especially feature LOCKING appeared unmanageable, because it changes the signature of 289 methods by introducing parameters such as *locker*, *lockMode*, or *lockType*. Decomposing the feature LOCKING would either result in utterly unreadable code or require a complete preliminary redesign of the whole database engine.

Together, workarounds for fine-grained extensions of statements, expressions, and parameters made the decomposition very difficult and the implementation tedious. Though it was possible to extract most features, code quality suffered and the resulting code base became hard to understand and maintain.

The optional feature problem. Features in Berkeley DB were not as independent in their implementation as we expected. Conceptually, most features are optional and independent; there are only 16 constraints between our 38 features in the feature model. However, their implementations often interacted, making decomposition difficult. With manual and automated source code analysis, we found 53 dependencies between the extracted aspects [Kästner et al., 2009c]. Due to such implementation dependencies, many variants that are valid according to the feature model cannot be generated. For example, even though STATISTICS and TRANSACTIONS are optional and independent in the feature model, the implementation of STATISTICS refers to the implementation of TRANSACTIONS, so we cannot generate variants with STATISTICS but without TRANSACTIONS.

Ignoring all implementation dependencies is not desirable, because this would restrict the ability to generate tailored variants drastically. In pure numbers the reduction from 3.6 billion to 0.3 million possible variants may appear significant but acceptable considering that still many variants are possible. Nevertheless, when having a closer look, we found that especially in the core of Berkeley DB, there are many implementation dependencies. For example, selecting only feature STATISTICS (which is optional and completely independent in the feature model) requires the implementation of TRANSACTIONS and of 14 other features due to direct and indirect implementation dependencies. Thus, features such as STATISTICS, TRANSACTIONS, MEMORY MANAGEMENT, or several database operations must be selected in virtually all variants. These implementation dependencies prevent many useful variants; so many feature combinations that are valid in the feature model cannot be generated. Thus, we have to use larger and inefficient variants in many scenarios. The remaining variability of 0.3 million variants is largely due to several small independent debugging, caching, and I/O features. Considering all implementation dependencies, this software product line has little value for generating variants tailored to concrete use-cases without statistics, without transactions, or as read-only database.

As described in Section 3.1.5, we could rewrite the source code to remove implementation-specific dependencies, for example, by adding additional modules. However, we found that such rewrites require much additional effort. We started with 9 additional modules to eliminate all direct implementation dependencies of the feature STATISTICS. The 9 modules alone required over 200 additional extensions. Of 1867 LOC of the statistics feature, we extracted 76 % into additional modules. The refactoring was tedious and required between 15 minutes and two hours for each additional module depending on the amount of code. Due to the high effort, we refrained from adding a module for every implementation dependency and left several dependencies in the source code, which was in contrast to our goal that variability should not be restricted by technical constraints [see Kästner et al., 2009c].

Modularity and tools.   The resulting implementation is modular in the sense that every feature is implemented cohesively in one (or multiple) aspects in a dedicated directory. Thus, we can directly *trace* a feature from the feature model to its implementation.

In literature, AspectJ is criticized for insufficient modularity [e.g., Sullivan et al., 2005; Aldrich, 2005; Steimann, 2006; Steimann et al., 2010]; several other compositional approaches have similar problems. From our experience with Berkeley DB, we can confirm this criticism. Although each feature's code is localized in a cohesive module, understanding a feature just by looking at its module is typically possible only for small features. To understand a larger feature (more than 100 lines of code or 10 extensions in our case [Kästner et al., 2007a]), typically, we have to look also at the base code and at other features and develop a mental model how they behave when composed. Tool support as the Eclipse plug-in *AJDT* [Clement et al., 2003] assists in this process by adding facilities to visualize the composition and navigate between code fragments of the base code and aspects. In Berkeley DB, we eventually *depended* on such tool support for understanding and maintenance.

In our experience, modularizing features was beneficial regarding traceability, but – at least in our implementation – not regarding information hiding or modular reasoning. To understand the implementation of a feature, we still had to read significant portions of the base code. We conjecture that there are better feature implementations, in which modularity plays to its strength. However, with regard to crosscutting features, extracted from a legacy application with many fine-grained extensions and several workarounds, we did not experience a substantial benefit from modularity but had to rely on tools anyway.

Discussion

All in all, our case study demonstrates that implementing software product lines with compositional approaches is feasible, even when crosscutting, fine-grained implementations are involved. However, at the same it shows that contemporary compositional languages like AspectJ cannot play to their strength. Modular implementation requires a high effort (especially when workarounds are required for fine-grained extensions and when features interact) and can be difficult to understand and maintain. Of the promised benefits of separations of concerns and modularity, only traceability is really achieved in our experience.

As discussed in [Kästner et al., 2007a, 2008a, 2009c], there are some threats to external validity, that is, whether our experience can be generalized to other product line projects. First, we feature-refactored features from an existing application; the legacy code might contribute to the high number of crosscutting and fine-grained extensions. Second, we decomposed very small features, to provide a highly configurable system, whereas in practice often larger subsystems are considered as features. Third, our case study covers one specific domain, which is known to be very complex. We believe that our decomposition of Berkeley DB might have been more challenging than usually, but crosscutting features and fine-grained extensions are common in software product lines in general. Our experience with other case studies (see Appendix A.1) and reports from other software product lines developed with compositional languages [e.g., Hunleth and Cytron, 2002; Batory et al., 2004; Tešanović et al., 2004; Zhang and Jacobsen, 2004; Lopez-Herrejon et al., 2005; Figueiredo et al., 2008] corroborate this view.

Finally, some limitations (granularity and multiple dimensions) are conceptual. New compositional languages will have the same fundamental limitations. Our experience with Berkeley DB motivated us to look into different implementation concepts, which we discuss next.

3.2. Annotative approaches

Annotative approaches implement product lines by annotating code fragments with features in a common code base. They generate variants mainly by removing annotated code fragments, which is sometimes described also as negative variability. In contrast to compositional approaches, features are not modularized. The most common form of such annotations are *#ifdef* and *#endif* directives of the C preprocessor *cpp* to conditionally remove feature code before compilation. For example, *cpp* is used to implement variability within the original C implementation of Berkeley DB, in which a user can configure 11 different features at compile-time. An excerpt from Berkeley DB with *#ifdef* directives for the features QUEUE and DIAGNOSTIC is shown in Figure 3.6.

```
1  static int __rep_queue_filedone(dbenv, rep, rfp)
2    DB_ENV *dbenv;
3    REP *rep;
4    __rep_fileinfo_args *rfp; {
5  #ifndef HAVE_QUEUE
6    COMPQUIET(rep, NULL);
7    COMPQUIET(rfp, NULL);
8    return (__db_no_queue_am(dbenv));
9  #else
10   db_pgno_t first, last;
11   u_int32_t flags;
12   int empty, ret, t_ret;
13 #ifdef DIAGNOSTIC
14   DB_MSGBUF mb;
15 #endif
16   // over 100 lines of additional code
17 #endif
18 }
```

Figure 3.6.: *Code excerpt of Berkeley DB.*

Historically, the C preprocessor *cpp* has been designed for metaprogramming. Of its three capabilities, file inclusion (*#include*), macros (*#define*), and conditional compilation (*#ifdef*), we focus only on conditional compilation, which is routinely used to implement variability. There are many preprocessors that provide similar facilities. For example, for Java ME, the preprocessor *Antenna*[5] is often used and supported in development environments such as *NetBeans*; the developers of Java's Swing library developed their own preprocessor *Munge*;[6] the languages Pascal, Fortran, and Erlang have their own preprocessors; and conditional compilation is a language feature in C#, Visual Basic, D, PL/SQL, Adobe Flex, and others. Additionally, there are several independent, partly configurable preprocessors (or more general software-configuration-management tools [Conradi and Westfechtel, 1998]) such as *GPP - Generic Preprocessor*,[7] *GNU M4*,[8] *SPLET* [Saleh and Gomaa, 2005], *XVCL* [Zhang and Jarzabek, 2004], or those included in the *Version Editor* [Atkins et al., 2002] or the commercial product-line tools *pure::variants* [Beuche et al., 2004] and *Gears* [Krueger, 2002].

Annotations do not only have to be textual preprocessor statements, but can be also stored separately as in FEAT [Robillard and Murphy, 2002] and our tool

---

[5]http://antenna.sf.net
[6]http://weblogs.java.net/blog/tball/archive/munge/doc/Munge.html
[7]http://www.nothingisreal.com/gpp/
[8]http://www.gnu.org/software/m4/

CIDE [Kästner et al., 2008a]. Annotations can not only mark source code, but also on other artifacts. For example, the tools *fmp2rsm* by Czarnecki and Antkiewicz [2005], *FeatureMapper* by Heidenreich et al. [2008b], and the model checking approaches by Lauenroth et al. [2009] and Gruler et al. [2008] use annotations on model elements. In these cases, variants of the model are generated by evaluating annotations and removing corresponding elements.

Finally, annotative approaches cannot only be used to configure variants statically before compilation, but also to enable or disable features at runtime. In the simplest case, the according code fragments are guarded by *if* statements (or other forms of annotations are transformed into *if* statements by a compiler). There are also annotative approaches that provide direct language support for such runtime changes, for example *rbFeatures* in Ruby [Günther and Sunkle, 2009b] and *FeatureJ* [Sunkle et al., 2009].

Annotative approaches, and especially traditional preprocessors, are easy to use, but have several problems, for which they are heavily criticized in literature as summarized in the claim "#ifdef Considered Harmful" [Spencer and Collyer, 1992] and in the colloquial term "#ifdef hell" [Lohmann et al., 2006]. Numerous studies discuss the negative effect of preprocessor usage on code quality and maintainability [e.g., Spencer and Collyer, 1992; Krone and Snelting, 1994; Favre, 1995, 1997; Ernst et al., 2002; Pohl et al., 2005; Adams et al., 2008]. Many academics recommend limiting or entirely abandoning the use of preprocessors in favor of compositional approaches. There is little work on how preprocessors could be improved. In the following, we provide a survey of the problems (indicated by "−") caused by contemporary annotative approaches (especially conditional compilation with preprocessors), but we also highlight their benefits (indicated by "+").

3.2.1. Separation of concerns (−)

Separation of concerns and related issues of modularity and traceability are usually regarded as the biggest problems of preprocessors. Instead of separating all code that implements a feature into a separate module (or file, class, package, etc.), a preprocessor-based implementation scatters feature code across the entire code base where it is entangled closely with the base code and the code of other features. For example, in a database management system, code to implement transactions (acquire and release locks, commit and rollback changes) is scattered throughout the entire code base and tangled with code responsible for recovery and other features. Even when feature code is roughly separated, and only annotations remain as marker where to include it, these annotations are scattered and tangled.

In literature, the reduced degree of separation of concerns is held responsible for a lot of problems. To understand the behavior of a feature, we need to search the entire code base instead of just looking into a single module; to understand a local

```
1  #if defined(HAVE_STACK_LIMIT) \
2     || (!defined(HAVE_SIGALTSTACK) && defined(HAVE_SIGSTACK))
3  # define HAVE_CHECK_STACK_GROWTH
4  ...
5  #endif
```

Figure 3.7.: *Example of scattered configuration knowledge in* Vim *(os_unix.c, Lines 635–639). Instead describing feature dependencies in a feature model, a feature is activate based on some condition in the middle of a code file.*

code fragment, we need to reason about the global program [Favre, 1995, 1997]. Even just removing an obsolete feature from the source code becomes a tedious task [Favre, 1997; Baxter and Mehlich, 2001]. Tangled code of other features distracts the programmer in the search. There is no direct traceability from a feature as domain concept to its implementation [Kästner et al., 2008b]. Tangled code also is a challenge for distributed development, because developers working on different concerns have to edit the same files. In general, Favre [1997] and Muthig and Patzke [2002] claim that annotations work fine in small projects, but do not scale to large software product lines with hundreds of features. Actually, annotations are used and maintained in many large scale product lines such as the Linux kernel in practice [Liebig et al., 2010]; but developers report many annotation-related problems [e.g., Tartler et al., 2009].

In contemporary preprocessor implementations, scattering does not only affect the source code, but also the configuration knowledge. Configuration parameters can be provided as parameters or as *#define* directives in a configuration file, but often *#ifdef* directives refer also to flags that are defined somewhere inside the source code, possibly depending on some other features, as exemplified in Figure 3.7. Such scattering of configuration knowledge can make it hard to understand when or why a certain code fragment is included in a variant [Favre, 1997; Pearse and Oman, 1997; Hu et al., 2000; Anastasopoules and Gacek, 2001; Muthig and Patzke, 2002; Singh et al., 2007]. Also consistency checks between feature model and features used inside annotations are often missing [Tartler et al., 2009].

3.2.2. Obfuscation (–)

Except for few languages (e.g., C#, D, Adobe Flex), annotations are not part of the language but added on top by an external tool. The host language and annotations are intermixed in the same file. Especially, when annotations are used at fine granularity and are strongly scattered, it can be difficult to follow the control flow in the host language [Pearse and Oman, 1997; Adams et al., 2008]. According to Lohmann et al. [2006], such source code is sometimes referred to as *"#ifdef hell"* among developers. Favre [1997] observed: "When human readers are not able to take into account all the variants at a time, they tend to go over the same piece

```
 1 class Stack {
 2   void push(Object o
 3 #ifdef SYNC
 4   , Transaction txn
 5 #endif
 6   ) {
 7     if (o==null
 8 #ifdef SYNC
 9     || txn==null
10 #endif
11     ) return;
12 #ifdef SYNC
13     Lock l=txn.lock(o);
14 #endif
15     elementData[size++] = o;
16 #ifdef SYNC
17     l.unlock();
18 #endif
19     fireStackChanged();
20   }
21 }
```

Figure 3.8.: *Java code obfuscated by fine-grained annotations with* cpp *[Kästner et al., 2008a].*

of code repeatedly, trying to understand only a few cases each time by means of partial readings. [. . .] This repetitive task is tedious."

Corresponding #*ifdef* and #*endif* directives may be hundreds of lines apart, and they can be nested arbitrarily. Already understanding the structure of annotations, without considering the annotated code, can be tedious [Favre, 1997; Pohl et al., 2005]. Long and nested annotations can even make it difficult to determine to which feature (or feature combination) a local code fragment belongs [Krone and Snelting, 1994; Pearse and Oman, 1997; Anastasopoules and Gacek, 2001].

When reading source code, many #*ifdef* and #*endif* directives distract from the actual code and can destroy the code layout [Pearse and Oman, 1997]. With *cpp*, every directive must be placed in its own line. There are cases, in which preprocessor directives entirely obfuscate the source code. For example, in Figure 3.8, we illustrate a preprocessor-based implementation of our fine-grained extensions from Figure 3.2 (p. 23). In this example, we need eight additional lines just for preprocessor directives. Together with additional line breaks, we need 21 instead of 9 lines for this code fragment. Although this example appears extreme at first, similar code can be found in practice. For example, in Figure 3.9, we illustrate the overwhelming amount of preprocessor directives in *Femto OS*,[9] a small real-time operating system.

---

[9]http://www.femtoos.org/

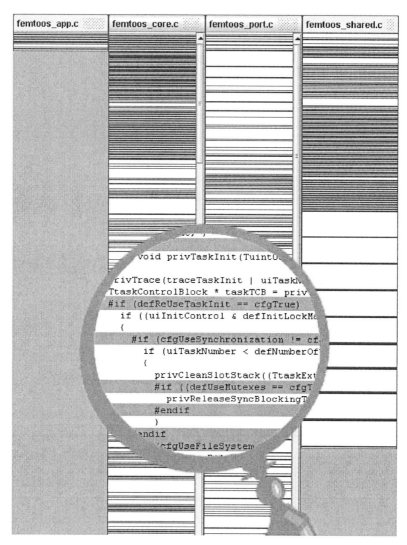

Figure 3.9.: *Preprocessor directives in the code of Femto OS: highlighted lines represent preprocessor directives such as #ifdef, white lines represent the remaining C code, comment lines are not shown.*

3.2.3. Error proneness (–)

Using annotations to implement optional features can easily introduce errors that can be very difficult to detect. The crosscutting nature of feature implementation is hard to understand and maintain, and thus prone to errors in general [Eaddy et al., 2008]. In contrast to compositional approaches, there is no way to check features in isolation. Furthermore, preprocessors cause additional challenges, even without considering macro expansion, which according to a study by Ernst et al. [2002] is a significant contributor to errors.

Contemporary preprocessors, such as *cpp*, make it difficult to detect even simple syntax errors. They operate at the level of characters or tokens, without interpreting the underlying code. Thus, developers are prone to simple errors, like annotating a closing bracket but not the opening one, as illustrated in the adapted code excerpt from Berkeley DB in Figure 3.10 (the opening bracket in Line 4 is closed in Line 17 only when feature HAVE_QUEUE is selected, all other variants contain a syntax error). We introduced this error deliberately, but such errors can easily occur in practice and are difficult to detect. The scattered nature of feature implementations intensifies this problem. The worst part is that compilers cannot detect such syntax errors, unless the developer (or customer) eventually builds a variant with a problematic feature combination (without feature HAVE_QUEUE in our case). However, since there are so many potential variants (2^n variants for n independent optional features), we might not compile variants with a problematic feature combination during initial development. Simply compiling *all* variants is also not feasible due to their high number, so even simple syntax errors might go undetected for a long time. The bottom line is that errors are found only late in the development cycle, when they are more expensive to fix. Beyond syntax errors, also type errors and semantic errors can occur, as we discuss in detail in Chapter 5.

Favre [1995] and Baxter and Mehlich [2001] argue that preprocessors, due to their simplicity, invite developers to make ad-hoc extensions and use "quick and dirty" solutions, instead of restructuring the code. Features are steadily added in a patch-by-patch fashion, but never removed or reflected in the design. Many feature combinations have never been tested, and often do not even make sense [Spencer and Collyer, 1992]. This problem applies to compositional approaches as well, but the ad-hoc nature of preprocessors intensifies it significantly. This leads to many annotations and deep nesting such that, according to Krone and Snelting [1994], "even experienced programmers will have difficulties to obtain some insight into the configuration structure, and when a new configuration variant is to be covered, the introduction of errors is very likely." Additionally, diagnostic tools are missing [Pearse and Oman, 1997; Hu et al., 2000].

```
 1  static int __rep_queue_filedone( dbenv, rep, rfp)
 2      DB_ENV *dbenv;
 3      REP *rep;
 4      __rep_fileinfo_args *rfp; {
 5  #ifndef HAVE_QUEUE
 6      COMPQUIET(rep, NULL);
 7      COMPQUIET(rfp, NULL);
 8      return (__db_no_queue_am(dbenv));
 9  #else
10      db_pgno_t first, last;
11      u_int32_t flags;
12      int empty, ret, t_ret;
13  #ifdef DIAGNOSTIC
14      DB_MSGBUF mb;
15  #endif
16      // over 100 lines of additional code
17  }
18  #endif
```

Figure 3.10.: *Adapted code excerpt of Berkeley DB, which contains a syntax error in variants without* HAVE_QUEUE.

3.2.4. Simple and uniform programming model (+)

Despite all criticism, there are several benefits of annotative approaches, to which some of their success in practice can be attributed. First, annotative approaches have a *simple programming model:* Code is annotated and removed. Preprocessor mechanisms are easy to use and understand. In contrast to compositional approaches, no new languages, tools, patterns, or processes have to be learned. Adoption is easy; developers are often already familiar with preprocessors. In many languages, preprocessors are already included; otherwise they can be added with lightweight tools.

Most annotative approaches are *language independent* and provide a *uniform experience* when annotating different code fragments and artifact types. The same annotation mechanisms can be used uniformly for annotating code fragments of different granularity, such as entire files, methods, statements, and parameters. Preprocessors, such as *cpp*, can not only be used on C code but also on Java code or HTML files. Instead of providing a tool or model for every language, each with different mechanisms (like AspectJ for Java, AspectC for C, Aspect-UML for UML), annotative approaches add the same simple model to *all* languages.

The simple and uniform programming model with lightweight tools is the main advantage of preprocessors which drives professionals to still adopt them despite all criticism [Favre, 1997; Clements and Krueger, 2002; Muthig and Patzke, 2002].

3.2.5. Fine granularity (+)

Another advantage of annotative approaches is that, conceptually, they can mark code fragments at arbitrary levels of granularity. They can annotate entire files, individual tokens, and everything in between. We simply introduce markers at the exact positions that should be extended. Although *cpp*-style preprocessors can annotate only whole physical lines, they are sufficient for even the finest extensions due to the ability to isolate language constructs in separate lines in most languages. In Figure 3.8 (p. 37), we illustrate how statements in the middle of a method and even parameters and parts of expressions can be annotated. Finally, compared to compositional approaches, annotations do not share the conceptual limitations regarding ordered statements and fixed signatures because they indicate the final position in the base code; there is no notion of a composition order.

3.2.6. Variability despite feature interactions (+)

Finally, preprocessors can handle multiple interacting optional features naturally [Kim et al., 2008]. Instead of being forced to create many additional modules, nested annotations provide an intuitive mechanism to include code only when two or more features are selected. In Figure 3.11, we show the annotation-based implementation of the expression problem (cf. Sec. 3.1.5). From this example, we can select every feature combination and can create all variants, without splitting the features into many small modules.

Furthermore, a (dominant) decomposition is still possible. Annotating code does not prohibit traditional means of separation of concerns. In fact, it is reasonable to still decompose the system into modules and classes and use preprocessors only where necessary. For example, in Figure 3.11, we decomposed the expression problem into classes *Add* and *Pow*. Preprocessors add additional expressiveness, where traditional modularization techniques come to their limits regarding crosscutting concerns or multi-dimensional separation of concerns.

3.3. Other approaches

There are some approaches, which do not fit into our classification of compositional and annotative approaches. For completeness, we give a brief overview.

First, there are a number of *hybrid approaches* that share characteristics of both compositional and annotative approaches. They are based mostly on a composition process, but use annotations to determine the location where to inject code. For example, AspectJ can advise Java 1.5 annotations [Kiczales and Mezini, 2005b]; advice is still woven in a compositional manner, but the location is picked by an explicit annotation. Similarly, invasive software composition can use annotations inside a module for composition [Aßmann, 2003]. Further examples of such hybrid

```
 1  #ifdef ADD                            21  #ifdef POWER
 2  class Add extends Expr {              22  class Pow extends Expr {
 3    Expr left, right;                   23    Expr base, exp;
 4    Add(Expr l, Expr r)                 24    Pow(Expr b, Expr e)
 5      { left=l; right=r; }              25      { base=b; exp=e; }
 6  #ifdef EVAL                           26  #ifdef EVAL
 7    double eval() {                     27    double eval() {
 8      return left.eval() +              28      return Math.pow(base.eval(),
 9          right.eval();                 29          right.eval());
10    }                                   30    }
11  #endif                               31  #endif
12  #ifdef PRINT                         32  #ifdef PRINT
13    void print() {                     33    void print() {
14      left.print();                    34      left.print();
15      System.out.print("+");           35      System.out.print("^");
16      right.print();                   36      right.print();
17    }                                  37    }
18  #endif                               38  #endif
19  }                                    39  }
20  #endif                               40  #endif
```

Figure 3.11.: *Preprocessor-based implementation of the expression problem (excerpt).*

approaches are *explicit programming* [Bryant et al., 2002] and *metaprogramming with traits* [Turon and Reppy, 2007]. Additionally, some approaches can exploit existing language facilities as implicit annotations. For example, deliberately introduced empty methods can be used as hooks for extensions (often used as workaround in compositional approaches, cf. Sec. 3.1.4), or naming conventions can be employed for extensions like "synchronize all methods starting with '*sync_*'". The hybrid approaches provide a trade-off between the respective advantages and limitations of both groups, they cannot achieve full modularity and traceability (annotations are still scattered), but they can make more fine-grained extensions and can be easier to use. We will come back to this trade-off in Chapter 6.

Second, in practice, sometimes *version control systems* are used to implement variability. Developers can use development branches or similar constructs to develop different variants [Conradi and Westfechtel, 1998]. However, such implementation approach is typically used only at a very early adoption level, because it does not scale well [Staples and Hill, 2004]. Instead of implementing features, developers implement variants. It is not possible to mix and match features to create a new variant. During development and maintenance, changes must be propagated to all variants (either manually or with merging tools of the version control system).

Third, *components* (and their modern distributed incarnation as *services*) can be used to build product lines [Bass et al., 1998; Pohl et al., 2005; Lee et al., 2008].

Domain engineering is used to determine which code fragments are to be reused in a domain and should therefore be implemented as a component (thus solving the problem how to find the right size of a component in one domain [Biggerstaff, 1994, 1998; Meyer, 1997]). Developers can then reuse these components when they implement a variant. In general, components can be classified as a compositional approach; they have the same benefits and limitations. However, in contrast to frameworks and other compositional approaches, each variant is implemented individually. There may be a high degree of reuse, lowering the development costs of each variant, but there is still significant implementation effort in application engineering. In line with generative programming [Czarnecki and Eisenecker, 2000], we focus on approaches that enable full automation in application engineering, therefore, we do not classify components as compositional approach.

Fourth, *generators*, *metaprogramming*, and *model-driven development* also can be used, such that a developer provides a specification as input (often in a domain specific language) and the generator produces an according variant. Depending of the point of view, most compositional approaches can be regarded as generator or model transformation (feature selection provides the input as model or domain-specific language), but there are more powerful tools with capabilities beyond just composing modules. For example, program transformation systems, such as *Stratego/XT* [Visser, 2004], *DMS* [Baxter et al., 2004] or the *Domain Workbench (a.k.a. Intentional Programming)* [Simonyi, 1995; Simonyi et al., 2006], can perform arbitrary modifications, typically including removal or complete restructuring. Similarly, template and frame engines, such as *XVCL* [Zhang and Jarzabek, 2004], *Spoon* [Pawlak, 2006], or template metaprogramming [Czarnecki and Eisenecker, 2000, Ch. 10], provide powerful (in some cases even Turing complete) mechanisms. Furthermore, they integrate well with other compositional approaches [Trujillo et al., 2007]. However, this expressiveness comes at a price of increased complexity; therefore, they are not frequently adopted in practice, except for few domains. Usability of generators or how to give certain safety guarantees are interesting research topics [e.g., Huang et al., 2005; Huang and Smaragdakis, 2008; Cordy, 2009], but outside the scope of this thesis. We focus on simpler and more restricted composition and annotation mechanisms.

Fifth, we can use various *build tools* to implement variability. For example, in tools such as *make* or *ant*, we can include or exclude files from compilation based on configuration options. For example, Staples and Hill [2004] use different build scripts and some variant-specific source-code files to compile different variants of a software product line. Furthermore, build tools can conditionally call arbitrary additional tools during the build process. The commercial product lines tools *pure::variants* and *Gears* also fall into this category. Depending on how they are used, we can classify build tools either as a very coarse grained compositional approach (assembling files), as a coarse grained annotative approach (excluding files), as just a tool to steer other variability mechanisms (calling preprocessors, composers, transformation engines, or compilers), or as a variability mechanism of its own.

Finally, although not aimed at software product lines, there are several approaches that aim at exploring crosscutting concerns in scattered implementations. For example, Robillard and Murphy [2002] propose concern graphs to explore and describe concerns in scattered implementations. In their implementation in *FEAT*, users can manage a list of concerns and assign code fragments to these concerns. The focus lies on assisting a developer in finding all code fragments belonging to a concern, but once they are assigned, *FEAT* displays a list of all scattered implementations assigned to a concern in a separate window so that developers can navigate between them. Similarly, users can tag code fragments with concerns as software plans in *Spotlight*, and subsequently navigate between tagged code fragments with special views [Coppit and Cox, 2004; Coppit et al., 2007]. Furthermore, code exploration tools, such as *AspectBrowser* [Griswold et al., 2001] and *JQuery* [Janzen and De Volder, 2003], use pattern expressions or queries to find code fragments belonging to a certain feature. With a suitable query, the search result describes the entire scattered implementation of a feature; a user can then quickly navigate between the search results. The main difference compared to annotation-based implementations is that in all these approaches annotations are not used to implement variability; these tools are not designed to generate variants. Instead, annotations are used only to document scattered concerns and to navigate between them. This raises problems similar to documentation in general. First, developers have little incentive to update annotations when the implementation changes. Second, incorrect or incomplete annotations have no immediate effect. In contrast, annotations used for product-line implementation are used primarily for variability; reusing them for views and navigation is a secondary goal. Incorrect or missing annotations result in errors in the generated variants; error detection mechanisms as described in Chapter 5 can be used to enforce consistency.

3.4. Summary, perspective, and goals

Compositional and annotative approaches are two large groups that cover not all, but most common product-line implementation approaches. Roughly, research focuses on compositional approaches to devise new languages to implement and compose modular features, whereas annotative approaches are pragmatic solutions commonly used in practice, in which code fragments are annotated and removed to generate variants.

In Table 3.1, we show a summary of the discussed benefits and limitations of both groups. It becomes apparent that both groups are almost complementary

Criteria	Compositional approaches	Annotative approaches
Modularity	achieved in some approaches (+/−)	no perceivable form of modularity (−)
Traceability	direct traceability to module (+)	scattered and tangled code (−)
Language integr.	direct language support, disciplined (+)	external ad-hoc tools, undisciplined, obfuscated (−)
Errors	modular error detection to some degree (+/−)	prone even to syntax errors (−)
Granularity	coarse granularity, often requires workarounds (−)	fine granularity (+)
Optional feature pr.	significant overhead, additional modules (−)	straightforward solution (+)
Uniformity	usually language dependent (−)	language independent (+)
Adoption	difficult adoption, new languages, new tools (−)	easy to use, lightweight tools (+)

Table 3.1.: *Overview of benefits and limitations of compositional and annotative approaches.*

regarding the discussed criteria. It remains important to point out that the table reflects our point of view as outlined before and depends on the criteria we selected (and their perceived impact) and on the groups we formed.

Our personal experience with Berkeley DB has discouraged us from using compositional approaches for practical product-line implementation. In our experience, they are hard to use and some promised benefits like modularity are not achieved to full potential; it is very difficult to convince industry to adopt compositional approaches. As discussed, some limitations of compositional approaches (granularity, optional feature problem) are even conceptual and cannot be solved with just a new language or composition tool.

Hence, instead of improving compositional approaches (which we still pursue with partners in a different, parallel line of research [e.g., Apel et al., 2008c,e, 2009b, 2010; Kuhlemann et al., 2009b; Steimann et al., 2010]), we take a different path in this thesis: Our goal is to improve annotative approaches that are already broadly used in practice. Annotative approaches have hardly received any attention in research. Many preprocessors were designed in the 70s and have not changed much since. We address most of the discussed drawbacks, and propose a novel perspective to see annotative approaches as *virtual separation of concerns*. Although, we cannot provide real modularity with benefits as separate compilation or modular type checking, we show how annotative approaches can be improved regarding traceability and obfuscation in Chapter 4, and regarding error detection in Chapter 5. In Chapter 6, we return to the comparison of compositional and annotative approaches and set the proposed improvements into perspective; finally, we discuss how and to what degree, we can integrate compositional and annotative approaches.

4. Views and visual representation

This chapter shares material with the ICSE'08 paper "Granularity in Software Product Lines" [Kästner et al., 2008a] and the ViSPLE'08 paper "Visualizing Software Product Line Variabilities in Source Code" [Kästner et al., 2008b].

In the previous chapter, we criticized annotative approaches for their suboptimal separation of concerns, missing traceability, missing language support to express variability, and tendency to obfuscate source code. All of these problems make it difficult to understand and maintain annotation-based implementations. In this chapter, we address these problems with different forms of tool support. Although, our approach still relies on scattered annotations, tool support emulates modularity.

We present and discuss a number of ideas to improve preprocessors. First, we integrate feature models into our preprocessor to encapsulate and document configuration knowledge. Second, we propose views to emulate benefits of modular implementations, so that a developer can directly trace a feature to its (scattered) implementation. Third, we propose a different visual representation for annotations to avoid the obfuscated source code often associated with preprocessors. We conclude with an empirical evaluation of selected facets of our suggestions. With these ideas and solutions we intend to initiate a discussion about better annotative approaches. In isolation, all proposed improvements are known in literature in some form (see discussion of related work in Section 4.5), but in their combination, we believe that we can lift annotation-based implementation to a level that can compete with compositional approaches.

We have implemented and integrated all discussed forms of tool support in our prototype product-line tool called CIDE (originally for *colored integrated development environment*). CIDE is an Eclipse plug-in that supports annotations on code fragments, but that also integrates a feature model to reduce scattering of configuration knowledge, provides views to emulate modularity, and represents annotations visually to reduce code obfuscation. CIDE is available for download at `http://fosd.de/cide`.

4.1. Integrating a feature model

A first problem, which is easy to fix, is the scattering of configuration knowledge in annotation-based implementations (cf. Sec. 3.2.1). In the C preprocessor *cpp*,

#ifdef directives refer to flags. Developers may or may not define flags in other code fragments, in central header files or configuration files, or as command line parameter to the compiler. There are no consistency checks for flags used in annotations. Without external documentation, it is not possible to distinguish whether a flag's definition is missing by accident or on purpose. Reasoning about annotations – for example, determining which decisions lead to a selection of a specific code fragment [Hu et al., 2000; Anastasopoules and Gacek, 2001] or whether a code fragment is included in at least one variant [Tartler et al., 2009] – is tedious and difficult to automate.

In software product lines, often feature models are used to describe features and their relationships (cf. Sec. 2.3). This way, configuration knowledge is coherently described in one model. For many forms of feature models, automated-reasoning approaches have been developed, which can, among others, determine valid feature combinations or dead features.

Many projects with annotation-based implementations do not maintain a feature model. Even if they do, the mapping between feature model and annotations in the source code is usually loose. Most preprocessors do not consider the feature model, and most feature modeling tools do not consider the implementation. For example, Tartler et al. [2009] report how variability (implemented with *cpp*) is managed in the Linux kernel: The kernel developers maintain a model of all features (referred to as configuration options) and their dependencies with the *kconfig* tool set. When generating a variant, a user selects features, then *kconfig* checks whether this selection respects all feature dependencies and writes a corresponding C file with a *#define* directive for every selected feature. This configuration file is used subsequently to compile the kernel variant. However, there are more flags used in *#ifdef* directives than defined in the feature model. Features are implemented first, and added only later to the feature model.

We address consistency problems with a more rigorous preprocessor. Possible variability must be documented in a feature model, and the preprocessor must be aware of this feature model. It must reject every annotation as error that refers to features not mentioned in the feature model. The other way around, source code editors can use the feature model to assist developers with annotations, for example, provide a list of all features or determine which features must be selected to include a specific code fragment. With such a preprocessor, we prevent the problems caused by scattered configuration knowledge.

4.1.1. Implementation

In our prototype implementation in CIDE, we strictly enforce consistency between feature model and implementation. By default, a user can annotate code fragments only with features that are part of the feature model (see Screenshot in Figure 4.1). To annotate a code fragment with a new feature, developers must first add this

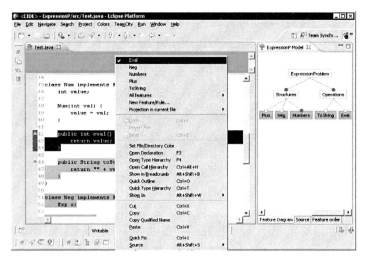

Figure 4.1.: *Annotations in CIDE are always based on the feature model (here shown in a window on the right). Users assign annotations using the context menu. They can select only from existing features, in this case* Eval, Neg, Numbers, Plus, *and* ToString; *the menu "New Feature..." adds a new feature to the feature model.*

feature to the feature model, before they can select it to assign an annotation. CIDE manages all annotations in its tool infrastructure.

CIDE is open for different kinds of feature models. In the simplest case, all features have only Boolean values (default case in CIDE). In a variant, each feature is either selected or not selected. This is equivalent to *cpp* annotations, in which only the predicates #*ifdef* and #*ifndef* are used. Automated reasoning about such annotations is possible and efficient with SAT solvers and tractable even for very large feature models [Batory, 2005; Mendonça et al., 2009] (which we use in Section 5.3). More complex feature models are possible, such as feature models with attributes. For example, to cover the *cpp* annotation "#*if SIZEOF_INT <= 2*", features can have numerical attributes. This expressiveness is supported by several kinds of feature models [e.g., Czarnecki et al., 2002; Benavides et al., 2005], and automated reasoning is still possible with constraint-satisfaction-problem solvers or others [e.g. Benavides et al., 2005]. In CIDE, we provide a plug-in to integrate the more expressive feature model of the commercial *pure::variants* product [Beuche et al., 2004]. With this plug-in, a user can specify more complex annotations in textual form, but still a dialog checks these annotations and accepts only well-formed ones that refer only to features that are defined in the feature model.

As alternative to an implementation of a new annotation mechanism in a controlled environment as CIDE, we could implement also a preprocessor for traditional textual annotations (e.g., *#ifdef* directives). Such a preprocessor would check consistency between feature model and implementation during the generation process. For example, since 2007, the source code of the Linux kernel contains a simple script to check this consistency for *#ifdef* flags [Tartler et al., 2009]. However, when implementing a backward compatible *cpp*-style preprocessor, it is necessary to consider that annotations in *cpp* are not used only for variability, but also for comments, to avoid redefinitions, to prevent multiple inclusion, and others [Pearse and Oman, 1997; Ernst et al., 2002]. In this line, Sutton and Maletic [2007] suggest namespaces or naming conventions for preprocessor flags to distinguish for which purpose preprocessor flags are used. Interestingly, the developers of the Linux kernel adopted such naming pattern and named all flags controlled by the feature model (a subset of all preprocessor flags) with the prefix "CONFIG_" [Tartler et al., 2009].

4.1.2. Discussion

In our experience, most developers do not document variability. There is rarely a list of all features in an annotation-based implementation, or even a feature model that describes the relationship between features. Annotations are mostly an ad-hoc mechanism.

In our search for open source Java ME applications implemented with the Antenna preprocessor, we found only a single application that documented variability: the academic product line *MobileMedia* [Figueiredo et al., 2008]. And even in this case, the feature model was not part of the source code distribution; the authors published an excerpt in [Figueiredo et al., 2008] and sent us the full model upon request. Even in this case, there was no explicit mapping between the name of a feature in the feature model and the preprocessor flag used in the implementation. For example, "Music" in the feature model was implemented with the flag "includeMMAPI". This way, the feature model can serve as a helpful documentation, but not to automatically generate variants, to check consistency, or for further analysis.

We see a tendency that some product-line developers are slowly picking up feature modeling. There are some recent industrial experience reports that describe how product-line developers structured their preprocessor flags and recently connected them to a feature model, for example, HP's Owen product line for printer firmware [Refstrup, 2009], Danfoss' product line of frequency converters [Jepsen and Beuche, 2009], or Wikon's product line of remote control systems [Pech et al., 2009]. Also the Linux kernel developers adopted an approach to describe features (configuration options in their terminology) and their dependencies to some degree [Tartler et al., 2009].

However, all these approaches integrate feature models only in one direction: For a feature selection, the used tools create a configuration file that defines the according preprocessor flags, but they do not check that the preprocessor flags used in the implementation conform to the flags used in the feature model. In such setting, it is still possible to use preprocessor flags that are not controlled by the feature model, either intentionally or by accident (e.g., caused by a typing error in the feature's name). We are only aware of one annotation-based implementation that checks this consistency: In the Linux kernel, a script checks whether all used preprocessor flags with the prefix "CONFIG_" are defined in the feature model. However, Tartler et al. [2009] report that the kernel developers apparently do not use the script and found at least 321 inconsistencies (conservative estimate). We argue that, due to the ad-hoc nature of annotations, consistency should not be left to the discipline of developers, but should be enforced directly by a rigorous preprocessor or compiler.

For all our case studies implemented with CIDE (see Appendix A.1 for a full list), we always provide a feature model. We require developers to model features and their dependencies; the, we enforce consistency between features in the feature model and annotations in the implementation. In our experience, maintaining the feature model adds only minimal effort and integrates well into the normal development process. It structures the problem, makes variability explicit, and enforces consistency. As a side effect, it allows automated reasoning about annotations, for example, we can detect dead code or determine which features we need to select to include a certain code fragment.

4.2. Views

One of the key motivations of modularizing features is that developers can find all code of a feature in one spot and reason about it without being distracted by other concerns. Clearly, a scattered, preprocessor-based implementation does not support this kind of lookup and reasoning, but the core question of traceability ("what code belongs to this feature") can still be answered by tool support in the form of views.

A *view* shows an excerpt of the source code and hides distracting parts that are not relevant for the task at hand. Furthermore, a view can contain code fragments which are physically located in different places (in different parts of a file, in different files, in different directories, etc.). This way, a developer can focus on the code fragment shown in the view.

We propose two kinds of views, *views on a feature* and *views on a variant* [Kästner et al., 2008b], discuss different design decisions, and present an implementation in our prototype tool CIDE.

4.2.1. View on a feature

A view on a feature (also called realization view by Heidenreich et al. [2008a]) shows the source code of one or more features (and some necessary context) and hides everything else. That is, it hides all files and directories that do not contain any code of this feature, and, inside files, it hides all code fragments that do not belong to this feature. Such view is roughly equivalent to a modularized feature in compositional approaches (without explicit interfaces).

In Figure 4.2b, we show a view on feature EVAL of a preprocessor-based implementation of the expression problem in Figure 4.2a (slightly modified from Figure 3.11 with an additional library that provides functionality for all variants). The view contains all files that include code fragments of feature EVAL, that is, classes *Add* and *Pow* are included, but not class *MathLib* since it does not contain any feature code. Inside the included classes, the view hides unnecessary code fragments (marked with "*[...]*"), and leaves only some necessary context (printed italic and gray).

Selecting the necessary amount of context information is a difficult design decision. With no or too little context, we cannot understand the code fragments in isolation. In our example, a view, just on both *eval* functions would probably not be very helpful in understanding the feature's implementation. Therefore, we leave the container class and annotations that affect the feature code as context. As additional context information, we furthermore leave markers to indicate hidden code. When the context information is not sufficient, a user can expand the view (i.e., include additional features) or switch back to the entire source code. We present a possible algorithm to determine the context in Section 4.2.3.

Note that the provided context is similar to the overhead required by compositional approaches. In compositional approaches, interfaces, method signatures, or pointcuts provide the context to understand a code fragment and its relationship to the remaining source code. For example, an implementation of feature EVAL with Jak would contain the class name in the declaration *"refines class Add"*, an implementation with AspectJ would contain the class name as part of an inter-type declaration or pointcut (cf. Fig. 3.1, p. 20). If such context information is insufficient, also developers of compositional approaches have to look into other modules (in analogy to expanding the view).

All in all, a view on a feature emulates some form of modularity. A developer can quickly trace a feature from the feature model to its implementation summarized in a view. It is also possible to provide a view on multiple features in the same way. Finally, views provide a natural form of multi-dimensional separation of concerns: A code fragment that belongs to multiple features (e.g., evaluating a plus expression) is part of multiple views.

```
1  #ifdef ADD
2  class Add extends Expr {
3    Expr left, right;
4    Add(Expr l, Expr r)
5      {left=l; right=r;}
6  #ifdef EVAL
7    int eval() {
8      return left.eval() +
9        right.eval(); }
10 #endif
11 #ifdef PRINT
12   void print() {
13     left.print();
14     System.out.print("+");
15     right.print(); }
16 #endif
17 }
18 #endif
```

```
19 #ifdef POWER
20 class Pow extends Expr {
21   Expr base, exp;
22   Pow(Expr b, Expr e)
23     { base=b; exp=e; }
24 #ifdef EVAL
25   int eval() {
26     return MathLib.pow(
27       base.eval(),
28       right.eval()); }
29 #endif
30 #ifdef PRINT
31   void print() {
32     left.print();
33     System.out.print("^");
34     right.print(); }
35 #endif
36 }
37 #endif
```

```
38 class MathLib {
39   static int pow
40     (int b, int e)
41   {
42     if (e<=0)
43       return 1;
44     return b *
45       pow(b, e-1);
46   }
47   //...
48 }
```

(a) Original source code.

```
1  #ifdef ADD
2  class Add [...] {
3    [...]
4  #ifdef EVAL
5    int eval() {
6      return left.eval() +
7        right.eval(); }
8  #endif
9    [...]
10 }
11 #endif
```

```
12 #ifdef POWER
13 class Pow [...] {
14   [...]
15 #ifdef EVAL
16   int eval() {
17     return MathLib.pow(
18       base.eval(),
19       right.eval()); }
20 #endif
21   [...]
22 }
23 #endif
```

(b) View on the feature EVAL.

```
1  #ifdef ADD
2  class Add extends Expr {
3    Expr left, right;
4    Add(Expr l, Expr r)
5      {left=l; right=r;}
6  #ifdef EVAL
7    int eval() {
8      return left.eval() +
9        right.eval(); }
10 #endif
11   [...]
12 }
13 #endif
```

```
14 class MathLib {
15   static int pow
16     (int b, int e)
17   {
18     if (e<=0)
19       return 1;
20     return b *
21       pow(b, e-1);
22   }
23   //...
24 }
```

(c) View on a variant with features ADD and EVAL.

Figure 4.2.: *Views on a annotation-based implementation of the expression problem. Omission inside a file are marked with "[...]", additional context is printed in gray and italics.*

4.2.2. View on a variant

A view on a variant shows the code of a given feature selection. This view contains all code of selected features and hides code fragments from deselected features. It is roughly equivalent to a variant generated by executing the preprocessor.

In Figure 4.2c, we exemplify a view on a variant in which only features ADD and EVAL are selected. This view includes the class *Add*, but without its method *print* (since feature PRINT is not selected). It hides the class *Pow* entirely, because it is not included in the variant. Finally, the view contains the class *MathLib*, because it is not annotated and hence included in all variants. In this view, we can directly see how features ADD and EVAL are connected. For example, in this case, the fields *left* and *right* are used in EVAL but declared in feature ADD.

A view on a variant is similar to a view on multiple features, but there are three differences.

1. Code fragments without annotations are included in all views on a variant, but never in views on a feature (except partly as context information). We can consider such code without annotations as part of a feature BASE that is included in all variants (and thus in all views on a variant).

2. A code fragment in nested annotations, which belongs to multiple features, is included in a view on a feature if *any* of the annotated features is selected, but included in a view on a variant only if *all* annotated features are selected. The rational is that a view on a feature shows the entire code of a feature, independent of any other constraints that might be necessary to include the code, and a view on a variant shows all code of a variant, which might not include the entire code of a feature. For example, in Figure 4.2, the method *eval* in class *Pow* is included in the view on a feature but not in the view on a variant. A view on a variant does not necessarily show the entire source code belonging to a selected feature, but only fragments that are relevant for the given variant.

3. Additional context is not necessary in a view on a variant; the variant always contains all relevant code. We could even hide all annotations from the view, as done in *Version Editor* [Atkins et al., 2002]. Nevertheless, we leave annotations and provide markers for hidden code to assist developers to keep the entire software product line in mind.

In compositional approaches, an application composed of multiple modules is roughly equivalent to a view on a variant. Although some compositional approaches such as Jak allow inspecting the composed code (and even propagating changes back to the software product line), most do not provide a distinct composed representation of the source code. A view on a variant can show how multiple features interact in the same file much more directly. A view on a variant plays to its strength as preview and for detecting problems in a specific variant, for example problems due to feature interactions that occur only when certain feature combinations are selected.

4.2.3. Design decisions

So far, we illustrated the basic concepts of views. When implementing them, there are a number of design decisions. We discuss different design options and justify our decisions for our prototype implementation in CIDE.

Implementation level. Views can be implemented at different levels. First, we can implement views at editor level, for example, inside an integrated development environment. That is, while the full source code is stored on disk, we extend existing editors to hide files and hide code fragments from the developer. Second, we can devise a separate tool that creates views in a separate location and propagates changes back again. Finally, we can even implement view functionality transparently inside the file system, so that already the operating system hides files or file content.

In CIDE, we implemented views on editor level in Eclipse, because this provides more flexibility and is less invasive. Developers can quickly switch between views, and we can provide visual markers instead of textual ones. View implementations at tool level and at file-system level have the advantage that they are independent of an editor, but the process to switch between views can be more difficult, because we have to generate new files and refresh them in all editors.

Editable views. Even though read-only views are certainly helpful to explore features in a software product line, we argue that source code shown in views should be editable, so that users can directly modify or extend the code of a feature or a variant without having to go back to the original code. However, making modifications in a view (especially in views on a variant) can result in ambiguities. When a developer inserts some source code next to a hidden code fragment, it is unclear whether the new code should be inserted before, after, in between, or even instead of the hidden code.

Implementation of editable views have been discussed intensively in work on updatable database views [e.g., Bancilhon and Spyratos, 1981; Stonebraker et al., 1990; Bohannon et al., 2006] and model round-trip engineering [e.g., Foster et al., 2007; Giese and Wagner, 2009; Hettel et al., 2009]. For CIDE, we adopt a simpler but still effective solution: We insert markers for hidden code as already exemplified in Figure 4.2. Thus, insertions occur before, after, or replacing the marker so that changes can be unambiguously propagated to the original code. A tool tip can show additional information about hidden code in the front end. Furthermore, markers make developers aware of additional code, which they might need to consider for a local change (e.g., by going back to the original code or by expanding the view). The marker solution works at all implementation levels: We can either provide graphical markers in an editor or generate textual markers in a file.

Determining necessary context. There are different ways to determine the context of a view on a feature, and there is no single obvious solution. From the provided context, a developer must infer where the code fragment is located and how it interacts with the base code and other features. If the context is too small, it is not possible to understand a feature in isolation; if the context is too large, the benefit of a view that hides irrelevant code is lost.

We found that the structural position of a code fragment is essential. For each annotated code fragment, we want to see in which method and class it is located. This is the necessary equivalent to information provided in interfaces of compositional approaches.

To determine a context that shows the structural position, we use a simple algorithm that considers the underlying structure of the source code and shows parents but not siblings. For example, in Java, we can consider classes, methods, fields and statements in hierarchical form. Whenever a code fragment is shown in the view, all parent elements must be shown as context, but siblings can be hidden. Thus, if a method is annotated, the view shows the class declaration, but may hide other methods in the class; if a statement is annotated, the view shows parent statements, the parent method, and the parent class, but may hide other statements and other methods. Even from structures shown in the context, the view can hide some information, for example, a class' name is sufficient, the view can hide the superclass declaration as in Figure 4.2b.

This mechanism to determine the context can be adapted to other languages, or at other granularity (e.g., considering additionally packages, parameters, and expressions; considering only classes, fields, and methods). Technically, in CIDE, we use a model of the underlying language, which provides parent-child relationships between elements, for details see [Kästner et al., 2008b]. We present this underlying model and how it can be extended for different languages in the context of disciplined annotations in Chapter 5.

So far, we provide only this very simple mechanism to provide structural information as context. In our experience, this is sufficient to roughly understand how the annotated code fragments relate to the remaining code. The representation is roughly equivalent to a class refinement or partial class. Still, many extensions are possible and should be provided as options to the user. For example, we can show a fixed frame of n lines (or n structural elements) before or after feature code, similar to the Unix *grep* utility; or we can enable or disable hiding code fragments that are more fine-grained than an entire line of source code. To find the best balance between hidden code fragments and necessary context for a practical tool, more user experience is necessary. An empirical evaluation in a controlled experiment is planned as future work.

4.2.4. Implementation

In our prototype CIDE, we implemented both kinds of views – views on a feature and views on a variant – for the file browser and for editors of file content. In order to select which features should be included in a view, we added an additional dialog *Feature List* (of course, also other representations to select features from the feature model are possible, e.g., a feature diagram). For views on a variant, this dialog also provides immediate feedback whether the current feature selection constitutes a valid variant.

First, we extended Eclipse's existing *Project Explorer*, which represents the file structure of a project. When activating the view with an additional button, CIDE hides all files that do not contain any code of the selected features (view on a feature) or all files that contain only code of deselected features (view on a variant). The view can be changed on the fly by selecting other features. In the screenshot in Figure 4.3, we illustrate a view on the feature Transactions on the file structure of Berkeley DB; the transaction code is still heavily scattered, but easier to locate since irrelevant files and directories are hidden.

Second, we provide views as code-folding strategies in Eclipse's source-code editors. When activated, irrelevant code fragments (even fragments inside one line) are hidden in the editor, and only graphical markers remain as illustrated in Figure 4.2. This implementation at editor level has the advantage, that internally the editor can still reason about the entire code (e.g., for syntax highlighting or type checking), but only portions of the code are visible to the developer. Again, switching between different views is possible on the fly by selecting other features.

4.3. Visual representation

Next, we address the representation of annotations. As discussed in Section 3.2.2, there are several problems that lead to obfuscated and difficult to understand source code. First, annotations in form of textual preprocessor directives and constructs of the host language are intermixed in the same file. Second, many pre-processors are line-based, forcing developers to introduce additional line breaks that can destroy the code layout, especially when fine-grained extensions are involved. Third, long annotations are difficult to trace; finding out whether a local code fragment may be affected by one or more annotations that started hundreds of lines earlier is tedious and error-prone. Finally, nesting adds additional complexity and can make it difficult to find out in which variants a local code fragment

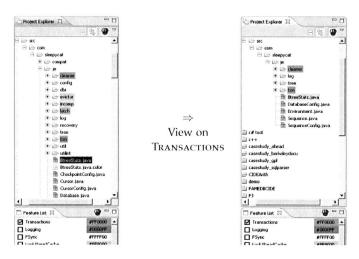

Figure 4.3.: *View on feature* Transactions *in the file structure of Berkeley DB [Kästner et al., 2008b]. The activated view on the right-hand side hides all files and directories that do not contain annotations of feature* Transactions.

is included.

There are many possible solutions that address one or more of these problems. A straightforward solution is to use textual annotations with a less verbose syntax that can be used within a single line (such as the preprocessor *Munge*) to avoid some obfuscation and unnecessary line breaks. Furthermore, visual enhancements to highlight preprocessor directives or annotated code can be used to make it easier to determine the scope of long, scattered annotations and easier to distinguish between the intermixed host language and annotations. For example, many C development environments display preprocessor directives in bold or colored font; the development environment NetBeans highlights annotated Java ME code fragments with a purple background color (independent of the feature to which the annotation belongs); for web development, which intermixes languages such as HTML, PHP, and CSS in a single file, several editors, such as *NuSphere PhpEd*,[1] can provide distinct visual representations (font styles or background colors) for each language.

We go one step further and visualize features in source code to enhance or even replace contemporary textual annotations. That is, we not only visualize that a code fragment is annotated, but we indicate also to which feature it belongs. This way, it should be possible to browse a long code fragment and quickly look for a

---

[1]http://www.nusphere.com

```
1   class Stack {
2     void push(Object o, Transaction txn) {
3       if (o==null || txn==null) return;
4       Lock l=txn.lock(o);
5       elementData[size++] = o;
6       l.unlock();
7       fireStackChanged();
8     }
9   }
```

Features: SYNCHRONIZATION

Figure 4.4.: *Annotations represented by a background color instead of textual annotations.*

visual representation of a feature. Since colors are processed preattentively,[2] the process should be faster than looking for textual annotations.

In the following, we first describe our initial solution in CIDE in Section 4.3.1, subsequently discuss limitations regarding scalability in Section 4.3.2, and finally present an empirical evaluation in Section 4.4.

4.3.1. Background colors

In CIDE, we abandon textual annotations and instead use background colors to represent annotations, one color per feature [Kästner et al., 2008a]. In contrast to font styles or foreground colors, background colors are not yet reserved in most source-code editors. To annotate a code fragment, a developer selects the code fragment in the editor and assigns a feature from a context menu. The code fragment is then shown with the background color of the according feature. In Figure 4.4, all code belonging to feature SYNCHRONIZATION is highlighted with a pale red background color. Technically, source code with existing textual preprocessor directives can be parsed and represented with colors in the editor, or annotations can be stored separately without modifying the underlying source code.

The use of background colors mimics our initial steps to mark features on printouts with colored text markers. When feature-refactoring Berkeley DB (cf. Sec. 3.1.7), we discussed different implementation patterns for difficult fine-grained extensions. To get an overview of the involved code fragments and their relationships, we marked all code that should be refactored into a feature module (an AspectJ aspect in that case) with a colored text marker on source-code printouts. When multiple features were involved, we used multiple colors, one color per feature. Colored text markers were a natural choice, we felt that textual modifications would have been distracting. We realized that instead of removing all

---

[2]Preattentive processing is an automatic and rapid stage of processing prior to processing with focused attention. At this early stage, humans can recognize a limited set of visual properties (e.g., line orientation, size, number, color) [Goldstein, 2002].

marked code and introducing it again using a feature module, we could simply interpret colors as conditional-compilation instructions, which could, for example, remove all red code. With CIDE, we implemented this color metaphor in an annotation-based product-line tool.

Especially for fine-grained extensions that require multiple additional and unnatural line breaks with contemporary preprocessors, annotations on the representation layer are more compact and easier to understand, in our experience. We do not intermix host language with annotation language, but separate annotations into the representation layer; the implementation in the host language remains unchanged. In Figure 4.4, we show the fine-grained extension from Figure 3.2 (p. 23), in which feature SYNCHRONIZATION is represented by a background color. This representation is shorter and more direct than the equivalent modular implementation in Figure 3.3 (p. 25) or the annotation-based implementation with *cpp* in Figure 3.8 (p. 37). At the other end of the spectrum, colors also scale for very coarse-grained annotations on entire files or directories. As shown earlier in Figure 4.3, we can represent annotations on entire files or directories with background colors in the resource navigator.

Annotations for different features are represented by different colors. A mapping is maintained by the tool infrastructure. For each code fragment, it is apparent to which feature it belongs, there is no need to search for the beginning or end of potentially very long annotations. Furthermore, it should be simple to find all code fragments in a file that belong to a specific feature, just by browsing the file. As explained above, colors are processed preattentively, that is, they are quicker to recognize and distinguish than textual annotations [Goldstein, 2002]. Since, according to Kersten and Murphy [2005], "programmers tend to spend more time navigating the code than working with it", a quicker recognition of features could significantly improve the speed of program comprehension.

Nevertheless, representing nested annotations poses a special challenge. Representing just the inner annotation is not an adequate representation, because developers would again have to search for possible outer annotations. In CIDE, we implemented two different solutions, and many other remain open to explore.

- In our first implementation, we naively *blend colors* of the involved features, for example code that is annotated by a red and a yellow feature is represented by orange, as illustrated in Figure 4.5a for an excerpt of the expression problem from Figure 3.11 (p. 42).[3] By blending colors, we add more colors that a user has to distinguish, which can make it difficult to scale this color scheme.

- Kim et al. [2008] extended CIDE to display only the innermost color, but add

---

[3]In this example, we blend yellow and red to orange and yellow and blue to green. Since colors are difficult to distinguish on some printouts, we provide a textual description of the colors in comments.

```
 1 class Add extends Expr { //yellow
 2    Expr left, right;
 3    Add(Expr l, Expr r)
 4       { left=l; right=r; }
 5    double eval() { //orange
 6       return left.eval() +
 7          right.eval();
 8    }
 9    void print() { //green
10       left.print();
11       System.out.print("+");
12       right.print();
13    }
14 }
```

(a) Blending colors.

```
 1 class Add extends Expr { //yellow
 2    Expr left, right;
 3    Add(Expr l, Expr r)
 4       { left=l; right=r; }
 5    double eval() { //red
 6       return left.eval() +
 7          right.eval();
 8    }
 9    void print() { //blue
10       left.print();
11       System.out.print("+");
12       right.print();
13    }
14 }
```

(b) Framing nested colors.

Features: ADD, EVAL, PRINT

Figure 4.5.: *Representing nested annotations with background colors.*

a left frame for each outer color as illustrated in Figure 4.5b. This way, they avoid blending colors, but some corner cases are more difficult to represent; for example, we would need some additional mechanisms such as colored borders to represent two congruent annotations on the same code fragment.

- Similarly, Coppit et al. [2007] use colored vertical bars to indicate concerns in the margin next to the editor in their tool *Spotlight*. Nested annotations are represented with multiple bars next to each other. Bars are more subtle and elegant, as long as annotations are separated into distinct lines of source code.

With the representation using background colors, we solve the problems outlined above. We no longer intermix host language with textual annotations; we do not require additional line breaks, even for long and nested annotations; and we see for every local code fragment to which feature(s) it belongs without searching for #*ifdef* and matching #*endif* directives.

4.3.2. Scalability of colors

Colors are a straightforward choice to represent additional information in a program, however there are limitations. Although humans can distinguish about two million colors in direct comparison [Goldstein, 2002], they can distinguish only few colors clearly in preattentive perception [Najjar, 1990; Rice, 1991]. Furthermore, there are differences in color perception between humans and color-deficient vision is not uncommon. Therefore, it is unrealistic to map 100 features of a medium-size software product line to 100 different colors and expect developers to distinguish them while browsing the source code.

Fortunately, a one-to-one mapping between features and colors is not necessary. In CIDE, we use a default of only 12 repeating colors,[4] which the user can change. That is, multiple features are represented by the same color; it is not possible to distinguish annotations only by color. Additionally, different developers may select different colors for the same feature. In CIDE, we offer a tool tip on annotated code that names the feature.

Despite repeating colors, the color metaphor is useful for a number of reasons:

- In our experience, there are rarely more than two or three features involved on a single page of source code (on a screen in the editor or on a printed page). Such low number of features can be distinguished clearly (more on this later).

- Even though multiple features are assigned to the same color, we never experienced annotations of two features with the same color in a single file in our case studies. When such clash occurs, the editor can detect it so that the developer can change one of the colors.

- In a large software product line, a developer would not learn all colors for all features anyway. Typically, a developer focuses on one or few features at a time (e.g., searching for all transaction code or debugging a problem regarding statistics about recovery). During the process, the developer learns (or assigns) the colors of the involved features, but looks up other colors when needed. Nevertheless, it is still possible to browse through a file and search for a single color.

- Except for the features the developer currently works on, colors serve merely as an indicator that a code fragment is annotated and where an annotation begins and ends. The concrete annotation can be looked up quickly or is often even apparent from the annotated code. For this reason, also naively blended colors for nested annotations as in Figure 4.5a work, even though colors often blend to some grayish/brownish tone.

The first argument – rarely more than three features are involved on a single page of source code – is the most important one, because it means that in most cases a low number of colors is sufficient. We therefore investigated this issue empirically.

---

[4]We selected bright and distinguishable colors in an ad-hoc fashion: yellow, orange, red, three shades of green, two shades of blue, purple, pink, brown, and gray. This selection was sufficient for our needs; optimizing a color selection and amount regarding human perception (e.g., optimizing hue distance, saturation and brightness levels) is an interesting task but outside the scope of this thesis.

Analysis: Annotations per page. To determine how many annotations of different features affect a typical page of source code, we analyzed four of our case studies with more than 10 features implemented as software product line with CIDE. MobileMedia (with 14 features) and the Graph Product Line (with 18 features) were developed by others as software product line from scratch; the Functional Graph Library (with 18 features) and Berkeley DB (with 42 features) were decomposed from an existing legacy application; for more details on these case studies, see Appendix A.1. Unfortunately, there are not many publicly available implementations of software product lines; therefore, we additionally analyzed the preprocessor usage in 40 open source C programs from different domains with different sizes, selected for a related study on preprocessor usage by Liebig et al. [2010]. For a description of the C programs including domain, version, lines of code, and number of features, see Appendix A.2. In contrast to our four case studies, the C programs usually were not developed as software product line. Still, according to Ernst et al. [2002], conditional compilation with the C preprocessor is often used in an ad-hoc fashion for variability in terms of features and portability in practice (other frequent uses of annotations are comments, avoiding redefinitions and preventing multiple inclusion). Already Liebig's study shows that annotations are used intensively in the selected C programs ($23 \pm 17\%$ of the source code is annotated; see Appendix A.2 for details). In addition to Liebig's study, we analyze how these annotations are distributed over *pages of source code*.

As a page of source code, we conservatively consider 50 consecutive lines in a file. That is the number on lines that fit on a single full-size editor in the default installation of Eclipse on a SXGA screen (1280×1024). We furthermore assume that we navigate by skipping half a page at a time. For example, a file with 78 lines will be divided into the pages 1–50, 26–75, and 51–78. For each page, we count how many annotations are shown on this page, including annotations that begin prior to the page and end after the page. Multiple annotations to the same feature (or feature combination) are only counted once, because they are represented by the same color. Nested annotations are counted separately, corresponding to the number of colors needed for a visualization that does not blend colors as in Figure 4.5b. Due to the size, we automated the analysis with an extension of Liebig's analysis tools. For comparability, we furthermore prepared the C programs by pretty printing, removing comments and empty lines, and removing inclusion guards (which are not a variability mechanism).[5]

---

[5]There are two technical issues that can cause our analysis tools to measure slightly more annotations per page than there actually are. First, to determine whether two *cpp* annotations refer to the same feature expression, we use a string comparison and simple heuristics. This detects most cases, but, for example, two annotations $A \wedge B$ and $B \wedge A$ can be considered equivalent but are recognized as separate annotations. Second, due to technical limitations of our analysis infrastructure, we only analyze the first 65 536 lines of each file. This excluded several pages from one file in *gcc* and from four files in *opensolaris*. We manually found that the ignored pages contain

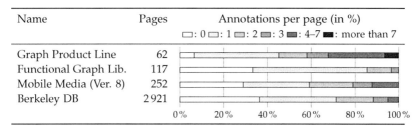

Name	Pages	Annotations per page (in %)
		□: 0 ▭: 1 ▦: 2 ▩: 3 ▨: 4–7 ■: more than 7
Graph Product Line	62	
Functional Graph Lib.	117	
Mobile Media (Ver. 8)	252	
Berkeley DB	2 921	

Table 4.1.: *Annotations per page in four Java ME product lines.*

As shown in Tables 4.1 and 4.2, already three colors are sufficient on most pages. In all case studies developed as software product line from scratch or by decomposing legacy applications, annotations occur in over 60 % of all pages, but more than three different annotations on the same page are rare. A page with more than seven annotations occured only in GPL (4 pages) and Berkeley DB (2 pages). In the analyzed C programs, most pages (67 %) do not contain a single annotation. Futhermore, 96 % of all pages can be represented with three colors; only 1.2 % of all pages would need more than seven colors. Nevertheless, in every C program, there is at least one page (typically in a header file) that contains more than seven annotations (up to 41 in *freebsd* and *gcc*). For these pages the color metaphor does not scale; instead, developers have to switch back to textual annotations. Still, for the far majority of annotations, few repeating colors are sufficient.

There are several threats to the external validity of our analysis, because publicly available source code of commercial-size software product lines are rare. We have only a small number of software product lines that were developed from scratch, and those have relatively few features. The C programs are larger and contain far more annotations, but have not been developed as software product line. They contain a significant amount of annotated code, but not all annotations refer to features in the sense of a software product line. Nevertheless, the analysis provides an overall impression that in fact few colors are sufficient to represent all features on – not all, but most – pages of source code. Some pages contain annotations for many different features, for those, the user should be able to switch back to textual annotations.

4.4. Experimental evaluation

Feature-model integration, views and visual representation, all aim at improving program comprehension of a software product line. The feature model modular-

---

mostly no or one annotation per page. For the overall results, we argue that these deviations are negligible.

Name	Pages	Annotations per page (in %)
		□: 0 ▭: 1 ▨: 2 ▩: 3 ▦: 4–7 ■: more than 7
apache	8 313	
berkeley db	7 267	
cherookee	1 989	
clamav	2 977	
dia	5 027	
emacs	9 448	
freebsd	231 674	
gcc	59 687	
ghostscript	17 291	
gimp	23 013	
glibc	30 944	
gnumeric	10 021	
gnuplot	2 986	
irssi	1 934	
libxml2	8 368	
lighttpd	1 515	
linux	233 534	
lynx	4 641	
minix	2 488	
mplayer	23 642	
mpsolve	392	
openldap	9 574	
opensolaris	336 061	
openvpn	1 358	
parrot	3 839	
php	22 623	
pidgin	10 510	
postgresql	17 674	
privoxy	933	
python	14 750	
sendmail	3 286	
sqlite	3 707	
subversion	20 164	
sylpheed	3 978	
tcl	5 314	
vim	8 968	
xfig	2 896	
xine-lib	19 392	
xorg-server	20 666	
xterm	1 964	

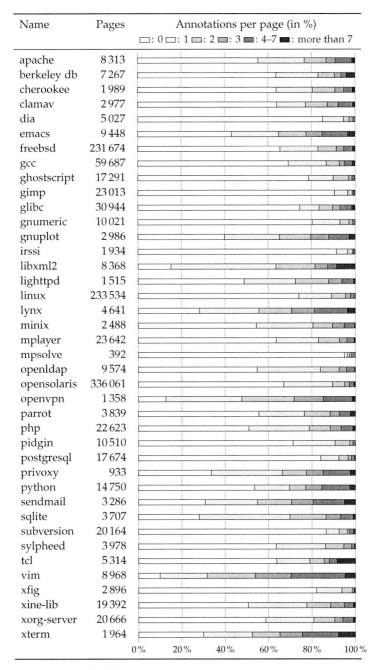

0 %   20 %   40 %   60 %   80 %   100 %

Table 4.2.: *Annotations per page in forty C programs.*

65

izes and documents configuration knowledge, so that features and their dependencies are easier to understand. Views emulate modularity, so that developers can directly trace a feature to its implementation. Visual representations decrease code obfuscation often associated with preprocessors. We provided an overview of possible mechanisms and design decisions to discuss a big picture of possible improvements of program comprehension. However, program comprehension is an internal cognitive process [Koenemann and Robertson, 1991]; hence, a thorough evaluation requires empirical evidence.

We implemented all improvements – feature-model integration, views, and visual representation – in our prototype product-line tool CIDE and conducted a series of case studies (cf. Appendix A.1). Our experience from case studies provides some first indication that the proposed mechanisms are feasible. Nevertheless, case studies are not sufficient to demonstrate soundly that they improve program comprehension compared to contemporary preprocessors (or even compared to modular implementations). Therefore, we approach an experimental evaluation.

Unfortunately, we cannot evaluate feature-model integration, views, and visual representation in their entirety. There are so many design decisions (editor level or tool level; editable views with markers or other mechanisms; how much context; which colors; blending colors versus frames versus colored lines; and many more), each of which would require experimental evaluation on their own. For example, just determining empirically the visual representation that supports program comprehension most would be a major research project. In the scope of this thesis, we can only take a first step. We evaluate only a single fundamental facet in a controlled experiment [Feigenspan et al., 2010]:[6]

Can colors improve program comprehension over textual preprocessors?

We focus on the visual representation with background colors because it is a significant change compared to traditional textual preprocessors. In contrast to views, especially views on a variant, which have already been evaluated to some degree in a different context (Atkins et al. [2002] measured that views on variants increase developer productivity by 40 %; see related work in Sec. 4.5), we are not aware of any empirical study on the influence of background colors on program comprehension. In demonstrations of CIDE colors were also the most controversial part of CIDE. Also in other contexts, colors have caused controversy; for example, the color coding in *Mylyn* was eventually dropped after it received mixed feedback and was perceived as visually loud by some [Kersten and Murphy, 2005]; Najjar [1990] remarks "A computer display that is lit up like a Christmas tree distracts users from their tasks and makes users feel like they are not being taken seriously." With our evaluation, we want to determine whether background colors are feasible at all and how they are perceived by users.

---

[6]The experiment was conducted by Janet Feigenspan as part of her Master's Thesis (Diplomarbeit) [Feigenspan, 2009] supervised in the context of this PhD project.

Specifically, we compare textual annotations in the style of the C preprocessor *cpp* with a graphical representation using only background colors, as implemented in our prototype CIDE. Here, we describe only the main design decisions and results of the experiment for brevity. For all information necessary to replicate the experiment, see [Feigenspan et al., 2010].

4.4.1. Experiment planning

Goal. The goal of the experiment is to assess the effect of colors on program comprehension, compared to textual annotations. To measure program comprehension – an internal cognitive process – there are several different methods available [see discussion in Feigenspan, 2009; Dunsmore and Roper, 2000]. We measure the correctness and response time for tasks that require an understanding of the program. Specifically, we use static tasks to examine the structure and maintenance tasks to fix a bug.

Static tasks represent the typical process of getting an overview of the source code or finding feature code, without examining its specific statements. Both representations, colors and textual annotations, carry the same information; hence, we expect no difference in correctness. Nevertheless, we expect that colors reduce the response time of static tasks, because colors are processed preattentively and thus considerably faster than text [Goldstein, 2002].

In contrast, *maintenance tasks* require a deeper understanding of the source code. For maintenance tasks, developers have to investigate the source code carefully. We expect that the benefit of colors on correctness or response time is negligible. After locating the code, developers focus mainly on the source code.

Additionally, we assessed the *opinion of subjects*: For each tasks, we ask subjects that worked with colors to estimate how they would have performed with textual annotations and vice versa. This way, we can detect concerns for adoption or a possible mismatch between perceived performance and actual performance (which can often be observed with new technology; for example, in a study by Henry et al. [1990] subjects performed better when introducing object-oriented programming, but perceived a reduced performance).

In summary, we state our expectations in four hypotheses that we evaluate in the experiment:

1. Colors as annotation increase response time in static tasks, compared to textual annotations.

2. There is no difference in response time between colors and textual annotation for maintenance tasks.

3. There is no difference in the number of correctly solved tasks between colors and textual annotations, neither for static nor for maintenance tasks.

4. For all tasks, subjects estimate a better performance with colors.

Subjects. As subjects, we recruited 43 students from the University of Passau that are enrolled in a lecture on product-line implementation.[7] Students of this course were already familiar with software product lines and their implementation. In one assignment, they have already implemented variability in a small program with the preprocessor *Munge*. Thus, the recruited students already had sufficient background knowledge so that we could minimize training for the experiment.

We split our sample into two groups: the first group (21 students) worked with textual annotations, the second group (22 students) worked with annotations represented by background colors. Subjects of both groups were matched by programming experience (measured with a preliminary questionnaire), gender, and age; one subject with color-deficient vision was assigned to the textual-annotation group; for details see [Feigenspan et al., 2010; Feigenspan, 2009].

Experimental material. For our tasks, we selected *MobileMedia*, a medium-sized software product line to manage multi-media data on mobile phones (see also Appendix A.1). It was developed from scratch as a software product line at the University of Lancaster for a study on design stability [Figueiredo et al., 2008]. MobileMedia is implemented with Java ME and the textual preprocessor *Antenna*; the implementation is code reviewed and published as open source. From the development history of MobileMedia, we use the fifth release with about 4000 lines of code in 28 classes and four optional features SMS, CopyPhoto, Favorites, and CountView.[8] This release is sufficiently complex, but not too large to be understood in a 2-hour experiment.

From the original implementation with textual annotations, we derived a second equivalent version that uses background colors instead of #*ifdef* and #*endif* directives. In Figure 4.6, we show a direct comparison. As colors, we selected bright and clearly distinguishable colors from CIDE: red for SMS, blue for CopyPhoto, yellow for Favorites, and orange for CountView; shared code between SMS and CopyPhoto is represented with violet (blend of red and blue). To minimize the effect of confounding parameters, we did not provide a version that mixes textual annotations and colors. We present the annotated code as HTML files to the sub-

---

[7]The German lecture "Moderne Programmierparadigmen" in Passau and their counterpart "Erweiterte Programmierkonzepte für maßgeschneiderte Datenhaltung" in Magdeburg are a joint project of Sven Apel, Christian Kästner, and Gunter Saake. Since 2007, we annually teach different product-line implementation techniques, including preprocessors, frameworks, feature-oriented programming, and aspect-oriented programming. Slides are available online: `http://wwwiti.cs.uni-magdeburg.de/iti_db/lehre/epmd/`

[8]To simplify the source code, we removed ten exception classes and two features for different screen resolutions from the original implementation.

```
21 public class PhotoListScreen extends List (
22
23    //add the core application commands always
24    public static final Command viewCommand = new
25    public static final Command addCommand = new C
26    public static final Command deleteCommand = ne
27    public static final Command backCommand = new
28
29    public static final Command editLabelCommand =
30
31    // #ifdef includeCountViews
32    public static final Command sortCommand = new
33    // #endif
34
35    // #ifdef includeFavourites
36    public static final Command favoriteCommand = 
37    public static final Command viewFavoritesComma
38    // #endif
39
40    /**
41     * Constructor
```

```
21 public class PhotoListScreen extends List (
22
23    //add the core application commands always
24    public static final Command viewCommand = new
25    public static final Command addCommand = new C
26    public static final Command deleteCommand = ne
27    public static final Command backCommand = new
28
29    public static final Command editLabelCommand =
30
31    public static final Command sortCommand = new
32
33    public static final Command favoriteCommand =
34    public static final Command viewFavoritesComma
35
36    /**
37     * Constructor
38     */
39    public PhotoListScreen() (
40       super("Choose Items", Choice.IMPLICIT);
41    )
```

Figure 4.6.: *Comparison of textual #ifdef directives and background colors as annotation (in the colored version Line 31 is annotated with orange background color, Lines 33 and 34 with yellow) [Feigenspan et al., 2010].*

jects, to exclude the influence of tool support such as code folding, type hierarchy, or outline view.

Tasks.   We assessed program comprehension with two static tasks (S1, S2) and four maintenance tasks (M1–M4):

- S1: First, subjects should determine which classes each feature affects. This represents the typical task to find all code of a feature.

- S2: Second, subjects should find all code fragments that are affected by more than one feature (shared code or glue code, cf. Sec. 3.1.5). Shared and over-lapping features are of special interest in the implementation of product lines, since they can represent feature interactions that are especially diffi-cult to maintain [Calder et al., 2003; Liu et al., 2006]. Searching such code is therefore a typical task for a developer.

- M1–M4: For the four maintenance tasks, we each introduced a defect into the code and provide a defect description. Each defect is located in the code of a single feature, and the defect description specifies this feature. For example, the description of M1 was *"If pictures in an album should be sorted by views, they are displayed unsorted anyway. Feature, in which the bug occurs:* COUNTVIEWS.*"* We checked that the defects were neither too difficult nor too easy to find in a pre-test and ordered the tasks by difficulty, M1 being the easiest.

See [Feigenspan et al., 2010] for a comprehensive list of all tasks.

Design.   We grouped the subjects into two groups. One group solved all tasks on the source code with textual annotations, the other group used the source code in which annotations were represented as background colors. Answers and times were collected with a web-based survey system.

In order to *reliably* measure the effect of different annotations (independent variable) on program comprehension (dependent variable), Feigenspan [2009] identified a series of confounding parameters and considered them in the experimental design. Among others, programming experience, domain knowledge, intelligence, education, gender, position effect, Hawthorne effect, tool support, programming language, coding conventions, difficulty, and many more were controlled in the experiment, as explained in detail in [Feigenspan, 2009].

4.4.2. Results

We show the distribution of response times in our experiment in a box plot[9] in Figure 4.7. For both static tasks, subjects in the color group were *significantly faster* than the group working with textual annotations (7 instead of 12 minutes and 5 instead of 6 minutes), which confirms our first hypothesis. For the maintenance tasks M1, M2, and M3, the differences in response time are *not statistically significant*; however, for M4, subjects in the color group were *significantly slower* (23 instead of 17 minutes). Therefore, we have to reject our second hypothesis and assume that colors do in fact have an influence on response time in some maintenance tasks.

In Figure 4.8, we show the results regarding the correctness of solutions. For example, in task M1 was solved correctly by 19 out of 21 subjects of ifdef group and by 21 out of 22 subjects of the color group. There are some differences, between the two groups, but the differences are *not statistically significant*. This result confirms our third hypothesis: The kind of annotation has no influence on the correctness of solutions.

Finally, in Figure 4.9, we show the subject's estimates of the performance with the other representation. Regarding static tasks, subjects of the color group estimated that they would have performed worse with textual annotations, and vice versa. For the maintenance tasks, subjects of the color group still estimated that they would perform worse with textual annotations (in contrast to the actual performance, which was the same or better), whereas subjects of the ifdef group responded with mixed estimates. Overall, there is a *statistically significant* difference in performance estimation in favor for colors for all tasks, which confirms our last hypothesis.

To test statistical significance (with a standard 5 % significance level), Feigenspan [2009] conducted a Mann-Whitney-U test for response times and the subjects' estimations, and a χ^2 test for correctness [for both tests, see Anderson and Finn,

---

[9]A box plot is a diagram to depict groups of numerical data and their dispersion. It plots the median as thick line and the quartiles as thin line, so that 50 % of all measurements are inside the box. Values that strongly deviate from the median are outliers and drawn as separate dots.

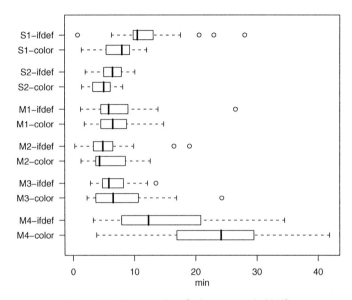

Figure 4.7.: *Response times [Feigenspan et al., 2010].*

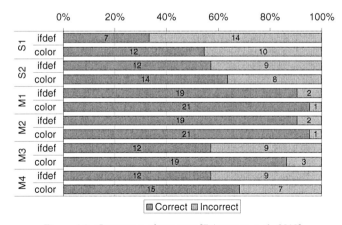

Figure 4.8.: *Correctness of responses [Feigenspan et al., 2010].*

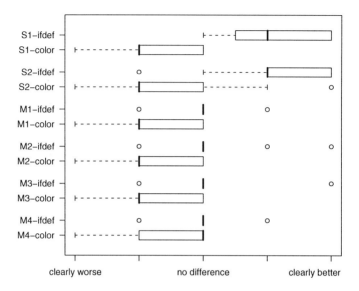

Figure 4.9.: *Subject's performance estimation with other version [Feigenspan et al., 2010].*

1996]. For detailed information on this choice and on the concrete test results, see [Feigenspan, 2009].

4.4.3. Interpretation

Our experiment confirms that colors instead of textual annotations speed up program comprehension in static tasks significantly (by 43 % and 23 % in our experiment), which we explain with the preattentive perception of colors. We suspect that the benefit in the second task is smaller because the subjects were already familiar with the source code and because they had to pay closer attention to the colors to detect blended colors. There is no significant difference in the correctness of answers though, both representations convey the same information; colors are only faster to recognize. We conclude that colors in general can help a programmer to understand a program when performing static tasks.

Regarding maintenance tasks, there was no significant difference for the first three tasks, which is in line with our expectation. Reading source code is the main focus when finding a defect in these tasks. In contrast to the time required for reading source code, the time for locating the according feature code is marginal. However, contrary to our expectations, subjects of the color group were significantly slower (-37%) performing the last and most difficult task M4.

A closer look at the source code reveals a possible explanation. The entire class, in which the defect was located, was annotated with feature SMS, so the entire file was represented with a bright, saturated red background color. That is, the subjects had to carefully read and understand a rather long code fragment with red background color. In contrast, the locations of the first three maintenance tasks were annotated with lighter colors: orange and yellow. We suspect that the saturated red background color was distracting and made it difficult to read the source code or might have even caused visual fatigue. That explanation is also supported by some comments, which the subjects were encouraged to enter at the end of the experiment.

Nevertheless, almost all subjects that worked with textual annotations estimated that they would have performed better with the color version. In the subjects' comments, we found that some subjects of the color group expressed that they were happy to get to work with it, whereas some subjects that worked with textual annotations wished they had worked with the color version. We assume that from the tedious static tasks, subjects developed a strong preference toward colors, which reflected in their performance estimation, even for tasks in which colors actually did not increase or even decreased performance. We interpret the results as indication that our subjects liked the color idea in general.

Overall, we conclude that subjects mostly prefer colors to textual annotations and that colors can significantly improve response time for static tasks. However, background colors can affect program comprehension also negatively. Instead of an ad-hoc mechanism to pick colors, we should carefully select the default colors, which remains an important task for future work. In our prototype CIDE, developers can adjust all colors, in contrast to our experiment, in which they were fixed. Additionally, it can be beneficial to allow developers to fade colors or switch between colors and textual annotations on the fly or optionally combine both representations. In ongoing work, we test our assumptions and evaluate different combinations in a follow up experiment.

Threats to validity. During the execution of the experiment, there were some minor deviations (subjects that were late, second room, missing question in final survey) as described in [Feigenspan et al., 2010], which might threaten internal validity, but we expect that the size of our sample is large enough to compensate for those deviations. Furthermore, we might have unintentionally shown our expectations to the subjects and influenced their performance (known as Rosenthal effect [Rosenthal and Jacobson, 1966]). Nevertheless, we intended to avoid this problem by keeping the introduction as neutral as possible and communication during the experiment to a minimum.

In our experiment, we have maximized our internal validity in order to feasibly and soundly measure the effect of different annotations on program comprehension. Thus, we have intentionally neglected external validity (i.e., ability to generalize our results to other subjects and settings). For example, we used students as subjects instead of professional developers, focused only on a single domain unknown to the subjects, had only few features, and specifically excluded tool support. Therefore, our results are only applicable to the setting of our experiment, but not necessarily to industrial practice with larger software product lines, more experienced developers, or other languages. To generalize our results, further studies are necessary. Especially, whether and how colors as annotations scale when hundreds of features are involved will be an interesting research topic. Nevertheless, since we could not build on prior experiments on program comprehension of product-line implementations, the narrow scope was a necessary first step to develop a sound base for future experiments.

4.5. Related work

There are several related proposals to improve preprocessors or to provide views or specific visual representations. We structure our discussion according to the structure of this chapter.

Integrating the feature model

Integrating a feature model into the implementation of a software product line is a well-known idea in product-line research. Although feature models were original designed for domain analysis [Kang et al., 1990] (see also Section 2.3), and not for implementations, *generative programming* made it popular to centralize all configuration knowledge and implement it in a generator [Czarnecki and Eisenecker, 2000, Ch. 5]. In generative programming, there is some mapping from features in the domain model to implementation artifacts, for example, to modularized feature implementations such as components, feature modules, or aspects. For a specific feature selection, the according artifacts are assembled. Generative programming describes an open framework; it is open for different domain modeling techniques, different ways to express configuration knowledge, and different implementation techniques.

Among others, the commercial product-line–development tool *pure::variants* follows this concept [Beuche et al., 2004]. A feature model is used to describe the domain, a second model, called family model, describes the mapping to implementation artifacts. For example, the family model describes which files to include when certain feature combinations are selected. Similar separations into domain model and implementation model with a mapping between the two are common in product-line research and product-line tools [e.g., Krueger, 2002; Metzger et al., 2007; Rabiser et al., 2007]

Feature-oriented software development goes yet a step further and established a one-to-one mapping between features and implementation artifacts [Prehofer, 1997; Batory et al., 2004; Apel and Kästner, 2009]. The concept of a feature from domain analysis is used directly at the implementation level, all configuration knowledge is stored in the feature model, and there is no additional mapping.

All these solutions can be applied straightforwardly to annotative approaches as well. In this case, features are not mapped to modularized implementation units, but to preprocessor flags. Depending on a feature selection, different preprocessor flags are defined for the preprocessor invocation. Both, a complex mapping, as in generative programming, or a direct one-to-one mapping, as in feature-oriented software development, are possible. Also our prototype CIDE supports both: By default, each annotation is mapped to exactly one feature in the feature model; with a *pure::variants* plug-in each annotation is mapped to a (possibly complex) rule over features in the family model.

However, in practice, especially for ad-hoc variability implemented with annotations, configuration knowledge is rarely documented in a feature model, in our experience. For example, HP's Owen product line is implemented with *cpp* and contains annotations to over 2000 different flags, none of which was documented in a feature model until recently [Pearse and Oman, 1997; Refstrup, 2009]. Even if a feature model and mapping to preprocessor flags exist, as in the Linux kernel, only some preprocessor flags are controlled by the feature model (or its mapping), others are still scattered in the source code. In such setting, reasoning about annotations becomes very difficult and requires techniques such as symbolic execution [Hu et al., 2000; Latendresse, 2004] or additional visualizations [Pearse and Oman, 1997; Vidács and Beszédes, 2003]. In contrast, CIDE enforces that actually all configuration knowledge is stored in the feature model or in the mapping, there is no equivalent to scattered *#define* directives. We are only aware of two other annotation-based product-line tools that enforce a mapping this strictly: *fmp2rsm* [Czarnecki and Antkiewicz, 2005] and *FeatureMapper* [Heidenreich et al., 2008b]. Both map features to elements of (UML) models. In both cases, as in CIDE, the mapping is maintained by the tool, and only mappings based on expressions over features defined in a feature model are possible.

Views on annotations-based product-line implementations

Views on selected parts of the source code have been explored in different contexts. While views on a feature are rare, several solutions exist to create *views on a variant*, especially for *cpp*-based implementations. Many source code editors, such as Emacs, Vim, Visual Studio, and Eclipse CDT, already support folding of *#ifdef* annotations. That is, a developer can manually fold or unfold each annotation. In Emacs' hide-ifdef-mode, there is even support to fold or unfold all annotations of one feature at the same time. However, in all these editors, there is no connection to a feature model, and folding has to be done per file. There is no means to create a view on an entire project.

The command line tools *unifdef*[10] and *sunifdef*[11] can partially evaluate *cpp* annotations. Given a partial feature selection (a list of selected and a list of deselected features), they evaluate annotations as far as possible and remove annotated code fragments that are excluded by the partial selection and remove annotations of code fragments that are always included by the partial selection. Annotations that cannot be included or excluded based only on the partial feature selection are left in the source code. Although these tools have been designed to clean source code from annotations no longer needed (e.g., to remove a feature), they can also be used to generate views on a variant at tool level (instead of editor level). However, they provide no means to propagate changes back to the original code.

Closest to our proposal are the views on a variant on *cpp*-based implementations with *CViMe* and *C-CLR* by Singh et al. [2006, 2007]. The authors describe the tools only vaguely, but the general idea is to recognize all preprocessor flags and create views for a configuration. They do not consider dependencies between preprocessor flags or a full feature model. As in CIDE, they use code folding in an editor to create a view on a variant, but there is no indicator of hidden code.

The *Version Editor* [Atkins, 1998; Atkins et al., 2002] provides an editable view on a variant for a proprietary textual preprocessor. Changes in the view are propagated back: Added code fragments are annotated to be included only in the selected variant, removed code fragments are annotated such that they are excluded from the selected variant. In an empirical evaluation, Atkins et al. [2002] found that views increase developer productivity by 40 % compared to standard editors without views. The main difference to views on a variant in CIDE is that annotations are not shown in the view, thus developers using the Version Editor might not even be aware that they edit a variant of a software product line instead of a standalone program. As a consequence, all information on features is lost in views. Instead of mapping code fragments to features, code added in a view is mapped to a variant. We argue that annotations provide useful context to developers. Even when working on a view on a variant, the developer is aware of the software product line and can decide whether a change (e.g., a bug fix) should affect only the selected variant or also other variants in the software product line. Therefore, we explicitly show annotations in our views as well.

In parallel to our work, Heidenreich et al. [2008a] discussed several views on annotated (UML) models and implemented them in their tool *FeatureMapper*. For a view on a variant, FeatureMapper draws all model elements that are not part of the variant in gray. Additionally, *FeatureMapper* is the only annotation-based product-line tool we are aware of that provides a *view on a feature*. A view on a

---

[10]`http://freshmeat.net/projects/unifdef/`
[11]`http://www.sunifdef.strudl.org/`; short for "son of unifdef"

feature (called "realization view") draws all elements that do not belong to the selected feature in gray. That is, the view still shows the entire model, but focuses the attention with visual means. Since elements are not hidden but only faded out, "the context of interaction between the feature realisation and the rest of the system is preserved" [Heidenreich et al., 2008a].

Other views

For compositional approaches, *pure::variants* [Beuche et al., 2004], a commercial product-line tool, can provide views on variants. The tool maintains a (potentially complex) mapping between features and artifacts and can provide an on-the-fly preview on all files that are included in a variant for a given feature selection. Due to a coarse-grained mapping of features to entire files, their views do not need to hide code fragments inside files, so editable views do not raise consistency issues.

Outside the context of software product lines, there have been approaches to separate concerns by creating *views on a concern*, for example, *visual separation of concerns* [Chu-Carroll et al., 2003], *effective views* [Janzen and De Volder, 2004], and the *concern manipulation environment* [Harrison et al., 2005]. First, *visual separation of concerns* builds views on top of the software configuration management tool *Stellation*. Views aggregate code fragments (at the granularity of methods) that are found by a query similar to a pointcut language. Additional context is not provided in the view, but the developer can quickly jump back to the corresponding location in the original code for further exploration. To support editable views, a view contains textual markers which are required to map changes back to the original code [Chu-Carroll et al., 2003]. Second, *effective views* provide a more sophisticated mechanism to create views. To create a view on a concern, instead of just hiding code fragments, their tool transforms (physically remodularizes) the source code to provide a virtual file with a modular implementation of that concern. That is, instead of just emulating modularity with views, effective views can provide views on real modules. However, to enable editable views *and* consistent transformations, effective views have only been implemented for a confined specialized language so far [Janzen and De Volder, 2004]. In a similar line, Ossher and Tarr [2000b] suggested on-demand remodularizations, which Harrison et al. [2005] later planned to provide with aspects in the *concern manipulation environment*; unfortunately, this project was stopped before views were implemented. We regard a physical remodularization as the better solution, however it is very difficult to achieve; a view by hiding feature code as proposed in CIDE is a pragmatic solution that can emulate modularity with similar effect.

More generally, views on a feature resemble cross-section views as in in 3D engineering or tomography. They hide all details unnecessary for the current task and let the user focus on a certain detail. An early example of such cross-section views in software engineering is the concept of *program slicing* by Weiser [1984]. A program slice is a read-only view that shows only relevant code fragments for a certain *control flow*, but hides everything else. The necessary context is determined from a control flow graph (or dynamic information in some extensions) such that the slice can reproduce the control flow. This way, program slicing helps to abstract from the complete program and to focus on a concrete, usually comprehension or maintenance related task. Similarly, Linton [1984] proposed an infrastructure for *relational views* on the underlying structure and call graph of a program.

Also in other contexts, views have been explored. A recent approach that has been quickly adopted for mainstream development is *Mylyn* [Kersten and Murphy, 2005, 2006], an Eclipse plug-in that creates task-based views on the source code, most notably on the file system. Depending on the task, only relevant files are shown in the project explorer. Effectively, Mylyn provides a view on the file system that is based on the context of the current task (which is collected in an internal model from development activity). Regarding the hiding entire files, CIDE's view and its implementation in Eclipse were inspired by Mylyn, but use feature annotations instead of a task-context model. Although Mylyn's model also includes information about classes and methods, views on file content in the editor are provided only in a basic form. Mylyn uses Eclipse's code folding capabilities on the level of methods: All methods that are not in the current context are folded by default; folding at statement level as in CIDE is not supported.

Visual representation of features

There is a huge body of work on program visualization (see [Diehl, 2007] for an overview) or on using colors for various tasks, such as error reporting [Oberg and Notkin, 1992] or merging [Yang, 1994]. We focus only on work that visualizes features in a software product line or scattered concerns.

Closest to our visual representation are again the annotation-based model editors *fmp2rsm* [Czarnecki and Antkiewicz, 2005] and *FeatureMapper* [Heidenreich et al., 2008b]. Both can – in addition to textual representations – represent some or all annotations with different colors. Each annotated feature expression is drawn with a distinct color. Overlapping annotations are not intended, but instead, for annotations constructed from multiple features (e.g., $A \wedge (B \vee \neg C)$), a new color is selected instead of blending colors. There is no empirical evaluation, but Czarnecki and Antkiewicz [2005] argue that models are usually split such that each fragment fits on a computer screen, and Heidenreich et al. [2008b] provide the possibility to enable coloring only for a subset of features. This way, both outline possibilities to handle also larger models with many features.

With the *AspectBrowser* [Griswold et al., 2001], developers can use search patterns to locate concerns (see discussion above). Search results are shown with background colors in source code editors, with a distinct color for every query. Additionally, they provide an overview of the entire code base in Seesoft style [Eick et al., 1992], again using colors to indicate query results. Griswold et al. [2001] evaluated their tool in a case study and found that the overview and highlighting with colors indeed support developers in maintenance tasks. However, they only evaluated scale regarding a large code base, not regarding many features, and they do discuss overlapping search results.

Spotlight [Coppit and Cox, 2004; Coppit et al., 2007] interestingly uses vertical bars in the left margin of the editor to visualize annotations. Again, different colors represent different concerns. Bars of different colors are placed next to each other. Compared to background colors, lines are more subtle and can represent nesting easily. Even saturated and dark colors can be used, because colors are not intermixed with the text. However, annotations are again restricted to entire lines of source code; annotations within a line cannot be represented. The authors do not discuss how this representation scales.

In contrast, existing mainstream development environments rarely use background colors for annotations. One notable exception is *NetBeans*, which shows all annotations with a purple background color, and all nested annotations (regardless of nesting depth) with a lighter purple background color. This makes it possible to quickly find top-level annotations and annotations on first nesting level, but it is not possible to recognize annotations on deeper nesting levels or to distinguish different features by colors.

Finally, there are approaches that do not visualize annotations in the source code, but separately with some other means. For example, the *Conditional Compilation Analyzer* [Pearse and Oman, 1997] visualizes the tree structure or preprocessor directives of a file in a separate window. From this visualization, a developer can follow nesting levels and get an overview of the complexity of annotations inside one file. Metrics help to compare files and establish guidelines. Similarly, Krone and Snelting [1994], Favre [1997], Hu et al. [2000], and Vidács and Beszédes [2003] all suggest some external or abstracted structures to visualize or reason about preprocessors. Such external structures are beneficial for many analyses, but we strive for a more direct integration. Still, the visualization of variability is largely an open research problem.

4.6. Summary

Annotative approaches are criticized for many different problems, including suboptimal separation of concerns, missing traceability, missing language support for variability, and tendency to obfuscate source code, which all make it difficult to understand annotation-based implementations. In this section, we have collected ideas how to address these problems with tool support and implemented them in our prototype CIDE. Although, we cannot eliminate all problems, we can mitigate many and can emulate some benefits of modular implementations.

First, we argued that annotations should be strictly integrated with the feature model of the software product line to avoid scattering of configuration knowledge, which can often be observed in ad-hoc implementations with traditional preprocessors. In CIDE, annotations are managed by a tool infrastructure, which allows only annotations based on features previously defined in a feature model.

Second, we proposed and implemented editable views on the source code to emulate modularity. Specifically, we distinguish between views on a feature, which show only the code fragments belonging to a feature and some necessary context, and views on a variant, which show all source code of a variant for a feature selected, similar to a generated variant. Even though the implementation of a feature is still scattered, in CIDE, a developer can quickly trace a feature from the feature model to its implementation.

Third, we discussed different visual representations of features to enhance or replace the common textual annotations. Background colors do not obfuscate the source code and can be used within a single line. Visual representations of annotations make explicit where annotations begin and end and how they are nested. They are quicker to recognize and can thus aid program comprehension, due to preattentive color perception. In a controlled experiment with 43 students, we found that colors instead of textual annotations can speed up program comprehension significantly for some tasks by up to 43 %. We addressed concerns of scalability by analyzing existing annotation-based software product lines and found that only a low number of distinct features annotated on each page of source code, so that also a low number of colors are sufficient.

The proposed solutions can be used in isolation but they can (and should) also be integrated. For example, views and visual representations can be constructed more efficiently, when annotations are strictly mapped to a feature model. Visual representations can be integrated with views, to make views even more compact. We combined all discussed improvements in our prototype tool CIDE. However, our implementation implies no definite suggestion on how to implement feature model integration, views, or visual representations. In fact, there are many alternatives and many design decisions, some of which we discussed, others which remain to explore. In this chapter, our main focus was to illustrate that annotative approaches, despite all criticism, are not beyond hope; they have just been ignored. We understand our research as encouragement for researchers to take another look at preprocessors and explore possible tool support, for tool builders to invest in better editors, and for developers in practice to demand better tool support. We will come back to a comparison of annotative approaches with our improvements and compositional approaches in Chapter 6.

5. Error detection

This chapter shares material with the TOOLS'09 paper "Guaranteeing Syntactic Correctness for all Product Line Variants: A Language-Independent Approach" [Kästner et al., 2009b] and the ASE'08 paper "Type-checking Software Product Lines – A Formal Approach" [Kästner and Apel, 2008b].

Software product lines are inherently complex and prone to all kinds of errors. The main problem is that certain errors only occur when a specific feature or feature combination is selected, potentially only in a single out of millions of possible variants. Errors may hide in the implementation until a customer eventually requests a problematic variant, possibly long after initial development. In contrast to compositional approaches, annotative approaches provide no means to check features in isolation; they are regarded as especially error prone. To avoid expensive maintenance late in the development cycle, we aim at error detection for the entire software product line (with all its variants) during initial development.

We see two causes of errors that are specific to annotative approaches and address them in this chapter. After introducing a brief taxonomy of error detection mechanisms to distinguish our approaches, we (1) prevent syntax errors with disciplined annotations and (2) detect type errors with a product-line–aware type system. Both syntax errors and type errors are challenging to detect in annotative approaches, due to the lack of modular error detection per feature. In both cases, the challenge is to raise existing mechanisms from checking individual variants to checking the entire software product line.

5.1. Taxonomy

To provide a common vocabulary for the following discussions of own and related solutions, we start with a taxonomy of different possible errors and error detection approaches summarized in the morphologic box in Figure 5.1 [Kästner et al., 2009b].

First, we distinguish three *kinds of errors*: syntactic errors, type errors and semantic errors (first row in Fig. 5.1).

- *Syntax errors* occur when a variant is ill-formed regarding the language's syntax, for example, when an opened bracket is not closed, as exemplified in Figure 5.2a.

5. Error detection

Kind of error	Syntax	Typing	Semantic
Error detection	Check variants		Check entire product line
Languages	Single	Multiple	Inter-language
Implementation	Annotative	Compositional	Other

Figure 5.1.: *Taxonomy of errors and corresponding checks in software product lines (morphological box).*

```
1  class DB {
2     ...
3  #ifdef X
4  }
5  #endif
```
(a) Syntax error.

```
1   class DB {
2      void insert(int o) {
3         this.put(o);
4      }
5   #ifdef X
6      void put(int o) {
7         ...
8      }
9   #endif
10  }
```
(b) Type error.

```
1  class DB {
2     void insert(int o) {
3        lock();
4        put(o);
5  #ifdef X
6        unlock();
7  #endif
8     }
9  }
```
(c) Semantic error.

Figure 5.2.: *Examples for three kinds of errors when feature X is not selected.*

- *Type errors* occur when a variant is ill-formed regarding the language's type system, for example, a statement invoking a method that is not defined in that variant as exemplified in Figure 5.2b.[1] In statically typed languages, type errors can be detected during compilation. To detect type errors, usually a syntactically correct program is required.

- *Semantic errors* occur when a variant behaves incorrectly according to some (formal or informal) specification. Semantic errors are most difficult to detect. For example, in Figure 5.2c, a lock is only released when feature X is selected, which can lead to a deadlock in variants without feature X. To detect semantic errors, a program must be executable, which typically requires the absence of syntax and type errors.

Second, we distinguish two general *error detection approaches*: check variants or check the entire software product line (second row in Fig. 5.1).

---

[1]Whether a specific error is a syntax error or a type error can be debatable to some extend. We use the following distinction: errors that are caught by a parser based on a (context-free) grammar are considered syntax errors, all errors detected with further static analysis in the compiler are considered type errors. One example of a borderline case are abstract methods in Java. Although it is possible to write a parser that rejects abstract methods in nonabstract classes, typical Java parsers use simpler grammars that accept programs with any kind of methods in abstract and nonabstract classes. In this case, a separate compiler pass enforces that nonabstract classes may not contain abstract methods. Depending on the *implementation* of the compiler different means are used to detect the abstract method error. Consequently, depending on the implementation, it can be classified as syntax or type error.

- In the first case, (some or all) *generated variants are checked* in isolation. A brute force strategy of generating and checking all variants is usually infeasible, because already with few features the number of variants that can be generated from a software product line explodes (for n independent optional features, there are 2^n distinct variants). In practice, this typically means that only some sampled variants or only those variants requested by customers are checked [Pohl and Metzger, 2006]. Errors in other variants may remain undetected until such variant is requested.

- In contrast, some approaches *check the entire software product line* and guarantee certain properties for all variants when this check passes [e.g., Czarnecki and Pietroszek, 2006; Thaker et al., 2007; Kästner and Apel, 2008b; Post and Sinz, 2008]. This means that the error detection mechanism is aware of product lines and has some ways of lifting the checks from a single variant to the entire software product line.

Third, we classify error detection mechanisms by their coverage of different *programming languages*: single language, multiple languages, and inter-language errors (third row in Fig. 5.1).

- Some checks are specific to a *single language*. For example, different languages require different type checks.

- Next, there are errors that can occur in *multiple languages* and can be addressed by the same tool or mechanism.

- Finally, there are errors that occur only at the *interaction of multiple languages*. One example of such inter-language error is a mismatch between the interface specification of a web service in a web service description language and its implementation in Java.

Fourth, different product-line *implementation mechanisms* on top of a programming language can require different error detection strategies (fourth row in Fig. 5.1). While some checks can be independent of the implementation, others rely on certain mechanisms. For this classification, we use the groups annotative approaches, compositional approaches, and others introduced in Chapter 3.

In the remainder of this chapter, we address first syntax errors (Section 5.2), then typing errors (Section 5.3) for the entire software product line for annotative approaches. Annotative approaches provide no means of modular syntax or type checking and are especially prone to such errors (cf. Sec. 3.2.3). In contrast, semantic errors are largely a common challenge to all product-line implementation mechanisms and are outside the scope of this thesis (see also discussion of related work in Section 5.4).

5.2. Disciplined annotations

Enforcing *disciplined annotations* is a solution that prevents syntax errors in software product lines developed with annotative approaches [Kästner et al., 2009b]. As shown in the taxonomy, syntax errors are the most fundamental category of errors that have to be addressed before typing or semantic errors. Furthermore, as discussed in Section 3.2.3, many annotative approaches are prone to syntax errors, since arbitrary code fragments can be annotated and checking features in isolation is not possible. In our experience, almost every product-line developer using preprocessors can tell a story how she searched for hours to fix a simple syntax error like a bracket mismatch.

In a nutshell, disciplined annotations are a subset of all possible annotations. Disciplined annotations are annotations on those code fragments that do not introduce syntax errors when deleted. Allowing only disciplined annotations limits expressiveness (without significant restrictions on practical usage scenarios as we will show) in exchange for certain safety guarantees for all variants. To determine which annotations are disciplined, we present a language-independent solution. In Figure 5.3, we show how disciplined annotations fit into our taxonomy.

Kind of error	Syntax	Typing	Semantic
Error detection	Check variants	Check entire product line	
Languages	Single	Multiple	Inter-language
Implementation	Annotative	Compositional	Other

Figure 5.3.: *Properties of disciplined annotations [Kästner et al., 2009b].*

5.2.1. Basic concept

The reason that preprocessor-based implementations, such as in Figure 3.6 (p. 34) or Figure 5.2a, are so prone to syntax errors is that most preprocessors consider the underlying source code as an arbitrary stream of characters. Thus, preprocessors can remove any lines, tokens, or even characters. This flexibility makes them very powerful, but also dangerous.

If we allow only annotations on entire methods in Java code, but no other constructs, we can trivially guarantee that removing code fragments will not introduce any syntax errors (of course type and semantic errors are still possible; more on this later). In Java, we can allow also to annotate entire classes, fields, and statements and guarantee that those annotations cannot cause any syntax errors. However, we cannot annotate the expression inside an *if* statement or the body of a *for* loop, because those might cause syntax errors when removed. We call annotations that cannot introduce syntax errors *disciplined annotations* and all others *undisciplined annotations.*

The general lesson is that a restricted preprocessor can avoid syntax errors, but, to do so, it needs an insight into the structure of the underlying source code. For example, the preprocessor (or an external tool to detect undisciplined annotations) must recognize classes and methods in Java source code to distinguish disciplined from undisciplined annotations.

In order to analyze the underlying structure and to reason about annotations, already the underlying source code must not contain any syntax errors. Disciplined annotations can only guarantee not to introduce *new* syntax errors. For the remainder of this section, we implicitly assume that the underlying annotated code is syntactically correct such that we can analyze its structure.

Finally, there is the question of how a tool determines which annotations are disciplined and which are not. Instead of deciding which kinds of annotations are disciplined in an ad-hoc fashion for each language, we design a solution that can automatically infer, from the grammar specification of a target language, which structural elements that can be annotated without causing syntax errors. That is, the same grammar that is used to define which code fragments are syntactically correct is used to determine which annotations are disciplined.

5.2.2. Detecting disciplined annotations

To detect which code elements can be annotated and removed safely, we consider the grammar of the target language. The grammar specifies which code sequences may appear in what order and where. From this information, we can derive which elements are mandatory and optional in the source code; the optional elements are those which can be annotated safely.

For illustration, consider the excerpt from a simple Java-like grammar in Figure 5.4 (in extended Backus-Naur form). It specifies that a compilation unit may consist of any number of type declarations. That is, from a syntax point of view, all type declarations are optional and can thus be annotated and deleted safely with regard to the syntax; an annotation on a type declaration is considered disciplined. In contrast, inside a type declaration, the *class* keyword, the name of a class, and the body with its opening and closing brackets are mandatory and must not be annotated. This distinction would already recognize the annotation in Figure 5.2a as undisciplined. The *extends* and *implements* clauses are again optional, so are the member declarations inside the class body. This way, we can infer from the grammar of a language which structural elements are optional.

Technically, we generate a parser from the grammar that propagates information whether structural elements are optional to the generated parse trees (for details on the implementation and tool chain, see [Kästner et al., 2009b]). That is, when the generated parser parses a Java code fragment, it creates a parse tree in which all optional elements are marked. We exemplify such generated parse tree for a small code fragment in Figure 5.5.

```
1  CompilationUnit : (TypeDeclaration)* <EOF> ;
2  TypeDeclaration : "class" <ID> ( "extends" <ID> )? ( ImplementsList )? ClassBody;
3  ClassBody       : "{" (Member)* "}" ;
4  Member          : Method | Field ;
5  ImplementsList  : "implements" <ID> ("," <ID>)* ;
```

Figure 5.4.: *Excerpt of a grammar of a Java-like language.*

```
1  class C implements D, E {
2    int x;
3    void m(){}
4  }
5  class F {}
```

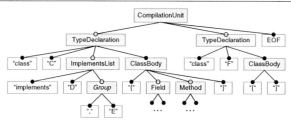

Figure 5.5.: *Source code fragment and corresponding parse tree. In analogy to feature diagrams, structural elements that are optional in the grammar are marked with an empty dot, mandatory structural elements are marked with a filled dot.*

A tool that enforces disciplined annotations must only compare whether the provided annotations match to optional elements in the parse tree. Specifically, we identified two rules to determine disciplined annotations [Kästner et al., 2008a, 2009b]:

- *Optional-Only Rule:* Only structural elements that are *optional* according to the language's grammar can be annotated and removed.

- *Subtree Rule:* When a structural element is removed all its children must be removed as well. For example, when a class is removed also its *class* keyword, name, *extends* and *implements* declaration, and body must be removed. Common preprocessors evaluate nested annotations from the outer to the nested inner ones and thus fulfill this rule automatically.

Our approach to determine disciplined annotations based on a grammar is language independent in the sense that it can be applied to every language for which a grammar specification exists.

In our implementation in our prototype CIDE, all these rules are enforced directly in the tool infrastructure. Instead of textual annotations as in *cpp*, CIDE manages all annotations internally. Annotations are only possible on code fragments that correspond to optional structural elements. For all other code fragments, CIDE refuses to add annotations. This way, CIDE enforces disciplined annotations and guarantees the absence of syntax errors in all variants.

5.2.3. From string removal to AST transformations

Disciplined annotations as described so far are simple, language independent, and backward compatible to existing preprocessors. Variants can be generated by simple string removal. However, as we will show in this section, we can improve the process regarding both expressiveness and ease of use. We therefore lift our analysis from parse trees to Abstract Syntax Trees (ASTs) and modify the variant generation process from string removal to AST transformations [Kästner et al., 2008a].

An AST is similar to a parse tree, but abstracts many details that are necessary for the technical parsing process. An AST is closer to the actual internal structure of the document than a parse tree. To illustrate this abstraction, in Figure 5.6, we show an AST that corresponds to our previous code fragment and parse tree of Figure 5.5. The AST hides all tokens necessary for parsing, such as the *class* keyword or commas.

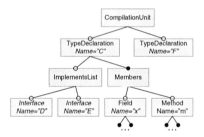

Figure 5.6.: *AST representing the underlying structure from Figure 5.5.*

Benefits of AST representation

The AST representation has three main benefits: improved expressiveness, easier use, and opportunities for extensions.

First, we improve expressiveness, since we can classify more annotations as disciplined with an AST than with a parse tree. For example, the grammar specifies that the *implements* list is optional inside the type declaration, but inside the list the first entry is mandatory due to special parsing requirements for the separating comma. Using the parse tree in Figure 5.5, a user can only annotate the second parameter or the entire list. However, intuitively all interfaces are optional elements

```
 1 class C implements
 2 #ifdef Feature1
 3   D
 4 #endif
 5   ,
 6 #ifdef Feature2
 7   E
 8 #endif
 9 {
10   ...
11 }
```

(a) Annotations based on structural AST elements.

```
 1 class C
 2 #ifdef Feature1 ∨ Feature2
 3   implements
 4 #ifdef Feature1
 5   D
 6 #ifdef Feature2
 7   ,
 8 #endif
 9 #endif
10 #ifdef Feature2
11   E
12 #endif
13 #endif
14 {
15   ...
16 }
```

(b) Backward compatible annotation of multiple list elements separated by comma.

Figure 5.7.: *Disciplined annotations mapped to optional AST elements are less verbose, but not backward compatible.*

in a list and it should be possible to annotate each of them, including the first one. The AST reflects this intuition and allows us to annotate every element separately.

Second, annotating AST elements is easier than annotating parse tree elements, since the developers do not need to care about the syntactic overhead. Following the previous example of the implements list, we annotate elements in the source code, but not the separating comma or the *implements* keyword. In Figure 5.7a, we show an example with annotations on both interface elements, but we can ignore the comma and *implements* keyword. An equivalent backward compatible annotation would require more and nested annotations, as shown in Figure 5.7b,[2] to get the syntactic overhead right in every variant. Of course this simpler annotation comes at a price that we need a different variant generation mechanism as explained below.

Finally, it is easier to reason about annotated AST elements instead of parse tree elements. AST elements are used for several other tasks anyway, such as type checking (see Sec. 5.3) and refactoring. Therefore, mapping annotations directly to AST elements is beneficial for those extensions.

---

[2]For the sake of concise examples, throughout this chapter, we allow *#ifdef* instructions inside a line, instead of breaking the source code into multiple lines. Additionally, we allow Boolean operators in the condition as "*#ifdef X ∧ Y*" and "*#ifdef X ∨ Y*" as alternative to nested *#ifdef* directives or "*#if defined(X) || defined(Y)*".

Technical realization

Using ASTs instead of parse trees raises two technical challenges. First, we need to produce ASTs and decide which AST elements are optional. This process should be safe and language independent as generating parse trees from a language's grammar. Second, we need to replace the variant generation process: Instead of removing strings between preprocessor declarations, we need a more sophisticated process based on AST transformations that takes care of the syntactic details.

Regarding the first problem, AST creation, many tools create an AST out of a parse tree as a separate step after parsing. Writing an AST back into a source code file is again implemented in a separate step. To guarantee syntactic correctness for all variants, both transformations must be performed safely without loss of information in every language.

To bridge this gap, we follow the lead of Wile, who used an extended grammar specification language to derive the abstract syntax directly from a grammar file [Wile, 1997]. Wile proposed a series of additional constructs in the grammar specification language, so that the abstract syntax and its relationship to the concrete syntax are directly specified in the extended grammar file. This way, we can extend our parser generator so that it directly produces an AST instead of a parse tree and still propagates all information about optionality. Wile further proposed a semi-automated process to transform an existing grammar describing a concrete syntax into the extended format. For example, to solve problems like the *implements* list described previously, he proposes a special list construct. In Wile's notation, the *ImplementsList* production is expressed as `ImplementsList: ID ^ ",";`, in which the ^ symbol is a special construct for lists followed by the token that separates list entries. Using this construct, the parser can interpret identifiers directly as lists and build the AST accordingly. We adopted Wile's concept and added those extensions to our tool chain (see [Kästner et al., 2009b]). This way, we can generate a parser that creates structural elements based on the target language's abstract syntax from a grammar file. Only a single tree is created, no manual mapping between parse tree and abstract syntax is required.

An alternative approach to bridge the gap between between textual syntax and AST, successfully applied in the context of aspect weaving, is to reuse an existing multi-language tool set that is responsible for a safe transformation, such as the commercial DMS Software Reengineering Toolkit [Baxter et al., 2004; Gray and Roychoudhury, 2004].

Regarding the variant generation mechanism, we can change the mechanism from removing strings to performing AST transformations. Instead of removing an annotated code fragment, we first parse the code file, identify the corresponding optional AST element, remove this element from the AST, and finally write the modified AST back into a file. During AST transformation, we still enforce the optional-only rule and the subtree rule; that is, we forbid removing mandatory

AST elements. Since tools for parsing a file into an AST and writing back an AST into a file are generated from a grammar, this process is safe: Writing an AST can never produce a syntax error. When elements in a list, such as the interfaces in Figure 5.7a, are written into a file, the necessary syntactic overhead is added automatically. For example, when both interfaces are removed in Figure 5.7, then the *implements* keyword is not written in the generated variant.

In our prototype implementation in CIDE, much of the complexity added by ASTs is hidden in the tool infrastructure. Since CIDE uses an own annotation mechanism instead of *cpp*-style textual annotations, CIDE is in full control of annotations and the variant generation mechanism [Kästner et al., 2009b]. Therefore it is simple, and even convenient, that only code elements, but not syntactic overhead has to be annotated.

5.2.4. Wrappers

Finally, experience has shown that there is another class of annotations that is classified as undisciplined so far, but needed to solve practical problems: wrappers. Wrappers are code fragments that wrap around other code fragments, such as the try-catch statement in Java. They are fundamental in many compositional approaches.[3] In some scenarios, wrappers should be removed, without removing the wrapped statements. In Figure 5.8, we show two examples of optional exception handling and optional null-pointer checks that require wrappers. Both the parse-tree–based and the AST-based solutions classify these annotations as undisciplined (the annotated code fragments do not correspond to optional structural elements; the subtree rule forbids excepting inner parts from an annotation).

There are some workarounds on how wrappers can be implemented with disciplined annotations, but they require boilerplate code and are counterintuitive.[4] Therefore, we introduce an additional mechanism for wrappers that can be used in any language, and we integrate it with our existing classification of disciplined annotations based on ASTs.

In our solution, specific AST elements can be marked as wrappers (technically, wrappers are specified with an attribute in our grammar specification language). When wrappers are annotated, specific child elements can be excluded from this annotation. For example, when annotating a try-catch statement in Java, we can exclude the child that represents the wrapped body from this annotation. When the wrapper is removed from the AST during variant generation, it is replaced by its wrapped child element. To ensure that no syntax error can occur in this trans-

---

[3]Wrappers are similar to method refinements in AHEAD or advice in AspectJ. For example, in AspectJ, *before* and *after* advice are not sufficient, some aspects wrap existing code with *around* advice.

[4]For example, in Java, the wrapper code can be specified in an overriding method, using a *super* call to invoke the wrapped code. To provide variability, the entire overriding method is annotated.

```
 1 class C {
 2   void foo() {
 3 #ifdef ExceptionHandling
 4     try {
 5 #endif
 6       this.bar();
 7 #ifdef ExceptionHandling
 8     } catch (RuntimeException e) {
 9       ...
10   }
11 #endif
12   }
13   void bar(C a) {
14 #ifdef NullPointerChecks
15     if (a!=null)
16 #endif
17       a.foo();
18   }
19 }
```

Figure 5.8.: *Wrappers, such as try, if, and for statements, cannot be annotated without annotating the wrapped elements.*

formation, a type-based mechanism secures wrappers during parser generation. For example, we ensure that a statement can only wrap other statements, but that it cannot wrap expressions or parameters. For further details, see [Kästner et al., 2009b].

5.2.5. Flexibility vs. safety

Disciplined annotations balance between two properties: flexibility and safety. By imposing a tree structure on a source code artifact, we attain *safety* (guaranteeing syntactic correctness for all generated variants). However, at the same time, we impose restrictions on what developers are allowed to annotate and thus reduce their *flexibility*, that is, developers have fewer possibilities to express variability: Compared to an implementation using the undisciplined C preprocessor, which works on token level, disciplined annotations can only annotate optional elements of the underlying AST. Hence, there are undisciplined implementations for which a corresponding implementation with disciplined annotations is difficult to find or requires boilerplate code. For example, defining a class with two alternative names is not possible with disciplined annotations since the name of a class is mandatory in the underlying structure (see Fig. 5.5), but we could create two copies of the class as a workaround.[5]

---

[5]It is always possible to replace undisciplined annotations by disciplined ones. In the worst case, we replicate the entire file for each variant, so that variability is reduced to annotations on files. This expansion mechanism is used, for example, by Vittek [2003] and on a finer level of granularity also by Garrido and Johnson [2005], see Section 5.4.

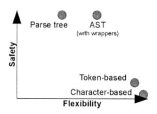

Figure 5.9.: *Safety versus Flexibility.*

Programming languages already define a certain structure for code artifacts by their language syntax. For example, the Java syntax defines a top-down structure for Java code (e.g., Java files contain classes, which contain methods, which contain statements). We expose this structure in the form of ASTs and exploit it with the subtree rule and the optional-only rule to prevent syntax errors. Different languages provide a different amount of structure in their syntax. For example, JavaScript artifacts only contain a list of statements or function declarations, grammar artifacts only contain a list of production rules with a simple inner structure, and XML nodes are nested completely arbitrarily.

This raises two questions. (1) How much structure does an artifact language need to enforce disciplined annotations? (2) Is the structure defined by a language's syntax a limitation when using disciplined annotations for other artifact types in the future?

To answer the second question first, consider a "README.txt" file. It is a valid artifact in a software product line, but will probably not provide any structure, at least none that is described by a context-free grammar. Fortunately, such artifacts, for which no specific language grammar is specified, can still be parsed based on a dummy grammar that accepts any file as a list of arbitrary optional tokens or even as a list of optional characters. With a dummy grammar, every character is optional with respect to the document; that is, every single character in this document can be annotated independently just as when using preprocessors. This shows that a required structure is not a limitation of our approach. Even if no structure is available, as in the "README.txt" file, we can still use the same mechanisms to annotate this file uniformly next to other artifacts in a software product line.

Nevertheless, structure is beneficial. When using a dummy grammar, the guarantee of syntactic correctness is lost, because *any* artifact (with a textual representation) adheres to this grammar. This shows that any structure – although it reduces flexibility – is beneficial for safety. The structure restricts the possible parts of the artifact that can be annotated and enforces reasonable annotations.

In Figure 5.9, we visualize the relative differences in safety and flexibility of all discussed approaches. For annotations based on a parse tree, we can guarantee syntactic correctness. We can give the same guarantee with more flexibility for annotations based on the AST, even when we introduce wrappers (see Sec. 5.2.3 and 5.2.4). In contrast, a character-based or token-based annotation – as with the dummy grammar or contemporary *#ifdef* preprocessors – provides the highest flexibility (every single character or token can be annotated) but no safety at all.

This discussion shows that a structure given by a grammar is not necessary for an artifact to be handled by a preprocessor that enforces disciplined annotations. However, when a reasonable grammar is provided, disciplined annotations can ensure syntactic correctness and take advantage of the artifact's structure to support the developer toward reasonable annotations. The ability to use the artifact's structure (if available) in every language to ensure syntactic correctness distinguishes preprocessors based on disciplined annotations from naive *cpp*-like preprocessors.

5.2.6. Evaluation

To evaluate expressiveness and flexibility of disciplined annotations, we target two questions:

- Can disciplined annotations be applied language independently? One of the key benefits of preprocessors is their language-independent and uniform application. Complicated language-dependent tools will likely not replace preprocessors, even with a guarantee of syntactic correctness.

- Are disciplined annotations sufficiently expressive in practice? Although many errors are caused by the high flexibility of preprocessors, if we overly restrict disciplined annotations, they would not be used.

Languages

Originally, our implementation of disciplined annotations in CIDE was tailored to the Java AST provided by Eclipse's Java development tools [Kästner et al., 2008a]. We then extended it to its current language-independent form, in which additional languages can be added as plug-ins and plug-ins can be generated from grammar specifications [Kästner et al., 2009b]. That is, CIDE is not entirely language independent, but it can be extended toward new languages quickly. Furthermore, it is always possible to disable disciplined annotations as a fallback solution for unsupported languages (e.g., by using a dummy grammar, as discussed earlier in Sec. 5.2.5).

We generated 17 language plug-ins based on grammars of various code and noncode languages. That is, in CIDE, we can enforce disciplined annotations for all these languages. In Table 5.1, we list all supported languages and some information describing optional structures, wrappers, and the number of production

Language	Optional structures	Wrappers	#Prod.
Featherw. Java*	methods, fields, parameters	-	16
Java 1.5[†]	members, stmt., parameters, ...	if, for, try, ...	133
C (plain)[†]	functions, stmt., parameters, ...	if, for, ...	80
C (pseudo)*	functions, stmt., preprocessor, ...	if, #ifdef, ...	46
C++ (pseudo)*	classes, methods, stmt., prepr., ...	if, #ifdef, ...	65
C#[‡]	classes, members, stmt., par., ...	if, for, try, ...	215
Haskell (pseudo)[†]	types, imports, data, classes, ...	-	54
Haskell 98*	types, imports, data, cl., par., ...	if	71
Python[†]	functions, stmt., parameter, ...	if, for, ...	94
JavaScript[†]	functions, statements, expr., ...	if, for, ...	111
JavaCC[†], Bali[†],			
ANTLR[‡]	productions, terminals, ...	[], ()*	14–166
Property files*	lines	-	1
Manifest files*	sections, attributes	-	3
HTML[†]	headings, paragraphs, list items, ...	\\, ...	11
XML*	nodes, parameters	-	13

*handwritten based on external specification, [†]adapted fr. JavaCC grammar, [‡]adapted fr. ANTLR grammar

Table 5.1.: *Generated language plug-ins in CIDE.*

rules each. The number of production rules can be used as a rough indicator of the complexity of the language. For most languages, the grammar was derived from an existing grammar in the JavaCC or ANTLR format (which required mostly just syntactic changes); this usually took less than one hour per language.

The language extensions for C and C++ were the most problematic, due to the existing preprocessor. Since our implementation of disciplined annotations does not cover macros (*#define*) or file inclusion (*#include*), C is very difficult to parse. To overcome this problem in CIDE, we wrote a pseudo parser, which does not actually parse the code based on the full language specification, but recognizes only important constructs, such as functions, variable declarations, and statements. For example, statements are recognized by the terminating semicolon, functions by the typical pattern for return type and parameter declarations. Preprocessor directives are recognized as part of the language, as long as they are used within certain limitations (e.g., *#include* must not occur inside functions). With a pseudo parser, we are able to use CIDE on many C projects, but we weaken the guarantee for syntactic correctness to some degree (see discussion in Sec. 5.2.5). The same pseudo-parser approach was used for C++ and also for an initial version of Haskell, because of Haskell's complex syntax and many extensions.

The XML grammar supports only plain XML files. All elements or attributes are optional and can be annotated. This guarantees that every variant is *well-formed* in the XML terminology. Guaranteeing that all variants of an XML artifact are *valid* based on the given document type definition or XML Schema description (e.g., determining that the *body* tag in XHTML is mandatory) requires additional information. This can either be done by providing a more specific grammar (e.g., a specific XHTML grammar) or by deferring some checks to a product-line–aware type system (cf. Sec 5.3). We prototypically generated a XHTML grammar from the XHTML specification; but in future work, we plan a more sophisticated mechanism to validate artifacts of XML-based languages.

All in all our experience shows that creating language plug-ins for new languages is simple for most languages. If a target language has a well-specified grammar, creating a language extension is a matter of few hours. All generated languages share the guarantee for syntactical correctness (with some limitations for pseudo parsers).

Expressiveness

To demonstrate that disciplined annotations provide sufficient expressiveness for practical application, we provide two kinds of evidence: (1) a number of case studies successfully developed with disciplined annotations in CIDE and (2) an analysis of how the preprocessor is currently used in existing Java ME and C projects.

First, we and others have used disciplined annotations in CIDE to annotate features in case studies such as Berkeley DB, Prevayler, FAME-DBMS, and an industrial product line of software for Water Boilers. In Table 5.2, we give a list of case studies and their size, grouped by languages. For details on those case studies, the respective development process, and their contributors see Appendix A.1.

The general experience in our case studies was that expressiveness was sufficient. There were a few cases, when we had to rewrite source code to make annotations disciplined, but these were only minor, obvious changes. For example, we split complex expressions into multiple statements or changed the branches of if-else constructs to apply wrappers. In our experience, disciplined annotations were not a limitation.

Second, Baxter and Mehlich [2001] argue that developers prefer disciplined annotations, even when they could use undisciplined ones, so that most annotations are in a disciplined form already. To support that theory with empirical data, we had a look at three existing Java ME projects that have been developed with the Antenna preprocessor, and 40 C projects that have been developed with the C preprocessor. All projects are open source and were developed independently from our analysis using a traditional undisciplined preprocessor.

All three Java ME projects (for more information on these projects, see Appendix A.1), were almost entirely disciplined as a manual investigation of all annotation revealed. As shown in Table 5.3, we found no undisciplined annotations

Artifact language	Case studies	Lines of code
Java	Berkeley DB Java Edition	84 000
	Graph Product Line	1 350
	Prevayler	8 000
C	Water Boiler	10 000
C++	FAME-DBMS	5 000
Python	Pynche	2 400
Haskell	Arithmetic Expression Evaluator	460
	Functional Graph Library	2 600
ANTLR grammar	SQL Parser	60
XML ANT build script	AHEAD Tool Suite	17 000
HTML documentation	AHEAD Tool Suite	28 000
	Graph Product Line	200
	Berkeley DB	120 000

Table 5.2.: *Case studies implemented with CIDE.*

in *Lampiro*, three undisciplined annotations in *MobileMedia* and eight undisciplined annotations in *Mobile RSS Reader*. All undisciplined annotations were very easy to transform into disciplined ones. In Figure 5.10, we exemplify one of these undisciplined annotations from *Mobile RSS Reader* and our transformation into a disciplined annotation.

```
1  if (sdate.length() > 0) {
2      date = new Date(
           Long.parseLong(sdate, 16));
3      //#ifdef DITUNES
4  } else {
5      ...
6      //#endif
7  }
```

(a) Original undisciplined annotation.

```
1  if (sdate.length() > 0) {
2      date = new Date(
           Long.parseLong(sdate, 16));
3  }
4  //#ifdef DITUNES
5      else {
6      ...
7  }
8  //#endif
```

(b) Equivalent disciplined annotation.

Figure 5.10.: *Example of an undisciplined annotation in* Mobile RSS Reader.

There are by far more C programs using a preprocessor for variability than Java programs. Therefore, we collected a large number of C programs for further analysis. Mirroring an earlier study of Liebig et al. [2010], we analyzed 40 open source C programs from different domains and of different sizes (together over 30 million lines of code; see Appendix A.2 for a description of the programs). Due to the number and size of the projects, we developed an automated analysis tool (an extension of Liebig's analysis tools).

Project	# annotations	# undisciplined annotations
Lampiro	108	0 (0.0 %)
MobileMedia (Rel. 8)	164	3 (1.8 %)
Mobile RSS Reader	1050	8 (0.8 %)

Table 5.3.: *Disciplined annotations in four Java ME product lines.*

An exact analysis of disciplined annotations in C code is difficult, as long a C code is interwoven with preprocessor directives (macros, includes, and conditional compilation). Our analysis tools use an approximation of the underlying structure, which is reflected also in the collected metrics. Therefore, we collect two distinct metrics regarding disciplined annotations.

- *TL&S.* Our metric *TL&S* counts the percentage of disciplined annotations, but considers only annotations on entire top level elements (such as functions and typedefs) and annotations on entire statements as disciplined. This metric produces many false negatives (many disciplined annotations are classified as undisciplined) but no false positives, it serves as a conservative lower bound.

- *DIS.* Our metric *DIS* counts the percentage of disciplined annotations as well, but is closer to our notion of disciplined annotations. We count annotations on entire parse subtrees as disciplined and we implemented a number of special handlers to recognize some wrappers like those in Figure 5.8 (p. 91). Nevertheless, this metric cannot be exact because of the underlying tools; both false positives and false negatives are possible. Still, in several sampled files, manual inspection confirmed that this metric recognizes disciplined annotations mostly correct.

Although not perfectly accurate, both metrics provide a sufficient overview to give a rough insight in how annotations are used in C projects. Additionally, we collect lines of code (after pretty printing and removing comments and empty lines for comparability) and number of annotations to give an insight into the size of these projects.[6]

We show the results of our analysis in Figure 5.4. The results confirm our expectations that most annotations are in a disciplined form anyway. The values differ from project to project; except for *mpsolve* all contain some undisciplined annotations, but in all cases by far most annotations are disciplined (on average 89 %). There is no significant correlation between the percentage of disciplined annotation and the size of the project.

---

[6]We excluded 21 file because the preprocessor declaration were not well-formed; there were not enough *#endif* directives to match the *#ifdef* directives.

Name	LOC	ANN	TL&S	DIS
apache	214 250	4 087	84 %	87 %
berkeley db	187 298	2 907	89 %	92 %
cherookee	51 719	805	84 %	88 %
clamav	75 210	1 361	90 %	91 %
dia	128 850	614	90 %	92 %
emacs	237 003	6 072	89 %	91 %
freebsd	5 923 123	85 431	87 %	90 %
gcc	1 615 639	16 438	85 %	88 %
ghostscript	441 411	3 415	91 %	93 %
gimp	587 277	1 836	91 %	94 %
glibc	747 047	12 981	84 %	88 %
gnumeric	254 578	1 548	81 %	86 %
gnuplot	75 978	2 054	81 %	85 %
irssi	49 661	151	90 %	91 %
libxml2	210 762	7 886	93 %	94 %
lighttpd	38 925	723	90 %	96 %
linux	5 973 183	46 757	93 %	95 %
lynx	117 692	3 765	80 %	84 %
minix	64 035	1 152	95 %	96 %
mplayer	605 573	6 320	82 %	87 %
mpsolve	10 170	30	100 %	100 %
openldap	245 907	2 744	87 %	92 %
opensolaris	8 615 530	82 728	77 %	80 %
openvpn	34 975	963	93 %	95 %
parrot	98 227	1 597	92 %	93 %
php	573 724	8 396	85 %	89 %
pidgin	269 178	2 162	89 %	91 %
postgresql	449 695	2 898	82 %	85 %
privoxy	24 038	686	77 %	81 %
python	373 961	8 726	91 %	92 %
sendmail	83 643	3 116	80 %	84 %
sqlite	94 419	1 509	88 %	89 %
subversion	509 171	3 927	80 %	81 %
sylpheed	101 435	1 074	88 %	90 %
tcl	135 078	3 903	87 %	88 %
vim	225 410	11 001	68 %	77 %
xfig	72 443	375	83 %	87 %
xine-lib	494 903	6 162	89 %	91 %
xorg-server	527 335	8 932	88 %	92 %
xterm	49 589	2 019	89 %	90 %
Sum/Average	30 588 045	359 251	87 (±6) %	89 (±5) %

LOC: lines of code, after normalization and removal of comments; ANN: total number of annotations; TL&S: conservative lower bound of disciplined annotations (percentage of annotations that cover top level constructs or statements); DIS: percentage of annotations considered as disciplined

Table 5.4.: *Disciplined annotations in forty C applications.*

Although most annotations are already disciplined in practice, it is still beneficial to *enforce* disciplined annotations with a tool and reject all undisciplined annotations. Already, a single undisciplined annotation in a large project can cause a hard to find syntax error in few variants. The high percentage of disciplined annotations in Java ME and C product lines are a good sign, since they mean that disciplined annotations are hardly a limitation in practice; refactoring legacy code to use only disciplined annotations will typically require only moderate effort.

All in all, our analysis shows that disciplined annotations are expressive enough to develop software product lines. They are still easy to use and language independent, thus keeping both important advantages of traditional preprocessors. At the same time, disciplined annotations can guarantee the absence of syntax errors.

5.3. Product-line–aware type system

Building on top of disciplined annotations, we now focus on detecting type errors in all variants of a software product line with a product-line–aware type system [Kästner and Apel, 2008b]. Such type system can detect many errors, beyond just syntax errors. For example, we can detect dangling method references or missing types, even if they occur only in one variant out of millions. Still, to detect type errors it is necessary that all variants are syntactically correct in the first place; thus, we build our type system on top of disciplined annotations. Additionally, disciplined annotations come in handy, since annotations are already mapped to the underlying abstract syntax tree (see Sec. 5.2.3), which we use also for type analysis. In Figure 5.11, we show how a product-line–aware type system fits into our taxonomy.

Kind of error	Syntax	Typing	Semantic
Error detection	Check variants	Check entire product line	
Languages	Single	Multiple	Inter-language
Implementation	Annotative	Compositional	Other

Figure 5.11.: *Properties of our product-line–aware type system.*

Since language-independent (or inter-language) type systems are still a research topic (with promising results, but without consensus), we focus on a product-line–aware type system for a single language. We first explain our type system for Featherweight Java (a subset of Java) and present a generalization to full Java, other languages, and inter-language typing afterward in Section 5.3.5.

5.3.1. Type errors in software product lines

Before we start with a formal discussion of our type system, we give a quick overview of different type errors that can occur and challenges for the type system.

We present a couple of examples, which are simplified for conciseness almost to the edge of triviality, but which stem from earlier experience in Berkeley DB (see Sec. 3.1.7).

Method invocations.   As a first example, consider the code fragment in Figure 5.12 of a class *Storage* used by another class *Database*. In a read-only database variant, setting values in the storage class is not supported, therefore the according code is annotated to be removed unless a feature WRITE is selected (*#ifdef*).

```
1  class Database {
2      void insert(Object key, Object data, Txn txn) {
3          storage.set(key, data, txn.getLock());
4      }
5  }
6  class Storage {
7  #ifdef WRITE
8      boolean set(Object key, Object data, Lock lock) { ... }
9  #endif
10 }
```

Figure 5.12.: *Ill-typed method invocation.*

While this code is well-typed for all variants that actually select the feature WRITE, the method invocation of *set* in Line 3 (underlined) cannot be resolved in variants in which WRITE is not selected. In such cases the method invocation is left without a method declaration. If read-only databases are not generated during development, this error might go undetected for a long time. In some cases, it might only be detected after development, when a customer actually requests a variant without WRITE. To type check the entire software product line, we need to make sure that the method invocation can *reach* a method declaration in *every* variant in which the invocation itself is not removed. One of many possible solutions to eliminate the error in our example is to annotate the *insert* method with WRITE as well.

Type references.   There are numerous similar type errors, for example, when an entire class is annotated as in Figure 5.13. If a database without transactions is generated, compilation will fail because the parameter's type *Txn* (underlined) cannot be resolved. Similar type errors can occur when the class is referenced as return type, when referenced as supertype of a class, when new objects are instantiated, and so on.

Parameters.   To fix the previous error, we could annotate the parameter *txn* of the method *insert* as well, as shown in Figure 5.14, so that in database variants without transactions *insert* has a different signature. To avoid a problem when accessing

```
1  class Database {
2      void insert(Object key, Object data, Txn txn) {
3          storage.set(key, data, txn.getLock()); }
4  }
5  #ifdef TRANSACTIONS
6  class Txn { ... }
7  #endif
```

Figure 5.13.: *Ill-typed type reference.*

the local variable *txn*, we annotate the invocation *"txn.getLock()"* as well. If a database without transactions is generated, typing this variant still fails, because the method invocation *"storage.set(...)"* has only two parameters, but the method declaration expects three.

```
1  class Database {
2      void insert(Object key, Object data #ifdef TRANSACTIONS, Txn txn#endif) {
3          storage.set(key, data #ifdef TRANSACTIONS, txn.getLock()#endif); }
4  }
5  class Storage { boolean set(Object key, Object data, Lock lock) { ... } }
```

Figure 5.14.: *Ill-typed method invocation due to annotation on parameter.*

Again, there are different solutions to make all variants in this example well-typed: we can annotate the *lock* parameter of *set* as well (and all occurrences in the method's body not showed here), or we can overload the method declaration of *set*. Either way, when type checking the entire software product line, we must ensure that the provided parameters match the expected formal parameters in all variants.

Considering the feature model and alternative features. The previous examples were relatively simple because they contained only annotations with a single optional feature. However, a software product line can have hundreds of features and not all combinations of features may make sense. For example, transactions are not necessary in a read-only database; therefore, we do not need to consider a variant with TRANSACTION but without WRITE during type checking. Furthermore, two features like PERSISTENT and IN-MEMORY for data storage can be alternative (mutually exclusive), so that every variant must select one of them, but not both at the same time. Even more complex relationships like "feature A can be selected only when B or C but not D is selected" can occur in practice (see Sec. 2.3).

Features and their relationships in software product lines are described in a *feature model*. There are different forms of how to describe such feature models; a common form is a feature diagram [Kang et al., 1990; Czarnecki and Eisenecker, 2000], but it is also possible to enumerate all valid variants, or to use logics to describe constraints on the feature selection [Batory, 2005; Benavides et al., 2005] (see Sec. 2.3). Based on a feature model, we can decide which feature combinations are *valid* and can be used to generate a variant. When type checking a software product line, we need to consider all valid variants.

In Figure 5.15, we show an example of a code fragment that is well-typed only if we know (a) that PERSISTENT and IN-MEMORY are mutually exclusive (otherwise a variant with both features would be ill-typed because class *Storage* would contain two methods with the same signature) and (b) that WRITE can only be selected if either PERSISTENT or IN-MEMORY is selected (otherwise an ill-typed variant could be generated with a method invocation of *set* but no according declaration). This illustrates that we need to consider relationships between features for type checking the software product line.

```
1  class Database {
2  #ifdef WRITE
3      void insert(Object key, Object data, Txn txn) {
4          storage.set(key, data, txn.getLock()); }
5  #endif
6  }
7  class Storage {
8  #ifdef PERSISTENT
9      boolean set(Object key, Object data, Lock lock) { /* implementation A */ }
10 #endif
11 #ifdef INMEMORY
12     boolean set(Object key, Object data, Lock lock) { /* implementation B */ }
13 #endif
14 }
```

Figure 5.15.: *Alternative implementations of a method declaration.*

5.3.2. Desired properties

There are two properties, which we want to achieve with a type system for software product lines: *generation preserves typing* and *backward compatibility*. The first is the necessary core of guaranteeing type safety for all variants and the second is an optional, tool-driven property, as we will explain.

Generation preserves typing.   We want to guarantee that every variant which we can generate from a software product line is well-typed. If a software product line allows ill-typed variants, we want an error message upfront, without actually generating a single variant. We call a software product line well-typed if all variants it can generate are well-typed.

Backward compatibility.   We want a software product line that we strip of all its annotations to be a well-typed program (not necessarily a variant with reasonable runtime semantics). For our work with Java, this implies two things: (a) our type system is an extension of Java's type system and not a replacement, and (b) we do not want to introduce new language constructs, because this would no longer be a Java program. This desired property might appear arbitrary but has a background from a tool developer's perspective. As soon as we introduce a new keyword, or just allow multiple methods with the same name, the existing tool infrastructure can no longer be used and must be rewritten. For example, this problem was experienced by the AspectJ-development-tools team and Scala team that provided commercial-quality Eclipse plug-ins for AspectJ and Scala. Because AspectJ and Scala extend the Java syntax, the existing editors including syntax highlighting, outline views, navigation, or code completion could not be reused; enormous effort was required to rewrite the entire tool infrastructure (often through "coping and editing") [Chapman, 2006; McDirmid and Odersky, 2006]. On the other hand, adopting a new language for software product lines without adequate tool support is difficult for developers that are used to the comfort of modern development environments.

Backward compatibility is not necessary and can be discussed controversially. On the one hand, if we drop backward compatibility, we can build a more expressive language, especially considering alternative features, as we will discuss in Section 5.3.4. On the other hand, if we retain backward compatibility and design a type system as extension, we can leave the existing type checker and tool infrastructure as is, and just add the additional conditions on top. From our perspective, backward compatibility is desirable; it influenced several design decisions, which we discuss in the respective sections.

5.3.3. Colored Featherweight Java (CFJ)

With Colored Featherweight Java (CFJ), we introduce a calculus of a language and type system for software product lines.[7] We designed CFJ for a subset of Java on top of disciplined annotations. It fulfills both desired properties: variant generation preserves typing and backward compatibility.

We decided to provide a formalization and proof for both properties, after an initial implementation of our type system for Java. We soon found that our implementation was incomplete: We could not give a guarantee and sometimes generated ill-typed variants because we forgot some checks. We found similar problems in other implementations (see related work in Section 5.4). At the same time, a formalization of our type checks for the entire Java language is not feasible because of Java's complexity. Instead, we formalize product-line–aware type checking mech-

---

[7]We presented CFJ first in [Kästner and Apel, 2008b]. Here, we present a refined and extended version of the type system. We made slight changes to increase flexibility regarding annotations on parameters. Thüm [2010] contributed some simplifications to reduce redundant checks.

anism for Featherweight Java (FJ), a subset of Java, and give an outlook how it can be extended toward full Java or other languages in Section 5.3.5.

Although CFJ is based on the existing language FJ (and CFJ's type system is an extension of FJ's type system, due to backward compatibility), CFJ must be considered as a separate language, not as an extended one, to describe an entire software product line instead of a single program. Software product lines written in CFJ are never directly executed, but are used to generate FJ programs, as we will show later.

Featherweight Java

FJ is a minimal functional subset of the Java language for which typing and evaluation are specified formally and proved type-sound with the FJ calculus [Igarashi et al., 2001; Pierce, 2002]. It was designed to be compact; its syntax, type judgments and operational semantics fit on a single sheet of paper. FJ strips Java of many advanced features such as interfaces, abstract classes, inner classes, and even assignments, while retaining the core features of Java typing. There is a direct correspondence between FJ and a purely functional core of Java, such that every FJ program is literally an executable Java program.

The motivation behind FJ was to experiment with formal extensions of Java, while focusing only on the core typing features and neglecting many special cases that would require a larger calculus, without raising substantially different typing issues. Because of its simplicity even proofs for significant extensions remain manageable. For the same reasons, we chose FJ over other calculi of Java subsets such as Classic Java [Flatt et al., 1998], Java$_{light}$ [Nipkow and von Oheimb, 1998], Java^s [Drossopoulou et al., 2000], or Lightweight Java [Strniša et al., 2007]. Besides many other examples, FJ was used to formally discuss an extension of Java with generics [Igarashi et al., 2001], to formally discuss inner classes [Igarashi and Pierce, 2002], and to reason about new composition techniques such as nested inheritance [Nystrom et al., 2004].

To save a tree, we do not repeat the FJ calculus, however its mechanisms will become clear from our formalization of CFJ as we highlight our modifications and repeat unmodified rules.

Syntax and annotations

First, we describe CFJ's syntax and how feature annotations are introduced in the calculus. For CFJ, we use the original FJ syntax without casts, as shown in Figure 5.16.[8] As in FJ, we use the following notational conventions: $\bar{x}$ denotes a

---

[8]An earlier version of our type system included casts [Kästner and Apel, 2008b]. Although casts were essential in the original Featherweight Java publication for the discussion about parametric polymorphism [Igarashi et al., 2001], casts do not add anything new for type checking product

$P ::= (\overline{L}, t, \overline{FM})$	CFJ program (SPL)
$L ::=$ class C extends C { $\overline{C\ f}$; K $\overline{M}$ }	class declaration
$K ::= C(\overline{C\ f})$ { super($\overline{f}$); $\overline{this.f=f}$; }	constructor declaration
$M ::= C\ m(\overline{C\ x})$ { return t; }	method declaration
$t ::=$	terms:
x	variable
t.f	field access
t.m($\overline{t}$)	method invocation
new C($\overline{t}$)	object creation

Figure 5.16.: *CFJ syntax.*

list of elements $x_1\ x_2 \ldots x_n$ and relations and operations on lists are applied to all entries; for example, $f(\overline{x}) = y$ is short for $\big(f(x_1) = y\big) \wedge \big(f(x_2) = y\big) \wedge \ldots \wedge \big(f(x_n) = y\big)$ and $f(\overline{x}) = g(\overline{y})$ is short for $\big(f(x_1) = g(y_1)\big) \wedge \big(f(x_2) = g(y_2)\big) \wedge \ldots \wedge \big(f(x_n) = g(y_n)\big)$. Finally, also as in FJ, we require elements of lists to be named uniquely; for example, there may not be two methods with the same name in a class.

As in FJ, a class table CT maps each class' name to its declaration and has the sanity conditions: (a) $CT(C) = $ class C... for every $C \in dom(CT)$; (b) Object $\notin dom(CT)$; (c) for every class name C (except Object) appearing anywhere in CT, we have $C \in dom(CT)$; and (d) there are no cycles in the subtype relation (see below) induced by CT.

Next, we need to define what code fragments can be annotated. Following our model of disciplined annotations (see Sec. 5.2), only optional code fragments, which can be removed without invalidating the syntax, can be annotated. In CFJ, these are (printed bold in Fig. 5.16) elements of the class list ($\overline{L}$), of field and parameter lists ($\overline{C\ f}$ and $\overline{C\ x}$), method lists ($\overline{M}$), term lists ($\overline{t}$), super call parameter lists ($\overline{f}$), or field assignments ($\overline{this.f=f}$). Restricting annotations and removal to only these elements guarantees syntactic correctness for all variants, but of course not yet the absence of type errors.

To introduce annotations into the calculus, there are many different possibilities. For example, we could change the syntax, such that we introduce #*ifdef* and #*endif* directives. Instead, we use a more general solution, which can be mapped to a specific surface syntax or tool. In our formalization, we introduce annotations using an *annotation table AT* that maps code fragments to their annotations,

---

lines. We decided to remove casts to streamline presentation and proofs.

We make slight modifications to the notation in [Igarashi et al., 2001]: We use $\overline{C\ f}$ instead of $\overline{C}\ \overline{f}$ to emphasize that it is a list of pairs rather than a pair of lists; the same for $\overline{C\ x}$ and $\overline{this.f=f}$. Note that this.f=f is one syntactic expression and not a relation between two. Additionally, although it is technically not a syntax rule in FJ, we explicitly introduce the program P into the syntax for symmetry in the generation process and proofs later.

similar to the class table CT. This corresponds directly to our mapping of annotations to AST elements, as discussed in the context of disciplined annotations in Section 5.2.3. When formalizing other preprocessors it is possible to parse textual annotations like #*ifdef* of some surface syntax into the annotation table and remove textual annotations from the product line's code base during type checking.

The annotation table is used the following way: $AT(\mathsf{L})$ returns the annotation of a class declaration, $AT(\mathsf{C}\ \mathsf{f})$ returns the annotation for a field, $AT(\mathsf{C}\ \mathsf{x})$ returns the annotation for a parameter, $AT(\mathsf{M})$ returns the annotation for a method, $AT(\mathsf{t})$ returns the annotation for a term, $AT(\mathsf{f})$ and $AT(\mathsf{this.f=f})$ return annotations for parameters and assignments inside the constructor. Furthermore, we use $AT(\mathsf{C})$ as syntactic sugar for $AT(CT(\mathsf{C}))$ to look up annotations on a class from a class name. Note that AT maps annotations from code elements (identified by their location) to annotations, not from names. For example, AT can map two methods *foo* in different classes to different annotations, the result of $AT(\mathsf{foo})$ depends which declaration of *foo* is referenced. The annotation table is equivalent to introducing annotations into the syntax, but makes the formalization easier to read.[9] Both annotation table and class table are provided by the compiler.

Reasoning about annotations

So far, we did not discuss the nature of feature annotations. As illustrated in our examples in Section 5.3.1, we are interested in reachability conditions like the following sentence *"whenever code fragment a is present, then also code fragment b is present"* based on their annotations. (We use the metavariables a and b to refer to arbitrary annotatable code fragments.) This is necessary, for example, to check whether a method invocation in code fragment a can always reference a method declaration in code fragment b, in all variants in that a is present. To answer such question we need to define both (a) what kind of annotations are possible and (b) how are they evaluated.

For annotations there are different approaches in different tools. In our implementation in CIDE, we even support different kinds of annotations through a plug-in mechanism. For a given variant with feature selection F this can be:

1. In [Thaker et al., 2007], each code fragment is (implicitly) annotated with exactly one feature; a code fragment is removed if the annotated feature is not selected in F.

2. In CIDE, by default, each code fragment can be annotated by one feature

---

[9]Actually, the annotation table is close to our implementation in our prototype CIDE, in which annotations are mapped to AST elements, which are identified by a unique ID. In contrast, for his formalization of CFJ with the proof assistant Coq, Thüm [2010] included annotations in the syntax, instead of adding an additional annotation table, which avoids keeping track of element locations or identifiers.

or a set of features. This is equivalent to *#ifdef* directives and nested *#ifdef* directives over single features. For a feature selection *F*, an annotated code fragment is removed if one of the annotated features is not selected in *F*.

3. In [Czarnecki and Pietroszek, 2006], arbitrary propositional formulas called *presence conditions* like *"(A or B) and not C"* are annotated. An annotated code fragment is removed if the formula evaluates to *false* for an assignment corresponding to the feature selection from *F*.[10]

4. Finally, in *pure::variants* (and also in CIDE when using the *pure::variants* connector) an annotation can be specified as Prolog expression or in a proprietary constraint language. Features can additionally have attributes (text, numerical values, etc.) and annotations can reason about these attributes (e.g., include code fragment only if text attribute *title* is not *"default"* or if numerical attribute *max-weight* < 4.25). Some other feature modeling tools also provide their own languages. Again, the code fragment is removed if the expression evaluates to *false* given the feature selection.

In our implementation, we use propositional formulas for feature models and for annotations, but in our formalization, we abstract from concrete formalisms. $AT(a)$ generally returns some expression that evaluates to *false* for a variant with feature selection *F* (i.e., $eval(AT(a), F) = false$) when the code fragment a should be removed, while each tool has to provide some implementation of *eval*. The empty annotation always evaluates to *true*, thus elements without annotations are never removed. Throughout this section, we use the term *'a code fragment is present'* for "the code fragment's annotation evaluates to *true*, therefore the element is not removed in the given variant(s)".

We can now define reachability between a and b as "whenever $AT(a)$ evaluates to *true* then also $AT(b)$ must evaluate to *true*" and denote it as follows:

$$AT(a) \rightarrow AT(b) ::=$$
$$\forall F \in \text{valid feature selections} : eval(AT(a), F) \Rightarrow eval(AT(b), F)$$

In other words, the variants in which code fragment b is included are a subset of (or are the same as) the variants in which code fragment a is included.

A naive approach of determining reachability by iterating over all valid selections does not scale, since there could be millions of valid variants. Still, there are several ways to evaluate the reachability formula efficiently using a SAT solver, a constraint-satisfaction-problem solver, or a Prolog engine, depending on how

---

[10]Complex presence conditions can also be encoded in CIDE by adding a new (dummy) feature to the feature model. In the feature model, a condition can express that the new feature is selected if and only if a certain condition on other features such as *"(A or B) and not C"* is fulfilled. Then the new feature can be used to annotate code, representing the more complex presence condition. We used this encoding in several case studies.

valid feature models, feature selections, and annotations are specified. In the common case that constraints between features can be represented by a propositional formula C_{FM} (e.g., most feature models can be transformed directly into propositional formulas [Batory, 2005; Thüm, 2008]), and when all annotations can be transformed into propositional formulas (which is possible in most tools), then we can automatically evaluate $AT(\mathsf{a}) \rightarrow AT(\mathsf{b})$ with a SAT solver as described by Thaker et al. [2007]: If the formula $\neg(C_{FM} \Rightarrow (AT(\mathsf{a}) \Rightarrow AT(\mathsf{b})))$ is not satisfiable then b is always reachable from a. For technical details how to reason about feature models and annotations using a SAT solver, see Batory [2005] and Thaker et al. [2007]. As Mendonça et al. [2009]Mendonça et al. and Thüm et al. [2009]Thüm et al. have shown, reasoning about feature models with SAT solvers is tractable for even very large feature models.

Annotation rules

Before we formally model the annotation checks as extensions in CFJ's type judgments, we first informally introduce the annotation rules that are to be checked. In general, we need to check code fragments that *reference* other code fragments. The code fragments – references and targets – must be annotated such that the target is *always reachable* from the reference. Otherwise, dangling references that typically result in ill-typed programs can occur. We start with this informal list of annotation rules, then model them formally in CFJ's type system (pp. 110ff), and later prove them to be complete (pp. 116ff). We have identified checks for thirteen different pairs of references and targets:[11]

(L.1) A *class* L can extend only a class that is reachable.

(L.2) A *field* C f can have only a type C of a class L that is reachable.

(K.1) A *super constructor call (i)* can pass only those parameters that are bound to constructor parameters and *(ii)* must pass exactly the parameters expected by the super constructor.

(K.2) A *field assignment* this.f=f in a constructor can *(i)* access only present fields C f in the same class and *(ii)* assign only values that are bound to constructor parameters.

(K.3) A *constructor parameter* C f can have only a type C of a class L that is reachable.

(M.1) A *method declaration* C m($\overline{\mathsf{C}\ \mathsf{x}}$) { return t; } can have only a return type C of a class L that is reachable.

---

[11]The names in this list reference the according productions in CFJ's syntax in Figure 5.16. For example, K.1 is the first check that addresses the constructor.

(M.2) A method declaration *overriding* another method declaration must have the same signature in all variants in which both are present.

(M.3) A *method declaration parameter* C x can have only a type C of a class L that is reachable.

(T.1) A *variable* x must be bound to a reachable parameter C x of its enclosing method.

(T.2) A *field access* t.f can access only a field C f that is reachable in the enclosing class or its superclasses.

(T.3) A *method invocation* t.m($\bar{t}$) *(i)* can invoke only a method M that is reachable and *(ii)* must pass exactly the parameters $\bar{t}$ expected by this method.

(T.4) An *object creation* new C($\bar{t}$) *(i)* can create only objects from a class L that is reachable and *(ii)* must pass exactly the parameters $\bar{t}$ expected by the target's constructor.

Furthermore, there are some rules that deal with the removal process of children from their parent element. For example, if a class is removed also all methods therein must be removed, if a method is removed also its parameters and its term must be removed. This is an instance of the subtree rule for disciplined annotations to properly propagate annotations from parent to child elements (see Sec. 5.2.2). These rules seem obvious and are actually enforced in *#ifdef*-like preprocessors by nesting annotations. However, when formalizing the calculus with arbitrary annotations, we either have to always take all parent annotations into considerations, or we have to make these rules explicit for all elements that can be annotated. We decide for the latter because it better integrates with wrappers in our implementation; we add the following subtree rules:

(SL.1) A *field* is present only when the enclosing class is reachable.

(SL.2) A *method* is present only when the enclosing class is reachable.

(SK.1) A *constructor parameter* is present only when the enclosing class is reachable.

(SK.2) A *super constructor invocation parameter* is present only when the enclosing class is reachable.

(SK.3) A *field assignment* in a constructor is present only when the enclosing class is reachable.

(SM.1) A *method parameter* is present only when the enclosing method is reachable.

(ST.1) A *method invocation parameter* is present only when the enclosing term is reachable.

$$C <: C \qquad \frac{C <: D \quad D <: E}{C <: E} \qquad \frac{\text{class C extends D} \{ \ldots \}}{C <: D}$$

Figure 5.17.: *CFJ subtyping.*

(ST.2) An *object creation parameter* is present only when the enclosing term is reachable.

In the remainder of this section, we highlight changes compared to the original FJ calculus for the annotation rules (L.1–T.5) in light gray and changes for the subtree rules (SL.1–ST.2) in darker gray.

Typing

Subtyping. CFJ's subtyping relation $<:$, shown in Figure 5.17, is identical to FJ's. Though we could check the annotation rule (L.1) here, we decided to postpone this check to FJ's type judgments instead (see T-CLASS).

Auxiliary functions. As in FJ, we need some auxiliary definitions for the type judgments shown in Figure 5.18. Although we try to perform most annotation checks in the type judgments, there are cases in which already the auxiliary functions – that are used in FJ to recursively look up fields or methods across the inheritance hierarchy – need to evaluate annotations. We use $\mathcal{A}$ as a metavariable for annotations (e.g., presence conditions in the form of a propositional formula) and use $\bullet$ to denote an empty sequence.

Field lookup. First, a field lookup determines all fields of a class C including fields inherited from superclasses. In CFJ, the function *fields* is identical to FJ. Annotations on fields are checked later in the type judgments.

Method lookup. Second, similar to the field lookup, the method lookup *mtype* finds methods with a given name m in a class C or its superclasses. In contrast to fields, the method lookup needs to be adapted because of the possibility of method overriding (in contrast to overshadowing fields, which is not allowed in FJ [Igarashi et al., 2001]). Thus, it could be possible that a method m in class C is not always reachable for a given annotation $\mathcal{A}$, but another method m in a superclass of C is. Therefore, we cannot check annotations only in the type judgments but have to adapt the auxiliary function *mtype* as shown in Figure 5.18.

In FJ, there are two possible cases, either the method is found in class C, then its signature is returned, or the method is not found, then the search proceeds to the superclass. In CFJ, we additionally have to distinguish whether

Field lookup

$$\boxed{\mathit{fields}(\mathsf{C}) = \overline{\mathsf{C}\,\mathsf{f}}}$$

$$\mathit{fields}(\mathsf{Object}) = \bullet$$

$$\frac{CT(\mathsf{C}) = \text{class C extends D} \{\,\overline{\mathsf{C}\,\mathsf{f}};\,\mathsf{K}\,\overline{\mathsf{M}}\,\}\quad \mathit{fields}(\mathsf{D}) = \overline{\mathsf{D}\,\mathsf{g}}}{\mathit{fields}(\mathsf{C}) = \overline{\mathsf{D}\,\mathsf{g}},\overline{\mathsf{C}\,\mathsf{f}}}$$

Method lookup

$$\boxed{\mathit{mtype}(\mathsf{m},\mathsf{C},\mathcal{A}) = \overline{\mathsf{B}\,\mathsf{x}} \to \mathsf{B}}$$

$$\frac{CT(\mathsf{C}) = \text{class C extends D} \{\,\overline{\mathsf{C}\,\mathsf{f}};\,\mathsf{K}\,\overline{\mathsf{M}}\,\}\quad \mathsf{M} = \mathsf{B}\,\mathsf{m}(\overline{\mathsf{B}\,\mathsf{x}})\,\{\,\text{return t};\,\}\quad \mathsf{M} \in \overline{\mathsf{M}} \qquad \mathcal{A} \to AT(\mathsf{M})}{\mathit{mtype}(\mathsf{m},\mathsf{C},\mathcal{A}) = \overline{\mathsf{B}\,\mathsf{x}} \to \mathsf{B}}$$

$$\frac{CT(\mathsf{C}) = \text{class C extends D} \{\,\overline{\mathsf{C}\,\mathsf{f}};\,\mathsf{K}\,\overline{\mathsf{M}}\,\}\quad \mathsf{M} = \mathsf{B}\,\mathsf{m}(\overline{\mathsf{B}\,\mathsf{x}})\,\{\,\text{return t};\,\}\quad \mathsf{M} \in \overline{\mathsf{M}} \qquad \neg(\mathcal{A} \to AT(\mathsf{M}))}{\mathit{mtype}(\mathsf{m},\mathsf{C},\mathcal{A}) = \mathit{mtype}(\mathsf{m},\mathsf{D},\mathcal{A} \wedge \neg AT(\mathsf{M}))}$$

$$\frac{CT(\mathsf{C}) = \text{class C extends D} \{\,\overline{\mathsf{C}\,\mathsf{f}};\,\mathsf{K}\,\overline{\mathsf{M}}\,\}\quad \mathsf{m} \text{ is not defined in } \overline{\mathsf{M}}}{\mathit{mtype}(\mathsf{m},\mathsf{C},\mathcal{A}) = \mathit{mtype}(\mathsf{m},\mathsf{D},\mathcal{A})}$$

Overriding

$$\boxed{\mathit{override}(\mathsf{m},\mathsf{C},\overline{\mathsf{C}\,\mathsf{x}} \to \mathsf{C}_0,\mathcal{A})}$$

$$\frac{}{\mathit{override}(\mathsf{m},\mathsf{Object},\overline{\mathsf{C}\,\mathsf{x}} \to \mathsf{C}_0,\mathcal{A})}$$

$$\frac{\begin{array}{c} CT(\mathsf{C}) = \text{class C extends D} \{\,\overline{\mathsf{D}\,\mathsf{f}};\,\mathsf{K}\,\overline{\mathsf{M}}\,\}\quad \mathit{override}(\mathsf{m},\mathsf{D},\overline{\mathsf{C}\,\mathsf{x}} \to \mathsf{C}_0,\mathcal{A}) \\ \mathsf{M} = \mathsf{B}_0\,\mathsf{m}(\overline{\mathsf{B}\,\mathsf{g}})\,\{\,\text{return t};\,\} \\ \mathsf{M} \in \overline{\mathsf{M}} \text{ implies } \overline{\mathsf{C}} = \overline{\mathsf{B}} \text{ and } \mathsf{C}_0 = \mathsf{B}_0 \text{ and } (\mathcal{A} \wedge AT(\mathsf{M})) \to (AT(\overline{\mathsf{C}\,\mathsf{x}}) \leftrightarrow AT(\overline{\mathsf{B}\,\mathsf{g}})) \end{array}}{\mathit{override}(\mathsf{m},\mathsf{C},\overline{\mathsf{C}\,\mathsf{x}} \to \mathsf{C}_0,\mathcal{A})}$$

Figure 5.18.: *CFJ auxiliary functions.*

found method is always reachable or not. Reachability is checked against a given annotation that is provided as a parameter $\mathcal{A}$ (i.e., $\mathcal{A} \rightarrow AT(\mathsf{M})$). In case the method is not always reachable, the search is continued in the superclass for the remaining variants with a reduced annotation $(\mathcal{A} \wedge \neg AT(\mathsf{M}))$. For technical reasons, we return the entire parameter list $\overline{\mathsf{B}}\,\mathsf{x}$ instead only their types, so that we can later (in rule T-Invk) reason about annotations on parameters. Note that auxiliary function *override*, as described below, checks that all these methods have compatible signatures; here, we check overridden methods only regarding reachability.

Overriding. Finally, the third auxiliary function *override* checks valid method overriding in FJ. In the presence of annotations, checking valid overriding is trickier than expected. We need to ensure that the return type and parameter types match in every variant in which two methods with the same name appear in the inheritance hierarchy of a class. This is complicated by allowing developers to annotate both methods and their parameters.

Method overriding is also the first and most important rule for which considerations regarding the desired backward compatibility – every CFJ program stripped of its annotation should be a well-typed FJ program – have influenced design decisions. We describe our solution fulfilling this property first and discuss possible alternatives later.

Our function *override* works in the following way: for a given method m with annotation $\mathcal{A}$ and type $\overline{\mathsf{C}} \rightarrow \mathsf{C}_0$, we iterate over all superclasses until we reach Object. Whenever we find a method in a superclass with the same name, we perform the two checks. First, for backward compatibility, the return type and all parameter types must match independent of any annotation ($\mathsf{C}_0 = \mathsf{B}_0$ and $\overline{\mathsf{C}} = \overline{\mathsf{B}}$); this implies also that both methods have the same number of parameters. Second, for (M.2), in all variants in which both methods are present (i.e., for which both $\mathcal{A}$ and $AT(\mathsf{M})$ both evaluate to true) the annotations on parameters must be equivalent (formalized as $(\mathcal{A} \wedge AT(\mathsf{M})) \rightarrow (AT(\overline{\mathsf{C}\,\mathsf{f}}) \leftrightarrow AT(\overline{\mathsf{B}\,\mathsf{g}}))$).[12] Taking both checks into account, we define the auxiliary function *override* as shown in Figure 5.18.

Due to our design decision for backward compatibility, our *override* function does not allow different signatures of a method in mutually exclusive features. For example, although the following code fragment generates only

---

[12] The formula is evaluated as follows:

$$\forall F \in \text{valid feature selections} : \big(eval(\mathcal{A}, F) \wedge eval(AT(\mathsf{M}), F)\big) \Rightarrow$$
$$\Big(\big(eval(AT(\mathsf{C}_1\,\mathsf{f}_1), F) \Leftrightarrow eval(AT(\mathsf{B}_1\,\mathsf{g}_1), F)\big) \wedge \cdots \wedge \big(eval(AT(\mathsf{C}_n\,\mathsf{f}_n), F) \Leftrightarrow eval(AT(\mathsf{B}_n\,\mathsf{g}_n), F)\big)\Big)$$

well-typed variants given that features X and Y are mutually exclusive, it is rejected by our *override* function.

```
1 class C extends Object { #ifdef X C foo(C x) { ... } #endif }
2 class D extends C       { C foo(#ifdef Y D y, #endif C x) { ... } }
```

Different type judgments would be possible that drop backward compatibility in exchange for increased expressiveness. In such case, we would need to check valid overriding only when two methods can occur in the same variant. Since we pursue backward compatibility, we keep our simpler version of *override*. For developers this restricted expressiveness is not limiting since simple workarounds can be used; in the code example above, we could add a parameter D y to the first method declaration and annotate it such that it is never present in any variant.

Type judgments. For term typing and well-formedness rules, we revisit each type judgment in FJ and adapt it for CFJ to incorporate annotations as shown in Figure 5.19. For brevity, we discuss only changes compared to FJ.

For all term type judgments, we need an environment that, compared to FJ, is extended for annotations. The environment Γ is a finite mapping from variables to pairs of a type and an annotation written $\overline{x} : \overline{C} \ with \ \overline{A}$. Additionally, the current annotation $\mathcal{A}$ is stored as environment. For the outermost term in a method, the current annotation is the annotation of a method (see T-METHOD), for inner terms the current annotation may change because parameters can be annotated individually (see T-INVK and T-NEW). The type judgment for terms has the form $\mathcal{A}; \Gamma \vdash t : C$ and reads "in the environment Γ with the current annotation $\mathcal{A}$, term t has the type C".

T-VAR. When typing a variable, we need to ensure that the variable is reachable in all variants in which x is accessed. This means that we check the current annotation of the variable access $\mathcal{A}$ against the annotation $\mathcal{A}'$ of the parameter (or this) passed through the environment Γ from T-METHOD.

T-FIELD. For typing field accesses, we require that the target field declaration is reachable (T.2). Therefore, we check the current annotation $\mathcal{A}$ against the annotation of the target field ($AT(C_i \ f_i)$). The type judgment for classes (see T-CLASS) ensures that the class corresponding to each field's type (C_i) is reachable (L.2).

T-INVK. For typing method invocations, we similarly check that the target method is present (T.3i) using the filtering of *mtype*. In method invocations, parameters can be annotated individually, so we need to check that the invocation parameters match the expected parameters of the method declaration in every variant (T.3ii). We use the same mechanism $\mathcal{A} \to (AT(\overline{t}) \leftrightarrow AT(\overline{D \ y}))$ as

Term typing $\boxed{\mathcal{A};\Gamma \vdash t : C}$

$$\frac{x : C \; \mathit{with}\; \mathcal{A}' \in \Gamma \quad \mathcal{A} \rightarrow \mathcal{A}'}{\mathcal{A};\Gamma \vdash x : C} \qquad \text{(T-Var)}$$

$$\frac{\mathcal{A};\Gamma \vdash t_0 : C_0 \quad \mathit{fields}(C_0) = \overline{C}\,\overline{f} \quad \mathcal{A} \rightarrow AT(C_i\, f_i)}{\mathcal{A};\Gamma \vdash t_0.f_i : C_i} \qquad \text{(T-Field)}$$

$$\frac{\mathcal{A};\Gamma \vdash t_0 : C_0 \quad \mathit{mtype}(m,C_0,\mathcal{A}) = \overline{D}\,\overline{y} \rightarrow C}{AT(\overline{t});\Gamma \vdash \overline{t} : \overline{C} \quad \overline{C} <: \overline{D} \quad \mathcal{A} \rightarrow (AT(\overline{t}) \leftrightarrow AT(\overline{D}\,\overline{y})) \quad AT(\overline{t}) \rightarrow \mathcal{A}}{\mathcal{A};\Gamma \vdash t_0.m(\overline{t}) : C} \qquad \text{(T-Invk)}$$

$$\frac{\mathit{fields}(C) = \overline{D}\,\overline{f} \quad AT(\overline{t});\Gamma \vdash \overline{t} : \overline{C} \quad \overline{C} <: \overline{D}}{\mathcal{A} \rightarrow AT(C) \quad \mathcal{A} \rightarrow (AT(\overline{t}) \leftrightarrow AT(\overline{D}\,\overline{f})) \quad AT(\overline{t}) \rightarrow \mathcal{A}}{\mathcal{A};\Gamma \vdash \mathsf{new}\; C(\overline{t}) : C} \qquad \text{(T-New)}$$

Method typing $\boxed{\text{M OK in C}}$

$$\frac{\begin{array}{c} M = C_0\; m(\overline{C}\,\overline{x})\;\{\; \mathsf{return}\; t_0;\; \} \quad AT(M) = \mathcal{A} \\ \mathcal{A} \rightarrow AT(C_0) \quad AT(\overline{C}\,\overline{x}) \rightarrow AT(\overline{C}) \quad AT(\overline{C}\,\overline{x}) \rightarrow \mathcal{A} \\ CT(C) = \mathsf{class}\; C\; \mathsf{extends}\; D\; \{\ldots\} \quad \mathit{override}(m,D,\overline{C} \rightarrow C_0,\mathcal{A}) \\ \Gamma = \overline{x} : \overline{C}\; \mathit{with}\; AT(\overline{C}\,\overline{x}), \mathsf{this} : C\; \mathit{with}\; AT(C) \quad \mathcal{A};\Gamma \vdash t_0 : E_0 \quad E_0 <: C_0 \end{array}}{\text{M OK in C}} \qquad \text{(T-Method)}$$

Class typing $\boxed{\text{C OK}}$

$$\frac{\begin{array}{c} K = C(\overline{D}\,\overline{g},\, \overline{C}\,\overline{f}')\;\{\; \mathsf{super}(\overline{g}');\; \overline{\mathsf{this}.f{=}f};\; \} \quad \overline{M}\; \text{OK in C} \quad \mathit{fields}(D) = \overline{D}\,\overline{g}'' \\ AT(C) = \mathcal{A} \quad \mathcal{A} \rightarrow AT(D) \quad \overline{C}\,\overline{f} = \overline{C}\,\overline{f}' \quad \overline{D}\,\overline{g} = \overline{D}\,\overline{g}'' \quad \overline{g} = \overline{g}' \\ AT(\overline{C}\,\overline{f}) \leftrightarrow AT(\overline{\mathsf{this}.f{=}f}) \quad AT(\overline{C}\,\overline{f}) \leftrightarrow AT(\overline{C}\,\overline{f}') \\ AT(\overline{D}\,\overline{g}) \leftrightarrow AT(\overline{g}') \quad \mathcal{A} \rightarrow (AT(\overline{D}\,\overline{g}) \leftrightarrow AT(\overline{D}\,\overline{g}'')) \\ AT(\overline{C}\,\overline{f}) \rightarrow AT(C) \quad AT(\overline{C}\,\overline{f}) \rightarrow \mathcal{A} \quad AT(\overline{M}) \rightarrow \mathcal{A} \quad AT(\overline{D}\,\overline{g}) \rightarrow \mathcal{A} \end{array}}{\mathsf{class}\; C\; \mathsf{extends}\; D\; \{\; \overline{C}\,\overline{f};\; K\; \overline{M}\; \}\; \text{OK}} \qquad \text{(T-Class)}$$

Product-line typing $\boxed{\text{P OK}}$

$$\frac{\overline{L}\; \text{OK} \qquad ;\vdash t : C}{(\overline{L}, t)\; \text{OK}} \qquad \text{(T-SPL)}$$

Figure 5.19.: *CFJ typing.*

for the *override* function (with the same implications for backward compatibility). Furthermore, when typing a parameter, the annotation context is set to the annotation of this parameter ($AT(t_i); \Gamma \vdash t_i : C_i$). Finally, the subtree rule (ST.1) is checked: There must not be a variant in which the invocation is removed but not its parameter ($AT(\bar{t}) \to \mathcal{A}$).

T-NEW. Typing an object creation term is similar to typing a method invocation. First, the target class must be present (T.4*i*), which is checked explicitly with $\mathcal{A} \to AT(C)$. Additionally for rule (T.4*ii*), we ensure that the provided parameters match the expected constructor parameters in every variant ($\mathcal{A} \to (AT(\bar{t}) \leftrightarrow AT(\overline{D\,f}))$). Finally, the subtree rule (ST.2) is checked.

T-METHOD. The type judgment for method declarations has the form M OK in C and reads "method declaration M is ok, when it occurs in class C". We make several extensions shown in Figure 5.19: First, we pass the method's annotation to *override* to check valid overriding in all variants (M.2). Second, we check that the class corresponding to the return type and all parameters of the method (C_0 and $\overline{C}$) are reachable (M.1, M.3).[13] Third, we provide the annotations of parameters in the type context to be checked in T-VAR later (T.1), and use the current annotation of the method $\mathcal{A}$ as annotation context. Finally, we check the subtree rule (SM.1).

T-CLASS. The type judgment for class declarations has the form L OK. At first, it appears very complex because it covers several annotation rules, but each rule by itself is simple. To distinguish the occurrences of $\bar{g}$ as constructor parameters, super invocation parameters, and fields of the superclass – which can all have different annotations – we distinguish $\bar{g}$, $\bar{g}'$ and $\bar{g}''$ but still assume that all $\bar{g}$'s are named the same ($\bar{g} = \bar{g}' = \bar{g}''$). The same for $\overline{C\,f}$ that is used both for fields and constructor parameters ($\overline{C\,f} = \overline{C\,f}'$).

First, rule (L.1) checks that the superclass is always reachable ($\mathcal{A} \to AT(D)$); thus, from every reachable class, we can reach all its superclasses. Second, rule (K.1) specifies that the super-constructor call receives exactly those parameters from the constructor's parameter list that are defined as fields in the superclass in all variants ($AT(\overline{D\,g}) \leftrightarrow AT(\bar{g}')$ and $\mathcal{A} \to (AT(\overline{D\,g}) \leftrightarrow AT(\overline{D\,g}''))$). Third, rule (K.2) specifies that the other constructor parameters match the field assignments and that those match the fields declared in the class ($AT(\overline{C\,f}) \leftrightarrow AT(\overline{\text{this.f=f}})$ and $AT(\overline{C\,f}) \leftrightarrow AT(\overline{C\,f}')$). Fourth, we check that the class corresponding to the type of each field in this class is reachable when the field is reachable ($AT(\overline{C\,f}) \to AT(\overline{C})$), which indirectly covers rules (L.2) and (K.3). Finally, subtree rules for fields, methods and constructor parameters (SL.1–2, SK.1–3) are checked.

---

[13]Thüm [2010] proved that the check $\mathcal{A} \to AT(C_0)$ is actually redundant. Still, we leave it for readability.

T-SPL. Finally, we are able to define when a software product line is well-typed (T-SPL): A software product line is well-typed if all of its classes are well-formed and the type judgment returns a type for the start term t (provided an empty environment with an empty annotation, written as ";$\vdash$ t : C").

Variant generation

Although technically possible, we do not execute product lines written in CFJ directly. Thus, there are no evaluation rules for CFJ, and it is not possible or necessary to prove type soundness with the standard theorems progress and preservation [Wright and Felleisen, 1994]. Instead, with a valid feature selection, we generate a tailored FJ programs by removing certain annotated code fragments. The resulting FJ program can be evaluated with FJ's evaluation rules [see Igarashi et al., 2001]. For FJ, Igarashi et al. [2001] already proved type soundness. Hence, we describe the variant generation mechanism and subsequently prove that generation preserves typing.

To generate a program variant, we define a function *variant* that takes a CFJ product line P and a feature selection F as input and returns an FJ program. The function *variant* descends recursively through the code of the product line and applies a function *remove* to all code fragments that can be annotated. The function *remove* evaluates possible annotations (as described in Section 5.3.3): those code fragments, for which the annotation evaluates to *false* are removed, all other code fragments remain in the code. In implementations based on disciplined annotations with ASTs as CIDE, *remove* is implemented using AST transformations, which ensures that separating tokens are placed correctly (see Sec. 5.2.3)

We define the generation rules (bottom-up) in Figure 5.20. For brevity, we write *variant*(a, F) as $[\![a]\!]$ and *remove*($\bar{a}$, F) as $\langle\!\langle \bar{a} \rangle\!\rangle$.

Properties of CFJ

In Section 5.3.2, we discussed two desired properties: backward compatibility and generation preserves typing. With the presented type system and variant generation rules, we can now prove both properties for CFJ. Backward compatibility is straightforward to prove. Generation preserves typing is more complex, so we performed the proof with the proof assistant Coq; for brevity, here, we describe only the theorem and proof strategy. For the interested reader, Thüm [2010] provides a detailed description of the proof, its structure, and its strategies.[14]

Theorem 5.3.1 (Backward compatibility). *Every well-typed CFJ product line stripped of the feature model and all annotations (without removing any code fragments) is a well-typed FJ program.*

---

[14]The machine-checked proof was developed by Thomas Thüm as part of his Master's Thesis (Diplomarbeit) supervised in the context of this PhD project.

$$\boxed{remove(\overline{a}, F), \text{ short } \langle\!\langle \overline{a} \rangle\!\rangle}$$

$$remove(\overline{a}, F) = \begin{cases} a_1, remove(a_2 \ldots a_n, F) & \text{if } eval(AT(a_1), F) \\ remove(a_2 \ldots a_n, F) & \text{else} \end{cases}$$

$$remove(\bullet, F) = \bullet$$

$$\boxed{variant(\overline{a}, F), \text{ short } [\![\overline{a}]\!]}$$

$$[\![x]\!] = x \tag{G.1}$$

$$[\![t.f]\!] = [\![t]\!].f \tag{G.2}$$

$$[\![t.m(\overline{t})]\!] = [\![t]\!].m([\![\langle\!\langle \overline{t} \rangle\!\rangle]\!]) \tag{G.3}$$

$$[\![\text{new } C(\overline{t})]\!] = \text{new } C([\![\langle\!\langle \overline{t} \rangle\!\rangle]\!]) \tag{G.4}$$

$$[\![C \; m(\overline{C \; x}) \; \{\text{return } t;\}]\!] = C \; m(\langle\!\langle \overline{C \; x} \rangle\!\rangle) \; \{\text{return } [\![t]\!];\} \tag{G.5}$$

$$[\![C(\overline{C \; f}) \; \{\text{super}(\overline{f}); \; \overline{\text{this.f=f;}}\}]\!] = C(\langle\!\langle \overline{C \; f} \rangle\!\rangle) \; \{\text{super}(\langle\!\langle \overline{f} \rangle\!\rangle); \; \langle\!\langle \overline{\text{this.f=f;}} \rangle\!\rangle\} \tag{G.6}$$

$$[\![\text{class } C \text{ extends } D \; \{ \; \overline{C \; f}; \; K \; \overline{M} \; \}]\!] = \text{class } C \text{ extends } D \; \{ \; \langle\!\langle \overline{C \; f} \rangle\!\rangle; \; [\![K]\!] \; [\![\langle\!\langle \overline{M} \rangle\!\rangle]\!] \; \} \tag{G.7}$$

$$[\![(\overline{L}, t, FM)]\!] = ([\![\langle\!\langle \overline{L} \rangle\!\rangle]\!], [\![t]\!]) \tag{G.8}$$

Figure 5.20.: *CFJ variant generation with* remove *and* variant.

Proof. CFJ has the same *syntax* as FJ. For stripping annotations, we assume that all annotations evaluate to *true* for all variants (i.e., $\forall F \forall a : eval(AT(a), F)$; called empty annotation). Now, we can prove that with empty annotations, the type systems of FJ and CFJ are equivalent: All reachability checks are always fulfilled; *mtype* in CFJ and FJ are equivalent considering that CFJ's *override* ensures the same method signature for all methods with the same name in a class hierarchy; and the remaining differences are straightforward to prove to be equivalent as well. $\square$

Theorem 5.3.2 (Generation preserves typing). *Every FJ program variant that is generated from a well-typed software product line P with a valid feature selection F is well-typed.*

$$\frac{P \text{ OK} \quad F \text{ is valid}}{variant(P, F) \text{ OK}}$$

Proof Strategy. We prove the theorem by induction on the structure of CFJ product lines, that is, induction over all possible CFJ class tables and all possible CFJ terms. Using induction, we recursively iterate over all elements of the CFJ class table (classes, methods, fields, parameter lists and terms) and the start term. For every CFJ element, if well-typed, we do an induction over the variant generation rules to determine all possibly generated FJ elements and prove that they are well-typed according to the FJ type system.[15] The proof that the generated element is a well-typed FJ element is specific for each different kind of element (e.g., class or method invocation). Generally speaking, we use the CFJ typing rules (including reachability conditions) and the variant generation mechanism to prove that all code elements needed to type a generated FJ element (e.g., referenced classes or methods) are part of the generated FJ program.

To illustrate the proof mechanism, consider the following example for the smallest element: an access to a variable. Variant generation for variables (G.1) is independent of the feature selection F and just returns this variable. Still, we have to prove that any generated FJ variable access is well-typed according to FJ's typing rules. FJ's typing rule T-VAR for variable access requires two conditions: (1) the provided environment Γ must not contain duplicates, and (2) the environment must contain the analyzed variable. For both conditions, we need to consider the FJ environment, which is formed by the enclosing generated method. Hence, we have to consider variant generation for methods, in which parameters can be removed (G.5). We can prove both conditions of FJ's T-VAR using induction on the environment:

1. CFJ's type system forbids duplicates in parameter lists (cf. Sec. 5.3.3); thus, it forbids duplicates in the CFJ environment; variant generation can only remove entries (cf. Fig. 5.20); hence, all parameter lists generated from well-typed CFJ product lines are duplicate free.

2. The generated variable always occurs in the FJ environment. This can be proved as follows: The variable access has been generated from a well-typed CFJ product line. In the well-typed CFJ product line, CFJ's T-VAR ensures that the variable occurs in the CFJ environment $\mathcal{A};\Gamma$ and that $\mathcal{A} \to \mathcal{A}'$, in which $\mathcal{A}'$ is the annotation of the corresponding CFJ method parameter. Additionally, we know that $eval(\mathcal{A}, F)$ is *true*, because otherwise we would not have reached the current point (G.1) of variant generation (variant generation would have stopped in G.3, G.4, G.7, or G.8). Consequently, reachability $\mathcal{A} \to \mathcal{A}'$ implies that $eval(\mathcal{A}', F)$ is also *true*, so the parameter is not removed during variant generation; it is part of the FJ environment.

The proofs for other elements follows a similar pattern. They are often more complex, because more context information (other classes, methods, and fields) has to be considered; nevertheless, the general proof pattern is the same: induction over well-typed CFJ elements and variant generation rules, proving that each generated FJ element is well-typed with information from the induction steps (and

---

[15]In line with FJ, to support Java's mutually recursive types, we assume a fixed CFJ class table. For the same reason, we also assume that the feature selection is fixed so that variant generation produces a unique, fixed FJ class table. Still, since the proof covers arbitrary CFJ class tables and arbitrary feature selections, it holds for all CFJ product lines and all feature selections.

often induction over other elements). Thüm [2010] provides the entire proof as script for Coq.

□

A third interesting property of CFJ's type system is completeness: Given a software product line P and given that *all* valid feature selections F yield well-typed FJ programs according to Theorem 5.3.2, is P well-typed according to the CFJ type judgments? Unfortunately, this property does not hold due to backward compatibility. It is possible to find an ill-typed CFJ product line, of which only well-typed variants are generated; for an example consider the discussion about overriding with different parameters in Section 5.3.3. That is, due to our decision for backward compatibility, CFJ is stricter than actually necessary. Nevertheless, as discussed before, we decided to enforce these restrictions for the benefit of tool developers. Still, with tests and our case studies (see Section 5.3.6), we confirm that CFJ is not too strict for practical applications.

5.3.4. Alternative features

In the formalization of CFJ, our roots in decomposing legacy applications are clearly visible. It is possible to make code fragments optional and to express annotations like *either FeatureA or FeatureB must be selected*. However, in CFJ it is difficult to have two alternative (mutually exclusive) implementations of the same class or method, similar to the persistent vs. in-memory storage example in Figure 5.15 (p. 102). Since we want CFJ to be backward compatible (see Sec. 5.3.2), we cannot simply allow multiple classes or members with the same name (or signature) because this is not supported by FJ (and Java). Nevertheless, alternative features are used in software product lines, when a common implementation expects to reach exactly one (of multiple alternative) implementations of a class or method. Thus, when using a product-line–aware type system for product-line development in general, we need to provide a way to implement and type check alternative features.

In CFJ, alternative features may influence the implementation in different locations:

1. **Alternative Classes:** Depending on the feature selection, there might be entirely alternative implementations of a class. Different implementations may contain different methods, common methods, or different implementations of the same method. They might even have nothing in common except the class's name, as long as both classes are annotated to be mutually exclusive. For example, in the original Jak implementation of the Graph Product Line (see Appendix A.1), different implementations of the classes *Graph*, *Edge*, and *Vertex* were used, depending of the feature selection [Lopez-Herrejon and Batory, 2001].

5. Error detection

```
1  public class Settings {
2    //#ifdef DCOMPATIBILITY2
3    public static final int MAX_REGIONS = 10;
4    //#else
5    public static final int MAX_REGIONS = 15;
6    //#endif
7    ...
8  }
```

(a) Alternative field declarations in *Settings.java*.

```
1  public boolean isItunes() {
2    //#ifdef DITUNES
3    return (m_itunes);
4    //#else
5    return (false);
6    //#endif
7  }
```

(b) Alternative return statements in *RssItunesFeed.java*.

```
1  //#ifndef DTESTUI
2  import javax.microedition.lcdui.List;
3  //#else
4  import com.substanceofcode.testlcdui.List;
5  //#endif
```

(c) Alternative imports in *PromtList.java*.

Figure 5.21.: *Three examples of alternative features in* Mobile RSS Reader.

2. **Alternative Members:** There can be different methods with the same name, but different bodies, parameters, or return types. Depending on the feature selection, a method may be implemented differently as illustrated earlier in Figure 5.15 (p. 102), even with different signatures. Similarly, alternative fields may be defined as shown in an excerpt from the Mobile RSS Reader case study (see Appendix A.1) in Figure 5.21a.

3. **Alternative Terms:** There can be different implementations of a method body, or alternative terms passed as parameters of a method invocation depending on the feature selection. Thus, it is also necessary to discuss alternative implementations of a term as in Figure 5.21b, rather than only of classes or methods.

In full Java and other languages, alternative features may influence other code fragments as well. For example, in 5.21c alternative import statements are used.

Reduction to alternative terms

There are different strategies how to deal with alternative features (in CFJ and in practice). One useful strategy is to reduce most alternative implementations to alternatives at the term level (respectively at statement level in Java). For CFJ, the reduction proceeds in two steps and can be done by the developer or be automated by a tool. Limitations of these steps are written in square brackets and discussed subsequently.

- When there are two or more classes with the same name [and same superclass, see below] but different implementations and annotations, they can be all merged into one class. The new class is annotated with a disjunction of all individual annotations ($\mathcal{A}_1 \vee \mathcal{A}_2 \vee \ldots \vee \mathcal{A}_n$), so that it is present in a variant if any of the original classes would be present. All members from the original classes are moved into the merged class and keep their annotations (the subtree rules (SL.1) and (SL.2) are automatically fulfilled). This step reduces alternative classes to alternative methods in a single merged class.

- When there are two or more methods with the same name [and return type, see below] in a single class declaration, they can be merged to a single method annotated with a disjunction of all previous annotations. Parameters also are merged and annotated with a disjunction of all previous annotations of each parameter. If their bodies are not the same, we need a way to represent alternative terms inside this method. Analogously, multiple fields with the same name [and type, see below] can be merged. This way, we reduce alternative methods to alternative terms.

In Figure 5.22, we show an example of this reduction. In practice this is very useful, for example, we applied it in the CIDE version of the Graph Product Line to eliminate the alternative classes and methods of the original Jak implementation.

```
1  #ifdef PERSISTENT
2  class Storage extends Object {
3      boolean save() { /* impl. A */ }
4      boolean clear() { /* impl. B */ }
5      boolean set(Object key, Object data, Lock lock) { return /* impl. C */; }
6  }
7  #endif
8  #ifdef INMEMORY
9  class Storage extends Object {
10      boolean clear() { /* impl. B */ }
11      boolean set(Object key, Object data) { return /* impl. D */; }
12  }
13  #endif
```

$$\Downarrow$$

```
1  #ifdef PERSISTENT ∨ INMEMORY
2  class Storage extends Object {
3  #ifdef PERSISTENT
4      boolean save() { /* impl. A */ }
5  #endif
6      boolean clear() { /* impl. B */ }
7      boolean set(Object key, Object data #ifdef PERSISTENT, Lock lock#endif) {
8          return #ifdef PERSISTENT/* impl. C */#endif #ifdef INMEMORY/* impl. D */#endif;
9      }
10  }
11  #endif
```

Figure 5.22.: *Reducing alternative classes and alternative methods to alternative terms.*

The reduction to alternative terms is limited regarding superclasses, return types, and field types. That is, if two alternative classes with the same name do not have the same superclass, if two methods with the same name do not have the same return type, or if two fields with the same name do not have the same type, they cannot be merged. We can either accept this limitation and disallow the three problematic cases, or we can search for mechanisms that support alternative implementations beyond alternative terms. To retain backward compatibility and since such cases are rare in practice (usually alternative implementations of a class still provide a common interface), we accept the limitation and suggest workarounds instead of new language features (such as multiple inheritance). A simple workaround, which works for all three problems, is to rename classes, methods, or fields with fresh names. By renaming the target declarations, variability is again propagated to alternative terms where depending on the feature selection either of the now distinguishable methods is invoked, either of the fields is accessed, or either classes is instantiated.For CFJ and our implementation for Java, we prefer this limitation – enforcing constant superclasses, return types, and field types in all alternative implementations of a class method or field – and use this renaming workaround (which can even be automated) for all other cases, instead of complicating the type system. Nevertheless, other solutions without these limitations but with more complex type judgments are possible, see Section 5.4.

Handling alternative terms

So far, we could reduce the problem to alternative terms (in CFJ) or alternative statements (in Java and many other languages). Now, we have to make sure that parser and type checker understand alternative terms/statements and check them accordingly.

In CFJ, the situation is especially problematic, since every method must contain exactly one return statement (i.e., a single term). We must make sure that in every variant exactly one (not none, not multiple) of these terms remains. In [Kästner et al., 2010], we discuss three solutions. Although the first two have significant drawbacks, we briefly summarize all three here:

1. *Method overriding.* Without changes to the CFJ calculus, we found only one way to implement alternative terms by using method overriding. The basic idea is to create an artificial superclass for each alternative term and use method overriding to provide different terms in different classes. In such an implementation, the target method has a different annotation in each subclass, and in a generated variant only one of these methods remains. Although this approach can be used without modification of CFJ and is backward compatible to FJ, it has the drawback of significantly obfuscating the source code with boilerplate code.

2. *New language constructs.* A whole group of solutions for alternative terms becomes available once we drop backward compatibility and decide to change the syntax or type judgments of CFJ. For example, we could simply allow two methods with the same name or a method with two return statements and adjust the syntax and type judgments to ensure that at most one of them remains in a generated variant. Another solution is to introduce new language constructs which allow refinements of classes or methods. That is, we could integrate language mechanisms such as mixins [Bracha and Cook, 1990; Flatt et al., 1998], class refinements [Batory et al., 2004; Apel et al., 2008c], virtual classes [Madsen and Moller-Pedersen, 1989; Ernst et al., 2006], aspects [Kiczales et al., 1997], classboxes [Bergel et al., 2005], nested inheritance [Nystrom et al., 2004], traits [Ducasse et al., 2006], hyperslices [Tarr et al., 1999], object wrappers [Jorgensen and Truyen, 2003], and others (cf. Section 3.1). These approaches are interesting when designing a completely new language, however in our work, we prefer a backward compatible solution.

3. *Metaexpressions.* Czarnecki and Antkiewicz [2005] suggested metaexpressions as a mechanism to support alternative values in a software product line of UML models. In their setting, they did not have the opportunity to change the syntax of UML but sought for another way to express alternatives. Metaexpressions are special annotations, stored separately, which specify one or more alternative values for a language construct. For example, they can specify alternative names for an UML association. Instead of changing the syntax, they specify alternatives externally by a tool. During variant generation, the generation mechanism selects which of the alternatives to include (or whether to remove the construct altogether). The key difference to additional language constructs is that alternatives are specified on a tool level, but still checked by the type system.

For CFJ, we have formalized metaexpressions [Kästner et al., 2010] and implemented an according solution in CIDE [Rosenthal, 2009].

Still, for full Java and most other languages, there are simpler workarounds because there can be multiple statements inside a method, so backward compatibility does not impose so many restrictions. Having two statements in a method with alternative annotations is still backward compatible. The only problematic exception in Java are return statements, because of Java's unreachable code detection (code after a return statement results in a compiler error). Still, simple workarounds are possible, for example, we can rewrite the code example from Figure 5.21b as shown in Figure 5.23a. As another trick in full Java, actually quite close to metaexpressions, we can use conditional expressions (which can be annotated disciplinedly as wrappers, see Sec. 5.2.4) as shown in 5.23b. In our experience with Java, almost all alternative features can be reduced to alternative statements and implemented with these simple workarounds.

```
1  public boolean isItunes() {
2      boolean result;
3      //#ifdef DITUNES
4      result = (m_itunes);
5      //#endif
6      //#ifdef ¬DITUNES
7      result = (false);
8      //#endif
9      return result;
10 }
```

(a) Alternatives as separate statements.

```
1  public boolean isItunes() {
2      return
3      //#ifdef DITUNES
4          true ? m_itunes :
5      //#endif
6          false;
7  }
```

(b) Conditional expression for alternatives.

Figure 5.23.: *Rewritten example of alternative return statements in Figure 5.21b.*

5.3.5. Beyond Featherweight Java

Our formalization is based on Featherweight Java because it allows proving the feasibility of a product-line–aware type system in a confined setting. Nevertheless, for a practical application, a product-line–aware type system should be provided for full Java or other languages (see Figure 5.24). Our experience with CFJ guides the way for a more general implementation in CIDE.

Kind of error	Syntax	Typing	Semantic
Error detection	Check variants	Check entire product line	
Languages	Single	Multiple	Inter-language
Implementation	Annotative	Compositional	Other

Figure 5.24.: *Multi-language and inter-language type checking in our classification.*

The formalization showed that backward compatibility is possible, so that we only have to add additional reachability checks between pairs (or triples or quadruples) of code fragments and their annotations. Interestingly, the mechanics of the *variant generation preserves typing* proof are very similar to our discussion that lead to the annotations rules (L.1–T.5) initially. We iterated over all generation steps and analyzed what additional checks have to be added to the type system to cover all possible annotations. This means, such a proof can be used constructively, to extend the type judgments of another calculus with annotation checks, be it of some FJ extensions such as FGJ [Igarashi et al., 2001] or FJI [Igarashi and Pierce, 2002]; or of a larger Java calculus such as Classic Java [Flatt et al., 1998], Java$_{light}$ [Nipkow and von Oheimb, 1998], or Java^s [Drossopoulou et al., 2000]; or even of a type system for completely different programming language.

On a practical level, to achieve language independence (or at least extensibility toward new languages) similar to disciplined annotations, we implemented a framework for product-line–aware type checking in CIDE that provides a general mechanism to iterate over a project, check reachability conditions, and report errors. Detected errors are shown like standard Java errors directly at the location of the type reference, method invocation, and others, and suggestions for fixing them can provided. This framework can be extended with plug-ins for specific languages. A plug-in is responsible to determine what reachability conditions are to be checked for a given language; for example, it looks up method invocations and corresponding method declarations. It is even possible check reachability conditions between elements of different languages (inter-language typing).

Currently, we provide the following type-checking plug-ins for CIDE:

- *Featherweight Java.* We implemented the CFJ type system in CIDE, including our metaexpression extension for alternative features (see Sec. 3). Specifically, Rosenthal [2009] implemented the entire type system natively without reusing an existing implementation.

- *Java.* For Java, we implemented all checks from Featherweight Java and several additional checks regarding local variables, interfaces, generics, imports, abstract classes, abstract methods, and others. This type system was implemented on top of Eclipse's type checks for Java, that is, we reused the existing lookup mechanisms and add only reachability checks on top. To be precise, we could not reuse all lookup mechanisms, but had to slightly adapt those that are equivalent to *mtype* and *override* in Section 5.3.3. Although our implementation is certainly not complete, we believe that we have covered the most important causes of type errors to be still useful in practice.

  The product-line–aware extension for Java is built on top of the standard Java compiler. Thanks to backward compatibility, the existing syntax- and type checking mechanisms, the internal Java model, and the background compilation process of Eclipse remain untouched. Therefore, Eclipse provides tool support such as syntax highlighting, code completion, and code navigation; and Eclipse already detects all type errors of standard Java, we only added reachability checks on top.

- *Bali.* Bali is a grammar specification language in the AHEAD tool suite [Batory et al., 2004], for which we added reachability checks between references to and declarations of productions and tokens. In this language, looking up pairs is straightforward with a simple name table. Still, the entire mechanism to check reachability in the context of a feature models is reused and shared with the other languages.

- *OSGi Manifest + Java.* As a demonstration of inter-language typing, we implemented a plug-in that looks up package references between a manifest file of an OSGi bundle [OSGi Alliance, 2009] and the bundle's implementation with Java. It again checks that the implementation is reachable from the according declaration in all variants, so that, in this case, no variant of an OSGi bundle can declare to export a package that it does not contain. So far, we implemented only checks for the *Export-Package* declaration as a proof of concept, but this can be extended easily to other checks between an OSGi manifest and Java or inter-language checks between other languages.

Together with an industrial partner, we are currently also implementing a product-line–aware type system for C that is largely backward compatible to the C pre-processor. This type system is developed outside CIDE, but follows the same mechanisms.

Finally, the mechanism to actually reason about feature models and annotations (to determine whether $AT(a) \rightarrow AT(b)$ holds for all valid variants) also is abstracted behind an interface so that different reasoning mechanisms can be plugged in. Currently, we have implemented two mechanisms: a very simple one based on set relations (which however supports only very simple feature models that can only express dependencies in form of parent-child relationships in a tree, but no alternatives) and one for full feature models, originally developed for FeatureIDE [Leich et al., 2005; Kästner et al., 2009d]. In the latter, which we use by default, reasoning is performed by transforming the feature model and reachability conditions into Boolean satisfiability problems as described by Thaker et al. [2007]; we subsequently solve the problem with the off-the-shelf SAT solver *sat4j*.[16]

To summarize, the formalization of CFJ is tailored to Featherweight Java, but the underlying mechanisms are general and can be transferred to other languages. Currently, the additional reachability checks for every language (and combination of languages in case of inter-language typing) are be provided manually using plug-ins. Whether these plug-ins can be generated automatically (e.g., from attribute grammars) is an open research question. Regarding inter-language typing, further research is needed to find the right abstractions or a suitable polylingual type system [e.g., Grechanik et al., 2004]. From a tool perspective, recent advances in inter-language refactorings in Eclipse can be used as possible starting point [Fuhrer et al., 2007].

5.3.6. Evaluation

To demonstrate practicality of a product-line–aware type system, we have performed a series of case studies with our Java type system in CIDE. Specifically, we want to answer the following questions:

---

[16]http://www.sat4j.org

- What performance can we expect from type checking a software product line (especially since SAT solvers are involved)?

- What are typical shapes of annotations?

- Does type checking detect relevant errors in software product lines?

We applied our type checking approach to four case studies. We selected Java programs that implement variability using some form of preprocessor. Since Java does not have a build in preprocessor, there are not as many projects as in C or C++, but, interestingly, providing variability is essential in the domain of software for mobile phones, so we found some open source projects that use the Java ME preprocessor *Antenna* (cf. Sec. 3.2). We selected the following software product lines (see also Table 5.5 and Appendix A.1):

1. *MobileMedia.* MobileMedia is a Java ME application to manipulate photo, music, and video files on mobile devices. It has been developed at Lancaster University as a software product line and has been used as case study in several studies on aspect-oriented software development [Figueiredo et al., 2008; Conejero et al., 2009]. The software product line has several optional features implemented with *#ifdef* directives, such as support for photos, music, video, SMS transfer, or favorites. We selected this software product line because the code is peer reviewed [Figueiredo et al., 2008] and because the development is well documented in several incremental releases (each added one or more features), which allowed us to analyze simple as well as more complex versions. Specifically, we look at two releases: Release 6 with nine features and the latest Release 8 with 14 features [cf. Figueiredo et al., 2008].

2. *Mobile RSS Reader.* Mobile RSS Reader is an open source project to implement a portable RSS reader for mobile phones on the Java ME platform. Variability is crucial to support different devices, therefore typical features refer to Java ME libraries: MIDP 1.0, MIDP 2.0, CLDC 1.1, JSR 75 (file system), and JSR 238 (internationalization). Additional features include support for devices with small memory capacity, logging and testing features, and several compatibility features for different RSS formats.

3. *Lampiro.* Lampiro is an instant-messaging Java ME client for the XMPP protocol developed by *Bluendo s.r.l.*, released as open source. Several features, such as COMPRESSION, ENCRYPTION (TLS), PROFILING and DEBUGGING, or SCREENSAVER, are implemented using *#ifdef* directives.

4. *Berkeley DB.* Finally, Oracle's Berkeley DB is an open-source database engine written in Java, which we decomposed into features in prior work [Kästner et al., 2007a, 2008a]. Berkeley DB is different from the preceding case studies

Name	LOC	#FEA	#ANN	Features
MobileMedia (Rel. 6)	4 600	9	88	PHOTO, MUSIC, SMS, SORTING, COPYMEDIA, FAVORITES, 128x149, 132x176, and 176x205
MobileMedia (Rel. 8)	5 700	14	164	PHOTO, MUSIC, VIDEO, SMS, SORTING, COPYMEDIA, FAVORITES, PRIVACY, CAPTUREPHOTO, CAPTUREVIDEO, PLAYVIDEO, 128x149, 132x176, and 176x205
Mobile RSS Reader	20 000	14	1 050	MIDP10, MIDP20, JSR75, JSR238, CLDC11, SMALLMEM, ITUNES, LOGGING, TEST, TESTUI, 4×COMPATIBILITY
Lampiro	45 000	11	108	MOTOROLA, TLS, COMPRESSION, BXMPP, SCREENSAVER, UI, GLIDER, BLUDENO, TIMING, SENDDEBUG, and PLAINSOCKET
Berkeley DB	70 000	42	1 825	TRANSACTIONS, STATISTICS, DELETEDBOPERATION, ENVIRONMENTLOCK, FILEHANDLECACHE, ...

LOC: approximate lines of code; #FEA: number of features; #ANN: number of annotated code fragments

Table 5.5.: *Size and features of our type-system case studies.*

in two ways. First, it was not originally developed as a software product line, but we later refactored it into features, such as TRANSACTIONS, STATISTICS, ENVIRONMENTLOCK, or DELETEDBOPERATION. Second, we annotated the code base with CIDE after having implemented an initial version of our type system. This gives a different perspective on the type system regarding the development of a new software product line from a legacy application.

Performance

To provide some intuition about the complexity and performance of type checking a software product line, we measure the time to compile a single variant (t_{Var}) and the time to check all reachability constraints in the software product line (t_{SPL}).[17] Additionally, we estimate the number of variants to illustrate what it would mean to check every variant in isolation.

We show the results of our measurements in Table 5.6. In a nutshell, our results show that our current implementation of the type system is about ten times slower than Eclipse's industrial-strength compiler. That means type checking the entire software product line takes only as long as type checking ten variants (ten variants are typically a fraction of the amount of potential variants in a software product line).

The slowdown is mostly caused by our algorithm to locate the pairs for reachability checks, such as method invocation and declaration, field access and declaration, type reference and declaration, and others. There are up to such 72 534 pairs in our case studies, as shown in Table 5.6. To enable quick *incremental* type checking on changes to the source code, to annotations, or to the feature model, we store also all checks for future reevaluation. We assume that an optimized implementation can significantly speed up this process. In contrast, the time needed to actually solve Boolean satisfiability problems is marginal. Many checks (60 % to 98 %) can be skipped without consulting an SAT solver either (a) because neither code element is annotated or (b) because both are annotated with the identical feature expression. For the remaining checks, the results for unique feature combinations can be cached, so that, in our case studies, only some hundred unique satisfiability problems remain to be solved. Solving all satisfiability problems requires less than 50 ms in each software product line.

Furthermore, there is evidence that indicates that the performance scales for even larger projects. Due to the typical shape of feature models, reasoning about them with SAT solvers is tractable even for very large feature models [Mendonça et al., 2009; Thüm et al., 2009]. Therefore, determining reachability does not pose problems in practice, even though it introduces satisfiability problems into the type-checking process.

All in all, this shows that, although reachability checks are required in all type judgments, they can be executed with reasonable performance that is acceptable for practical development. Our current implementation slows down type checking by a factor of ten, which means that for every software product line with more than ten potential variants, it is faster to check the entire software product line than to check every variant in isolation. Type checking is still reasonably fast that it can be executed in the background during development to find errors as early as possible.

---

[17]We measured all times on a standard 2.66 GHz lab PC with 4 GB RAM, Windows Vista, Sun Java VM 1.6.0.03, and Eclipse 3.5.

Name	t_{Var}	t_{SPL}	#Variants	#Checks	#SAT	#USAT
MobileMedia (rel. 6)	0.2	1.3	144	5714	1924	39
MobileMedia (rel. 8)	0.3	1.8	2784	7359	3569	111
Mobile RSS Reader	0.6	8.3	2048	35094	10684	127
Lampiro	2.0	19.0	2048	72534	780	26
Berkeley DB	2.6	21.0	3.6 billion	70316	19517	324

t_{Var}: time to compile a single variant in seconds; t_{SPL}: time to evaluate all reachability checks in seconds; #Variants: approximate number of potential variants; #Checks: number of performed reachability checks; #SAT: number of satisfiability problems solved; #USAT: number of unique satisfiability problems solved

Table 5.6.: *Performance of type checking in our case studies.*

Shape of annotations

Most annotations in our case studies were simple and consisted only of a single feature *(#ifdef X)* or a negated feature *(#ifndef X)*, however, nesting was quite common (up to level 4 in Mobile RSS Reader). Beyond single features and nesting, only MobileMedia used some pattern like $A \wedge B$ or $A \vee B$ (the most complex annotation we found was "(Music $\wedge$ Photo) $\vee$ (Music $\wedge$ Video) $\vee$ (Video $\wedge$ Photo)" in MobileMedia Release 8). Usually it is quite easy to reason about reachability manually and to interpret the errors reported by the type system. Nevertheless, automatically checking reachability constraints in a type system is helpful due to the sheer number of reachability constraints.

In all software product lines that were developed with *#ifdef* directives originally, we found alternative features or alternative implementations depending on whether a feature is selected. Alternatives generally occurred on the level of statements or for setting initial values of constants. In Mobile RSS Reader, also alternative superclasses were used, so that a class inherits from different classes depending on whether feature TestUI is selected. To avoid complexity, we forbid alternative superclasses (see discussion in Sec. 5.3.4) and rewrote the corresponding implementation. In general, we found three alternative code fragments in MobileMedia Release 6, eight in MobileMedia Release 8, 70 in Mobile RSS Reader, and 10 in Lampiro that could all be reduced to alternative statements as explained in Section 5.3.4.

Detecting errors

To our surprise, we found inconsistencies or type errors in all case studies except Berkeley DB. Berkeley DB is not relevant in this context, because it was already developed with CIDE and an early version of our type system; thus, we already eliminated all type errors in Berkeley DB during development. In all other case studies that were developed without a product-line–aware type system, we checked existing annotations in released source code.

In MobileMedia Release 6 (and Release 8), we found that a variant with SMS but without PHOTO would not compile. On closer inspection, we found that feature SMS actually depends on PHOTO, it is only meant to send photos, rather than music or video. This dependency was neither shown in the simplified feature model published in [Figueiredo et al., 2008], nor in a feature model provided by the authors on request, nor was any description about the relationship of features shipped with the source code. After adding this dependency to the feature model, CIDE indicates that all variants are well-typed. This detected mismatch between feature model and implementation is a typical example of the strength of product-line–aware type systems.

In Release 8, MobileMedia has five additional features, and annotations became more complex. CIDE initially indicated several type errors, because we inferred an incorrect feature model from the source code; we could easily fix this when we received a complete feature model from the authors and added the constraint between SMS and PHOTO as discussed earlier. Still, there were two remaining type errors caused by incorrectly annotated import statements (import statement are not part of the CFJ calculus but checked in the Java type system in CIDE). Although the target class and its references were correctly annotated, the import statements were not annotated. This causes a Java type error in several variants because a removed class is imported (e.g., in variants with SMS but without CAPTUREPHOTO and without VIDEO, or in variants with COPYMEDIA but without PHOTO). A product-line–aware type system can point out even such seemingly insignificant errors.

In Mobile RSS Reader, our type system found also inconsistencies: Variants with both MIDP20 and SMALLMEM and variants with TESTUI but without MIDP10 contain type errors. Our domain knowledge is not sufficient to judge whether these are undocumented constraints or incorrect implementations. As an easy fix, adding the constraints "$\neg(\text{MIDP20} \wedge \text{SMALLMEM})$" and "$\text{TESTUI} \Rightarrow \text{MIDP10}$" to the feature model reduces the number of possible variants, but all variants are well-typed. It is up to the developers and domain experts to either change the implementation or the feature model.

Additionally, we found some dead code fragments in Mobile RSS Reader that would require a feature selection that is not allowed by the feature model. Although, such analysis is not part of the type system (dead code is always well-typed regarding reachability constraints), we can easily add a warning to our implementation to point out dead code.

Finally, in Lampiro, we already had difficulties to create a single Java version of the source code with all features (for backward compatibility). We found that feature SCREENSAVER is dead (since the first revision in the project's repository)

```
1   // #ifndef GLIDER
2   setTitle("Lampiro");
3   Image logo = Image.createImage("/icons/lampiro_icon.png");
4   UILabel ul = new UILabel("Loading_Lampiro...");
5   // #endif
6   UILabel up = new UILabel(logo);
7   up.setAnchorPoint(Graphics.HCENTER | Graphics.VCENTER);
8   uvl.insert(up, 1, logo.getHeight()+10, UILayout.CONSTRAINT_PIXELS);
9
10  ul.setAnchorPoint(Graphics.HCENTER | Graphics.VCENTER);
11  uvl.insert(ul, 2, UIConfig.font_body.getHeight(), UILayout.CONSTRAINT_PIXELS);
```

Figure 5.25.: *Code excerpt from* Lampiro (SplashScreen.java, Lines 79–89) *with type errors when accessing local variables* logo *and* ul *in lines 6, 8, and 11 in variants with* GLIDER.

and must never be selected: Its implementation calls methods that do not exist, introduces duplicate methods, and contains both missing and duplicate import declarations. Similarly, feature GLIDER is dead; it is obvious from code fragments as shown in Figure 5.25 that it makes no sense selecting this feature (otherwise local variables *logo* or *ul* are not declared before used). Since GLIDER was only introduced in the last revision in the repository; we assume that it is an incomplete part of an upcoming feature. Our type system in CIDE points out these problems immediately. It forces developers to document in the feature model that certain features are incomplete and must not be selected.

All in all, we did not expect to find many errors, because all software product lines released their code, and because the number of features is still manageable small. We were surprised to find inconsistencies or type errors in every software product line that was annotated with *#ifdef* directives. In all cases these were only minor problems (undocumented dependencies, forgotten annotation on an import statement, dead code), nothing significant and all easy to fix. Nevertheless, this shows how easy subtle errors can be introduced into well-developed software product lines and how product-line–aware type systems can help to maintain consistency and fully document all implementation-relevant dependencies between features. In Berkeley DB, our type system helped to achieve consistency during the development process.

5.4. Related work

There is a large body of research to detect errors in software product lines. We structure our discussion according to our taxonomy as follows: First, we review approaches that check individual variants instead of the entire software product line, known as product line testing. Second, we discuss approaches that check the entire software product line for (a) syntax errors, (b) type errors, and (c) semantic errors.

Product-line testing

A first group of approaches focus on product-line *testing* [Tevanlinna et al., 2004; Pohl and Metzger, 2006]. Testing can be applied to different implementation mechanisms, different languages, and can detect even inter-language defects. Tests primarily address *semantic errors* during the execution of a variant, but since variants are compiled in the process, testing can find also syntax and type errors.

There are different ways a software product line can be tested. If possible, subsystems representing certain features can be tested in isolation. However, many errors occur only in the combination of features in a variant, therefore also integration tests and whole system tests of the final variant are necessary [McGregor, 2001; Pohl et al., 2005].

As described earlier, typical software product lines can have millions of feature combinations, so testing all valid variants is not feasible. Testing strategies therefore typically sample certain variants, including those variants which are currently requested by customers. Research on product-line testing focus mainly on reuse of test cases between variants [e.g., McGregor, 2001; Tevanlinna et al., 2004; McGregor et al., 2004; Gälli et al., 2005; Pohl and Metzger, 2006].

Product-line testing is a pragmatic approach, common in current product line practice. However, tests are not exhaustive and cover only a relatively small number of variants. For each generated variant, at least some manual effort for testing is required. Product-line testing scales only to software product lines with a limited number of variants or customers. In industrial practice, most software product lines produce only such limited amount of variants (despite a high feature number that could theoretically be combined into millions of variants), developers ignore the remaining variants until needed. For example, in HP's Owen product line with over 2000 features, less than 100 variants which are needed for their current printer hardware are compiled and tested [Refstrup, 2009]; Nokia's Mobile Browser product line has only four variants, which are compiled in nightly builds to catch syntax and type errors while still all variants are tested independently [Jaaksi, 2002].

In our work, we target an automated synthesis of variants allowing the full variability identified in domain analysis (see Sec. 3.3). Therefore, testing features in isolation and testing few sampled variants may detect important problems, but we focus primarily on error detection approaches that cover the entire software product line with all its variants. Nevertheless, there is a trade-off between checking only those variants currently needed and checking the entire software product line. On the one hand, covering the entire software product line requires a higher effort during development, since consistency is enforced even for variants which are probably never built. On the other hand, new variants are easier to produce and maintenance costs are not delayed until late in the development cycle, when they are more expensive to fix. We argue for early consistency, especially when it can be achieved with simple mechanisms as disciplined annotations and product-line–aware type checking.

Syntax errors

Syntax errors are typically a problem of annotative approaches. In compositional approaches, typically each feature's implementation can be checked for syntax errors in isolation, and the composition engine enforced syntactically correct input and transforms it into output that is, by construction, always syntactically correct. Recent composition tools that support multiple languages in a uniform way, such as the AHEAD tool suite [Batory et al., 2004] and FeatureHouse [Apel et al., 2009b], can even check the product line's syntax for multiple languages. Furthermore, for (language-specific) generators, there have been approaches to check the generator, to ensure syntactical correct output for any input [Huang et al., 2005]. In contrast, annotative approaches are often so general that they work only on plain text; although there is some work on safe macro expansion [e.g., Leavenworth, 1966; Kohlbecker et al., 1986; Weise and Crew, 1993; McCloskey and Brewer, 2005], detecting syntax errors related to annotations (especially conditional compilation) is largely unexplored.

Interestingly, there are some annotative tools that – as a byproduct, by the way they are constructed – ensure syntactic correctness for some languages by transforming and annotating software artifacts on a higher level of abstraction. One example is Czarnecki's tool *fmp2rsm* to generate variants of annotated UML models [Czarnecki and Antkiewicz, 2005]. Using this tool, syntax errors (e.g., a class without a name) cannot occur because annotations and variant generation is not performed on the textual representation of the model, but on an abstract level with the Rational Software Modeler engine, which does not allow transformations that would invalidate UML syntax. Heidenreich's *FeatureMapper* is a similar example for annotated models in Eclipse's modeling framework [Heidenreich et al., 2008b]. In our approach to prevent syntax errors with disciplined annotations, we employ the same mechanism: We abstract from plain text and remove code fragments from this safely from the underlying structure.

Also in other fields of software engineering, this abstraction principle is applied to source code. For example, refactorings in development environments such as Eclipse are usually not performed directly on the textual source code, but on an abstract representation such as an abstract syntax tree [Fuhrer et al., 2007]. Similar, many general-purpose program transformation systems, such as Stratego/XT [Visser, 2004] and DMS Software Reengineering Toolkit [Baxter et al., 2004], work on abstract syntax trees to prevent syntax errors and avoid dealing with separating commas or similar syntactic overhead. Work on Intentional Programming drives this abstraction to an extreme and stores all program code in a tree structure [Simonyi, 1995; Simonyi et al., 2006]; instead of editing a textual representation, developers use a sophisticated tree editor. For disciplined annotations, we use the same abstraction principle to ensure syntactic correctness in software product lines.

Finally, disciplined annotations have already been proposed in different contexts, independent of syntax errors. Source code with undisciplined annotations can not only be very hard to understand (see Sec. 3.2.1 and 3.2.2), but also difficult to manipulate by tools [Stroustrup, 1994; Favre, 1997; Ernst et al., 2002; Garrido and Johnson, 2005]. For example, refactorings of C or C++ code are much more difficult to automate due to the preprocessor than refactorings of Java or Smalltalk code [Garrido, 2005; McCloskey and Brewer, 2005]. There are three general strategies to deal with annotations:

1. *Enforce disciplined annotations.* Disciplined annotations restrict possible annotations to a level that can be understood and manipulated by a tool. All undisciplined annotations are rejected by the parser and it is the developer's responsibility to refactor the annotations into a disciplined form.

   This strategy is used by the DMS transformation system [Baxter and Mehlich, 2001], such that *#ifdef* directives are allowed only in certain disciplined locations. Disciplined annotations are needed in this context to understand and manipulate C source code safely. The authors claim that this strategy covers 85 % of unprocessed C source files in large, real source system and that manually rewriting a system with 50 000 lines of code into a disciplined form will typically take only "an afternoon." Baxter and Mehlich [2001] further report that developers oppose undisciplined annotations anyway: *"The reaction of most staff to this kind of trick is first, horror, and then second, to insist on removing the trick from the source."* Our analysis in Section 5.3.6 corroborates this experience.

   Additionally, a new generation of programming languages has learned from the problems caused by undisciplined annotations and provides conditional compilation in a disciplined form directly as language constructs. For example, in D, ASTEC [McCloskey and Brewer, 2005], PL/SQL, and Adobe Flex, constructs corresponding to *#ifdef* directives are part of the grammar and can be used at certain disciplined locations only, such as on methods and statements. Annotations are evaluated directly in the compiler (after parsing), rather than in a separate preprocessor step. Similarly, with FeatureJ and rbFeature, Sunkle et al. [2009] and Günther and Sunkle [2009a,b] integrated disciplined annotations into Java and Ruby and additionally even make information about features available at runtime. With our approach, we provide disciplined annotations in a uniform way for multiple languages, without designing annotations for each language.

In our approach, we enforce disciplined annotations to prevent syntax errors. We use a fine granularity as defined by the language's grammar. From our experience and analysis, we can confirm that disciplined annotations are sufficiently expressive and undisciplined annotations can be quickly rewritten into a disciplined form.

2. *Ignore undisciplined annotations.* Instead of rejecting undisciplined annotations, some approaches can simply ignore them and reason only about the remaining disciplined annotations. However, this is only suitable for some analysis approaches, but not for source code transformations, since transformations can break ignored undisciplined annotations. Nevertheless, Adams et al. [2009] receive sufficiently accurate results even when they ignore undisciplined annotations during analysis of preprocessor usage in legacy systems (to evaluate potential refactoring toward aspects).

3. *Expand undisciplined annotations.* Finally, approaches that want to be fully backward compatible must understand all possible annotations. An approach, taken by Garrido [2005] and Vittek [2003], is to expand undisciplined annotations to disciplined annotations. For example, a method with two alternative return types (annotating a return type is usually not disciplined) can be expanded into two annotated methods that only differ in the return type. This way, fine-grained undisciplined annotations are expanded into coarse-grained disciplined annotations, at the cost of code replication. Changes in the expanded code are then traced back to the original code. Both systems require sophisticated rewrites and significant overhead (in the case of [Vittek, 2003], using expansion is almost identical to a brute force approach that generates and parses all valid variants). These approaches can also be used to check for syntax errors (and to build a type system on top), but the complexity and overhead is overwhelming compared to enforcing disciplined annotations.

Type errors

Product-line–aware type systems. The concept of checking type safety for an entire software product line (instead of only for a single program) emerged from research on generative programming.

First, in an influential approach, Huang et al. [2005] ensure that Java code generated by their tool *SafeGen* is well-typed. Though their tool is used for metaprogramming in general, rather than as product-line technology, the basic idea is similar to proving the variant generation process to be safe in CFJ. Using first-order logics and theorem provers, they check whether generators written in their confined metalanguage (with selection and iteration operators) produce well-typed output for arbitrary Java input. However, checks cover only some of Java's type judgments; there is no *guarantee* that the output is well-typed. In recent work, they introduced a newer metaprogramming language *MorphJ* with similar constructs that supports modular type checking and has been proven type sound [Huang and Smaragdakis, 2008].

The work on checking the generation mechanism instead of individual input programs in *SafeGen* influenced Czarnecki and Pietroszek [2006] to check an entire software product line instead of individual variants. Specifically, they target product lines of UML models in their tool *fmp2rsm* and guarantee well-formedness for all variants. Their tool extends an existing UML editor so that a user can annotate *presence conditions* to UML elements, such as classes or associations; a variant of the UML model is generated by removing elements of which the annotation evaluates to false for a feature selection. Czarnecki and Pietroszek [2006] then describe a mechanism for this tool environment to check that all variants conform to certain well-formedness rules of UML – for example, "an association in UML class diagrams connects exactly two elements." These well-formedness rules are similar to type judgments in programming languages and can be specified in UML's metamodel formally (and machine-readable) using constraints written in the object constraint language OCL. Their tool transforms presence conditions, the feature model, and constraints into a propositional formula, which can be solved by an off-the-shelf SAT solver in a single step. Error messages are reconstructed from the SAT solver's result. Well-formedness can only be guaranteed with regard to those constraints that have been specified as machine-readable constraints. For UML those must be first inferred from the informal, textual UML specification, which is similar to how Java's type judgments must be inferred from the textual Java Language Specification. The authors do not discuss completeness of their inferred constraints. The metaexpression solution for alternative features was first described for their tool [Czarnecki and Antkiewicz, 2005], however metaexpressions have not (yet) been considered in their well-formedness checks [Czarnecki and Pietroszek, 2006].

Regarding alternative features, Aversano et al. [2002] sketched an early type checking mechanism for alternative variable declarations in C. Depending on a feature selection, a variable can have alternative types, which they store in an extended symbol table. This work mainly addresses low-level portability issues in C (such as different integer types), not on product line implementation in general. Since Java abstracts from most low-level portability issues, alternative declarations were not important in our case studies, we could always achieve backward compatibility and reduce alternatives to the statement level as described in Section 5.3.4.

Beyond annotations on existing languages, there have been approaches to type check software product lines implemented using compositional approaches. Some compositional approaches can check feature modules in isolation, similar to components, so that only their combination into variants need to be checked [e.g., Ossher and Tarr, 2000a; McDirmid et al., 2001; Warth et al., 2006; Huang and Smaragdakis, 2008; Bettini et al., 2010]. The first type checking approach to cover an entire software product line for feature composition was *safe composition* by Thaker et al. [2007]. They analyze language semantics of Jak [Batory et al., 2004]. To type check software product lines, they identify six constraints that need to be satisfied, which their tool maps to propositional formulas and checks with an SAT solver in one step. One constraint deals with references to fields and methods (roughly corresponding to T-FIELD and T-INVK), two deal with abstract classes and interfaces (no correspondence in FJ), and three deal with specific constructs of the Jak composition mechanism (no correspondence in FJ). Their checks are not claimed or even proved complete, and in fact – compared to CFJ – checks that ensure the presence of types uses in signatures such as (M.1), (M.3) are missing. In recent work, safe composition was eventually formalized and proved type-sound with a machine-checked model by providing an algorithm to reduce it to Lightweight Java [Delaware et al., 2009].

Kim et al. [2008] ported Thaker's implementation of safe composition to annotations in CIDE, in parallel to our work. As Thaker's implementation, it is incomplete and checks only six selected constraints. Additionally, in line with Thaker et al. [2007] and Czarnecki and Pietroszek [2006], it solves all constraints in a single step and reconstructs a single error message from the SAT solver's result, in contrast to small checks in CFJ, which allow better error reporting. CFJ can report multiple errors in the same software product line and trace them to a distinct method invocation, type reference, or other language construct.

In a parallel line of research, we have formalized a calculus Feature Featherweight Java (FFJ) for class refinement and module composition [Apel et al., 2008c] and extended it toward checking entire software product lines [Apel et al., 2010]. In this work, we entirely drop backward compatibility since the host language with its composition semantics is already incompatible to Java and there is no sophisticated tool support, yet. Instead, we aimed at flexibility so that even alternative classes with different supertypes or alternative fields with different types and alternative methods with different return types within the same class hierarchy are possible. Compared to CFJ the formalization is much more complex, because a term in the software product line may have different types and even the subtype relation may change in different variants depending on the feature selection. CFJ and FFJ tackle type checking software product lines for different implementation mechanisms and from different perspectives: CFJ targets at annotations and tool support, whereas FFJ targets module composition and explores maximum flexibility.

Conditional language constructs

Independent of product-line research, the programming language community developed several type systems that support type conditions on methods or other language constructs. So, invoking a conditional method is only well-typed when the condition is satisfied in the context of the invocation. Conditional language constructs are discussed in the context of parametric polymorphism. For example, in a collection class, such as *List*, clients should only be allowed to invoke a method *print* if the class is parametrized with a type that can be printed; a collection should only implement the interface *Printable* if the type parameter implements this interface as well. Conditional language constructs have been explored in object-oriented languages at least since CLU [Liskov et al., 1981] and have been studied, for example, in extensions to Cecil [Litvinov, 1998], Java [Myers et al., 1997; Huang et al., 2007], and C# [Emir et al., 2006]. In all these languages, type constraints are structural constraints (parameter X contains method Y) or subtyping constraints (parameter X is a subtype/supertype of Y).

Conditional methods with type constraints and CFJ are related, because both restrict the access to methods in some variants (#ifdef vs. condition on type parameter) and both statically ensure that all variants are well-typed. So, in some sense, we could replace #*ifdef* directives on statements by conditions on type parameters and instead of generating a variant by removing code, we could instantiate the program with a suitable type parameter. However, there are four important differences:

- *Code removal vs. multiple instances.* Our work addresses conditional compilation in the context of product lines, such that code is actually removed in a generation step. In contrast, all languages with conditional methods we are aware of do not generate variants but check that a present method is never called when the condition on the type parameter evaluates to *false*. Type conditions have the benefit that different instances of a class with different configurations may be used in the same program, but they does not remove code and thus does not reduce binary size as sometimes desired in product-line development, especially for embedded systems [Beuche et al., 1999; Lohmann et al., 2006; Rosenmüller et al., 2009].

- *Expressiveness of conditions.* Compared to a full feature model, the expressiveness of type conditions is restricted. In languages with structural constraints, they can express part-of relationships; in language with subtyping constraints, they can express simple parent-child relationships (similar to our initial 'set relations' implementation, see Sec. 5.3.5). Most type conditions have the benefit that reasoning can be performed without a SAT solver; however, more expressive feature constraints are needed in product-line practice (see Sec. 5.3.6), such as alternative features, negated features

($\neg$A), or propositional expressions (e.g., A $\vee$ $\neg$B $\wedge$ C).

- *Granularity.* Annotations and type conditions provide different levels of granularity. In contemporary languages with type conditions, typically conditions can only be placed on methods (and sometimes fields and supertypes); type conditions aim primarily at providing flexible libraries. In contrast, *#ifdef* directives and annotations in CFJ and CIDE are more flexible and can annotate entire classes, individual statements, or even method parameters, which is typically not needed in libraries. Our work targets at variability in applications and product lines, in which also the behavior of an individual method may change depending on the feature selection. Of the four case studies in Section 5.3.6, only the first can be implemented and checked with type conditions of contemporary languages.

- *Backward compatibility.* Finally, to add type conditions to Cecil, Java, or C#, all approaches introduce new language constructs. In contrast, we aim explicitly at backward compatibility to reuse the existing tool infrastructure.

These differences are mostly design decisions for a specific language. It is possible to develop conditional language constructs that are similar to CFJ (backward compatible, at finer granularity, with more expressive conditions) or product-line–aware type systems with characteristics of conditional language constructs. However, so far the product-line community and the programming language community pursued different goals (product-line development by code removal, backward compatibility, flexible annotations, and alternative implementations vs. expressive type system for libraries and multiple instances), which lead to different design decisions. With contemporary conditional compilation constructs, our case studies would be very difficult to implement. We argue that both approaches are complementary and may eventually converge. In this context, we contribute a different perspective with different design decisions and their trade-offs for conditional language constructs.

Semantic errors

Regarding semantic errors, most developers rely on tests of features and some variants (see above). Recently, there have been a number of early approaches toward checking an entire software product line instead of individual variants by adapting formal methods for product-line engineering. In general, the idea is similar to product-line–aware type checking: Existing mechanisms are extended to understand and reason about annotations. Detecting semantic errors is beyond the scope of this thesis, but may be a valuable extension in future work. Therefore, we give only a brief overview.

Model checking can be adapted for software product lines in different ways. Lauenroth et al. [2009] extend a CTL model checking algorithm to understand annotations inside the model. In contrast, Post and Sinz [2008] and Gruler et al. [2008] encode annotations into the model before checking, so that they can use an off-the-shelf model checker. Fisler and Krishnamurthi [2001] and Classen et al. [2009] adapt a model checking approach similarly for model composition.

Additionally, other formal verification approaches have been explored regarding software product lines. For example, Poppleton [2007] extended the specification language Event-B for features, Fisler and Roberts [2004] explored ACL2 to describe and verify feature-oriented compositions. Integration with a feature model to verify the entire software product line is still an open research topic. There is still much research necessary to scale these approaches to realistic product lines. So far, none of them has been evaluated for nontrivial examples.

5.5. Summary

Annotative approaches are regarded as error prone (see Sec. 3.2.3). In software product lines, where errors may potentially occur only in a single out of millions of variants, such errors can be very difficult to detect. Errors may hide in the implementation until a customer requests a problematic variant, possibly long after initial development, when fixing them is expensive. We see two causes of errors that are specific to annotative approaches and addressed them each in this chapter.

First, most annotative approaches work on plain text without an understanding of the underlying code base. Therefore, it is easy to introduce syntax errors that occur only in some variants with incorrect or incomplete annotations. As a solution, we propose disciplined annotations. Disciplined annotations (a subset of all annotations) cannot cause syntax errors, variants with and without the annotated code fragment are syntactically correct. To decide which annotations are disciplined, we consider the underlying structure. Only optional code fragments in this structure (such as entire classes and entire methods, but not individual brackets, or just the return type of a method) may be annotated. Disciplined annotations are less expressive (for some extensions, workarounds are required), but as we have shown, still expressive enough in practice. In fact, not all but most annotations we found in practice are already disciplined. Thus, with some automated analysis as implemented in CIDE and with only minor restrictions to the way developers can annotate code, we can prevent annotations from causing syntax errors altogether.

Second, annotative approaches support no form of modular type checking. Instead, only individual variants are type checked. Checking only variants again raises the problem that type errors, such as dangling method invocations, may remain undetected until a problematic variant is eventually generated. As solution, we propose a product-line–aware type system on top of disciplined annotations, that type checks all variants of the software product line in a single step. The basic idea is to check for every pair of method invocation and according method declaration (and many other pairs) by comparing their annotations, so that, whenever the method invocation is included in a variant, also the according method declaration must be included. With CFJ, we have developed a formal calculus and proofed that all variants generated from a well-typed product line are well-typed. We have implemented an according type system for Java in CIDE and found type errors in some variants of several existing software product lines, which were developed with traditional preprocessors.

With disciplined annotations and a product-line–aware type system, we can detect syntax and type errors in the entire software product line. This way, we enforce consistency for all valid variants, even for variants which are currently not deployed. Although this enforced consistency increases effort during initial development, it reduces maintenance costs later on and reduces the costs for generating additional variants.

6. Comparison and integration

*This chapter shares material with the McGPLE'08 paper "Integrating Composi-
tional and Annotative Approaches for Product Line Engineering" [Kästner and Apel,
2008a] and the GPCE'09 paper "A Model of Refactoring Physically and Virtually
Separated Features" [Kästner et al., 2009a].*

After discussing five improvements of annotative approaches in the previous
chapters, we take a step back to look at the big picture. We integrate the proposed
improvements as *virtual separation of concerns* and compare them with compositional approaches. Finally, we outline their integration to combine their respective
advantages.

We name our concept of an improved annotative approach with tool support *virtual separation of concerns*, because – even though we do not *physically* decompose
concerns (or features) into modules – we provide some form of *virtual* separation with tool support. Although annotations are scattered in the implementation,
tools can provide views on features or variants on demand. Integrating the feature model, disciplined annotations, and a product-line–aware type system ensure
consistency and completeness of annotations, which is necessary to make views
and other tool support efficient. A visual representation of features addresses the
obfuscation often associated with annotations. We summarize virtual separation
of concerns as follows:

Virtual separation of concerns = annotations + tool support

6.1. Comparison

We revisit our comparison of annotative and compositional approaches from
Chapter 3 and additionally include our concept of virtual separation in this comparison. We discuss each criterion and conclude with a grade of either good support "(+)", partial support "(+/−)" or weak/no support "(−)". Again, the grades,
in this brevity, reflect our point of view and are debatable; they are meant to give
a quick overview.

6.1.1. Modularity

Modular implementations of features are possible with compositional approaches,
but not all languages enforce modularity strictly (see Sec. 3.1.1). In contrast, contemporary annotative approaches do not support modularity, code of a feature

is usually scattered. A virtual separation with views can emulate modularity to some degree, but cannot reach true modularity and its benefits.

On the positive side, tool support offers several improvements compared to contemporary annotative approaches. It simplifies many tasks that were previously tedious with contemporary preprocessors. Modular reasoning is possible to some degree in a view (at least in a nonmonotonic form as discussed for aspect-oriented programming [Ostermann, 2008; Kiczales and Mezini, 2005a]). Views hide distracting tangled code of other features and emulate cohesion; they ease the previously tedious task of searching for feature code. Context information shown in views plays the role of interfaces in modular implementations. Additionally, all configuration knowledge is encapsulated. With tool support including a feature model and disciplined annotations, we can always reason about annotations and determine the condition to include a code fragment. Removing an obsolete feature, which was criticized as especially tedious without modularity [Favre, 1997; Baxter and Mehlich, 2001], is straightforward with tool support.

Despite all improvements, virtual separation of concerns cannot provide real modularity with well-defined encapsulated modules that provide benefits such as separate compilation, separate testing, parallel development, and black-box reuse. For example, since different views work on the same code base, multiple developers may work on the same file in parallel, which requires integration later on.

Nonetheless, we need to emphasize that virtual separation of concerns does not require dropping modularity completely. There are different degrees of modularity (independent of how variability is achieved). On the one end of the spectrum, we can decompose a concern entirely and encapsulate it in a strictly modular form. On the other end of the spectrum, we can find entirely scattered implementations of a concern that are not decomposed at all. In between, there are many further degrees of modularity (see excursus below). Many annotation-based implementations are partially modularized, at least by small-scale means as functions and classes provided by the host language. While only a strict modularization provides the full benefit of modularity, we still gain some advantages of modularity with a partial modularization. For example, we can test the modularized parts in isolation and we can reuse modularized parts (even in a black-box fashion). That is, we cannot test or reuse an entire feature implementation, but the main parts of this implementation. Partially modularized features also reduce potential conflicts during parallel development. In the best case, a feature is mostly modularized, only some invocations – which can be regarded as glue code – remain scattered and have to be tested in variants or rewritten when the feature's implementation is reused.

With our discussion partial modularization, we want to stress that virtual separation of concerns does not automatically mean that modularity is entirely lost or reuse is not feasible. Annotations added in an ad-hoc fashion will probably not benefit from modularity, but even with annotations it is possible to develop largely modularized features. It depends entirely on how developers implement features.

Summary: Modularity	
Compositional approaches	good support in some approaches (+/–)
Contemp. annotative approaches	no perceivable form of modularity (–)
Virtual separation of concern	modularity emulation only (–)

Excursus: Degree of modularity. In this brief excursus, we give an in-depth explanation of partial modularization and different degrees of modularity. We illustrate different degrees of modularity by means of an example from Berkeley DB. Readers familiar with this idea may skip to Section 6.1.2.

The highest degree of modularity with a strictly modular implementation separates a concern entirely and decouples it from the remaining concerns (typically via an interface). Many languages, including some but not all compositional approaches, support strict modular implementations with some language mechanisms. As discussed in Section 3.1.1, some compositional languages provide a lower degree of modularity; they implement concerns in a cohesive form (subclass, feature module, aspect, etc.), but they are less strict regarding encapsulation and interfaces, resulting in a loss of separate compilation and in difficulties regarding modular reasoning and reuse. The same holds for hybrid forms of compositional and annotative approaches discussed in Section 3.3 and our integration later in Section 6.2.

At the other extreme, there are implementations that are entirely scattered, which are not even decomposed with small-scale means such as functions or classes. After decades of software-engineering education teaching separation of concerns, it can be difficult to imagine implementations that do not even use the most basic forms of decomposition. As example, consider a concern that is represented only by some entirely scattered statements in various methods. Annotations are typically used on top of some host language that already supports at least some hierarchical form of decomposition into functions, classes, or some form of modules. Even noncode artifacts are typically structured in some form. Thus, even in many annotation-based implementations, we find some partial decomposition.

Let us illustrate different degrees of modularity on the example of the crosscutting feature STATISTICS in the database engine Berkeley DB (see Sec. 3.1.7). The feature maintains over 100 counters to collect various statistics of different parts of the system, such as size of the cache, number of open transactions, and open files. Consider these different implementations:

- In an implementation without any means of modularity, we can entirely distribute counters and code to adjust these counters (in the form of isolated statements) in different parts of the program. In such implementation, there is no decomposition at all, not even on a small scale in terms of functions; STATISTICS is entirely intertwined with the base code.

- In the actual implementation of Berkeley DB (and also in our annotation-based implementation with CIDE), counters and code to adjust them are still scattered, but there is an additional infrastructure to collect statistics from these counters and to present them to users in an aggregated from. This infrastructure is implemented in eight classes (scattered over different packages) and several methods (scattered over several classes). Although there is still massive scattering, and even the classes and methods are scattered, at least some parts of the statistics system are decomposed from the base implementation in terms of methods and classes. This achieves a low degree of modularity.

- With an advanced compositional language as Jak or AspectJ (see Sec. 3.1), we could refactor also the scattered methods of the infrastructure into class refinements or an aspect. We could group these refinements or the aspect together with the other classes of the feature STATISTICS in a module (e.g., package or feature module). This way, we increase the degree of modularity. There is still severe scattering of counters and corresponding code, but already the entire infrastructure is decomposed. Note that the discussion of granularity is independent of the variability mechanism: We can either include or exclude the infrastructure module in a compositional manner, or we can annotate the module to be conditionally removed before compilation.

- We can further increase the level of modularity by refactoring additionally all local counters and all code to adjust them into class refinements or aspects, as we did in our AspectJ implementation of Berkeley DB [Kästner et al., 2007a]. This way, we decompose all code related to statistics from the base code and encapsulate it in a single module (again independent of the variability mechanism).

- As discussed above, aspects written in AspectJ are not considered to be strictly modular; for example, separate compilation is not possible. To achieve strict modularity, we can implement the feature with one of the more modular extensions of AspectJ [e.g., Sullivan et al., 2005; Aldrich, 2005; Steimann et al., 2010], as we did in [Steimann et al., 2010], or with some other modular implementation mechanism.

When we look at annotation-based implementations, they are often decomposed to some degree. The implementations of many features are completely scattered, but many other features are partially modularized. There are many examples of partially modularized feature implementations among our case studies (see Appendix A): In Berkeley DB, statistics are partially modularized, as discussed above; similarly the majority of the transaction system's implementation is scattered, but some parts are decomposed into several classes in a single package and a number of scattered methods. In MobileMedia (release 6), 67 % of feature SMS is decomposed into a distinct package, further 20 % are modularized in two additional classes, so that only some method declarations and invocations are scattered (13 %). In contrast, (academic) software product lines with modern composition languages that support crosscutting concerns usually pursue a high degree of modularization [e.g., Hunleth and Cytron, 2002; Zhang and Jacobsen, 2003; Batory et al., 2004; Tešanović et al., 2004; Apel and Batory, 2006; Kästner et al., 2007a; Figueiredo et al., 2008; Rosenmüller et al., 2009; Bettini et al., 2010; Apel, 2010].

6.1.2. Traceability

In contrast to modularity, traceability can be fully achieved with tool support. In compositional approaches, there is a more or less complex mapping from features to modules. In the simplest case each feature is mapped to a single module, so that traceability is trivially provided. With consistent annotations (integrated with the feature model), we can similarly trace a feature to all related code fragments. Views can additionally make even complex mappings easy to trace.

Note that keeping traceability links up to date is not a problem in virtual separation of concerns. In contrast to external traceability links as in FEAT [Robillard and Murphy, 2002], Spotlight [Coppit et al., 2007], or AspectBrowser [Griswold et al., 2001] (see discussion in Sec. 3.3) or traceability links in tools of the requirements-traceability community [e.g., Cleland-Huang et al., 2003; Mäder et al., 2008], feature annotations in a software product line are required to generate variants. Additionally, we enforce consistency of annotations with disciplined annotations and a product-line–aware type system. Hence, we can expect that developers maintain even scattered annotations and keep them up to date.

Summary: Traceability	
Compositional approaches	direct traceability to module (+)
Contemp. annotative approaches	scattered and tangled code (–)
Virtual separation of concern	tool-supported traceability (+)

6.1.3. Language integration

Compositional approaches use a language mechanism to implement variability, whereas annotative approaches usually use external ad-hoc tools that do not consider the underlying language. Compositional approaches offer limited but disciplined mechanisms to express variability; having variability or composition mechanisms as part of the language is beneficial, because the compiler or other tools can reason about variability and the composition process without external overhead. In contrast, contemporary annotative approaches use annotations in an undisciplined way on top of a host language, which obfuscates the source code with external annotations and makes reasoning (e.g., for refactoring or static analysis) about a product-line implementation difficult.

Virtual separation of concerns provides a form of disciplined annotations that are harmonized with the language. By restricting annotations to disciplined annotations, we can map annotations to language elements of the underlying language. This way, annotations can be integrated seamlessly into the type system and into various tools. For example, refactoring a software product line with disciplined annotations is much easier than with undisciplined annotations [Garrido, 2005]; we come back to this in Section 6.2.3. We can even provide disciplined annotations as part of a language, as in FeatureJ [Sunkle et al., 2009] and rbFeature [Günther and Sunkle, 2009a,b] or in D, PL/SQL, and Adobe Flex (see Sec. 5.4), but even when we implement disciplined annotations with a separate tool, we can consider them as language extension.

With some additional overhead, we can even design a language with disciplined annotations that can access information about features at runtime; we can implement dynamic feature activation and deactivation with annotations, as demonstrated by Sunkle et al. [2009] and Günther and Sunkle [2009a,b].

Another question is how to present annotations to the user. We can (a) use conventional *#ifdef* directives or similar textual syntax, (b) develop a syntax for disciplined annotations that integrates well into the host language (e.g., D, Adobe Flex, FeatureJ, rbFeature), or (c) even use graphical representations, such as background colors. Note that variability mechanisms in compositional approaches also require some overhead in a more or less verbose syntax. For some compositional languages such as AspectJ, there is even sophisticated tool support to visualize the effect of language constructs [e.g., Clement et al., 2003]. In this regard, virtual separation and compositional languages are quite similar.

Summary: Language integration	
Compositional approaches	direct language support, disciplined (+)
Contemp. annotative approaches	undisciplined ad-hoc tools (−)
Virtual separation of concern	seamlessly integrated disciplined ann. (+)

6.1.4. Errors

While compositional approaches support modular syntax checking of features and often also modular type checking and separate testing of modules, the scattered nature of implementations in contemporary annotative approaches prevents such local error detection mechanism; only generated variants can be checked. With disciplined annotations and a product-line–aware type system, virtual separation of concerns overcomes many problems of contemporary annotative approaches and even improves error detection beyond what is possible in most compositional approaches.

Regarding syntax errors, disciplined annotations bring virtual separation to the same level as compositional approaches. As in compositional approaches each code artifact can be checked in isolation. If the artifact is syntactically correct and all annotations are disciplined, no syntax errors can occur during generation.

Regarding type errors, several compositional languages can type check a module in isolation (including black-box frameworks and components, *Hyper/J* [Ossher and Tarr, 2000a], *Jiazzi* [McDirmid et al., 2001], *MorphJ* [Huang and Smaragdakis, 2008], and *Traits* [Bettini et al., 2010]). That is, the internals of the module are checked against its interface. When composing modules, it is still necessary to check the individual composition (e.g., whether interfaces match and whether all dependencies between modules are met). When variants are generated by composing modules in different combinations, type errors can still occur. With exception of the work of Thaker et al. [2007] and Apel et al. [2010] which also introduce a product-line–aware type system (see Sec. 5.4), we are not aware of any compositional approach that provides a mechanism to check whether all valid feature selections can be composed without type errors. Our product-line–aware type system skips modular checks and directly checks the entire product-line implementation against a feature model. Thus, without enforcing any additional interfaces between feature modules, our type system can determine whether all variant generated from the product line are well-typed. Thus, we argue that virtual separation of concerns can detect type errors at least as effectively as compositional approaches, or even better compared to most contemporary compositional approaches.

Regarding semantic errors, we do not see a major difference between compositional approaches, contemporary annotative approaches, and virtual separation of concerns. Although the modularization in compositional approaches allows local tests, a similar (partial) modularization is also possible with annotative approaches. Of course scattered implementations are difficult to test, but testing modular implementations of crosscutting concerns in compositional approaches is a challenge as well [Elrad et al., 2001; Parizi and Ghani, 2007]. From our perspective, semantic errors caused by the combination of the behavior of different features (known as feature interactions [Calder et al., 2003]) are the most critical semantic errors in product lines; they only occur in specific variants and cannot be detected modularly. We argue that semantic errors in variants are equally difficult to detect in compositional approaches and annotative approaches. Researchers currently explore solutions for different approaches of product-line implementation; for example, they adopt formal methods for both compositional and annotative approaches (see Sec. 5.4).

All in all, error detection in software product lines is difficult and many issues remain open. Nevertheless, we argue that virtual separation of concerns brings error detection for annotations to a level that can be compared to (or even improves over) error detection in compositional approaches.

Summary: Errors	
Compositional approaches	modular error detect. to some degree (+/−)
Contemp. annotative approaches	prone even to syntax errors (−)
Virtual separation of concern	product-line–wide error detection (+)

6.1.5. Granularity

Compositional approaches provide only coarse-grained extensions, which can lead to verbose workarounds for some extensions. In contrast, annotative approaches are usually fine-grained and can change lines, tokens, or even characters in an artifact; they are very expressive. With disciplined annotations, virtual separation of concerns provides a granularity in between: finer than in compositional approaches, but coarser than in annotative approaches. With a visual representation of annotations, we provide also suggestions how to cope with obfuscation caused by many fine-grained annotations with traditional textual annotations.

Disciplined annotations restrict granularity, so that developers can annotate only code fragments that represent optional elements in the underlying structure. Nevertheless, they still provide finer granularity than compositional approaches: Disciplined annotations typically include statements and parameter; as in contemporary annotative approaches, there are no conceptual limitations regarding fixed signatures or position and ordering (cf. Sec. 3.1.4).

As discussed in Section 5.2.6, despite slightly reduced granularity, disciplined annotations hardly impose any restrictions compared to traditional preprocessors in practice. Most annotations are in a disciplined form already, or can be easily refactored into one. Compared to compositional approaches, a virtual separation with disciplined annotations is still very fine-grained and can express most extensions without workarounds.

Summary: Granularity	
Compositional approaches	coarse granularity, req. workarounds (−)
Contemp. annotative approaches	fine granularity (+)
Virtual separation of concern	fine granularity (+)

6.1.6. Optional feature problem

The optional feature problem (or feature interaction problem, or more generally the tyranny of the dominant decomposition) describes the difficulty to modularize two interacting features. The code that connects both features should only be included when both features are selected. A typical strategy of compositional approaches is to encapsulate it in an additional module (see Sec. 3.1.5), which causes additional effort and makes the system more difficult to understand. In contrast, annotative approaches use nested annotations to describe that a code fragment belongs to two features and should only be included when both features are selected.

In this context, the views of virtual separation of concerns play their strength. As discussed in Section 4.2, a code fragment that belongs to multiple features is shown in multiple according views. A physical on-demand remodularization has been proposed to address such multi-dimensional views with compositional approaches [Ossher and Tarr, 2000b; Janzen and De Volder, 2004; Harrison et al., 2005], but they are very difficult to implement (see discussion in Sec. 4.5). In contrast, virtual separation provides a straightforward virtual remodularization that is pragmatic and easy to implement and adopt. Again, disciplined annotations and product-line–aware type system support views by enforcing consistent annotations.

Summary: Optional feature problem	
Compositional approaches	sign. overhead, additional modules (–)
Contemp. annotative approaches	straightforward solution (+)
Virtual separation of concern	straightforward solution + views (+)

6.1.7. Uniformity

A software product line typically contains artifacts of many different (code and noncode) languages. Still, compositional approaches are usually tied to one specific language. For example, even for a general concept as pointcut and advice mechanisms in aspect-oriented programming, developers must learn different tools for different languages, each with a different concrete syntax. Additionally, many (especially noncode) languages might not even be supported. In contrast, most annotative approaches consider all artifacts as a stream of characters or tokens and ignore the underlying language; hence they can be used language independently. Developers can use the same tool in a uniform way for multiple artifact languages.

Virtual separation of concerns uses the underlying structure of an artifact for several purposes, which makes it language-dependent. For example, we need to understand the structure of an artifact to decide which annotations are disciplined; type checking requires details on the semantics of a language to check; and even our algorithm to determine the context for a view on a feature use the underlying structure.

Nevertheless, in each step, we specifically designed the mechanisms such that they can be extended toward new languages. We defined disciplined annotations and views on an abstract structure that can be provided for different languages (we even automate the generation of new language plug-ins from a grammar specification). This way, the same tool infrastructure (variant generation, visualization, views) can support several languages in a uniform way. For type checking, we need more language-specific information, but still, we have shown how existing type systems can be extended and we implemented product-line–aware type checking in CIDE such that new languages can be plugged in. Even though virtual separation of concerns is not language independent, we can still apply it to many languages *in a uniform way* – as demonstrated for Java, C, C++, Python, Haskell, Bali, XML, and HTML (see case studies in Sec. 5.2.6, 5.3.6, and Appendix A.1).

Summary: Uniformity	
Compositional approaches	usually language dependent (–)
Contemp. annotative approaches	language independent (+)
Virtual separation of concern	uniform support for multiple languages (+)

6.1.8. Adoption

Compositional approaches are difficult to adopt for product-line development in practice, because they introduce novel concepts, languages, tools, or processes. Modularity is a long-term investment, which causes higher initial effort but provides little short-term benefits, which makes it difficult to convince developers and management. In contrast, annotative approaches have a very simple programming model, which is flexible, easy to understand, and easy to use: Code is annotated and removed. Annotations can be introduced in an ad-hoc fashion into existing projects.

With virtual separation of concerns, we keep the simple model of annotations. Although we enforce a disciplined form of annotations and slightly change the variant generation process from string removal to AST transformations (see Sec. 5.2.3), the general variability mechanism is as simple as before. On the one hand, we slightly restrict expressiveness, on the other hand, we even simplify annotations so that developers to not have to deal with syntactic elements like separating commas.

We provide immediate feedback of type errors, which is helpful to achieve consistency and can reduce the amount of variant-specific error checking. Error messages for type errors for variants that the developer is currently not working on might be demanding at first use and increase initial development effort. In exchange we reduce maintenance effort and guarantee that a change does not break other variants at syntax and type level. We additionally designed our type system in a backward-compatible fashion, so we conserve existing tool support, to which many developers became accustom.

Finally, views and visual representation provide an immediate improvement over contemporary preprocessors, which fosters adoption of virtual separation [cf.

Atkins et al., 2002; Feigenspan et al., 2010]. Subjects in our experiment preferred the improved representation.

Overall, we expect that the benefits of additional tool support outweigh the minor increase in effort for consistent and type-safe annotations. The big picture of simply annotating and removing source code is the same as for contemporary annotative approaches.

Summary: Adoption	
Compositional approaches	difficult adoption, new languages/tools (–)
Contemp. annotative approaches	easy to use, lightweight tools (+)
Virtual separation of concern	easy to use + tool support (+)

To conclude, we give an overview our evaluation, reduced to approximate grades, in Figure 6.1. It becomes apparent that virtual separation of concerns keeps all benefits of annotative approaches and addresses most of their weaknesses compared to compositional approaches. Nevertheless, we still cannot achieve strict modularity, but at most partial modularity. Since modularity is a very important criterion, missing modularity can be critical and outweigh benefits such as easy adoption or being language independent. Therefore, we conclude this thesis in the next section with a discussion on how we can integrate virtual separation of concerns with compositional approaches to leverage the respective advantages.

Criterion	Compositional approaches	Contemporary annotative approaches	Virtual separation of concerns
Modularity	+/–	–	–
Traceability	+	–	+
Language integration	+	–	+
Errors	+/–	–	+
Granularity	–	+	+
Optional feature pr.	–	+	+
Uniformity	–	+	+
Adoption	–	+	+

+: good support, +/–: partial support, –: weak/no support

Table 6.1.: *Summary of our comparison of compositional approaches, contemporary annotative approaches, and virtual separation of concerns.*

6.2. Perspective: Integrating compositional and annotative approaches

Despite all improvements, compositional approaches and annotative approaches (respectively our improvement as virtual separation of concerns) still have complementary benefits. We cannot generally choose one over the other. At the same time, there are many similarities; we can typically rewrite an annotation-based implementation into an implementation with a compositional language (sometimes straightforward, sometimes with some demanding code changes). In this section, we provide a perspective on how we can integrate both compositional and annotative mechanisms and explore challenges and opportunities of such integration. Specifically, we discuss automated refactorings between both representations.

6.2.1. Spectrum between physical and virtual separation

We regard the discussed compositional approaches and (improved) annotative approaches as two ends of a spectrum between a pure physical separation (variability by adding and composing modules, no annotations) and pure virtual separation (variability by removing annotated code fragments, no composition mechanism).[1] In between, we find implementations that use both composition and annotation mechanisms, for example, annotations inside plug-ins, inside feature modules, or inside aspects.

We visualize this spectrum and show some code examples in Figure 6.1. In this example, in a pure virtual separation, we use only two annotations to conditionally remove a method declaration and a statement depending on the feature selection. In a pure physical separation, we use two feature modules implemented in Jak, and we generate variants by including or excluding the second feature module from composition. In one of many possible combinations in between, we again use two feature modules, but one of them still contains annotations. Variants are generated both by conditionally removing annotations and conditionally including the second module, both depending on the feature selection. All three implementations are equivalent; they expose the same behavior in all variants.

Technically, integrating physical and virtual separation is straightforward: We simply use annotations inside modules. Since annotations are language independent – or can be extended toward new languages quickly – we can annotate class

---

[1]The discussion of variability mechanisms between physical separation and virtual separation is independent of our discussion of different degrees of modularity in Section 6.1.1. In approaches with a high degree of modularity, a module (e.g., an aspect) either (a) can be located in a feature module that is included or not included in the composition process depending on a feature selection or (b) can be annotated and removed or not removed before compilation depending on a feature selection. In both cases the implementation is modularized, but the variability mechanism differs. In this section, we focus only on the variability mechanism.

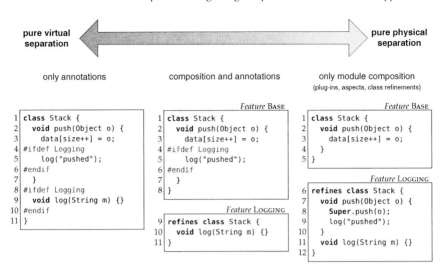

Figure 6.1.: *Spectrum between physical and virtual separation of concerns.*

refinements (including method introductions and method refinements), aspects (including pointcuts, advice, and inter-type declarations), or other novel compositional language constructs without technical problems. During variant generation, either we evaluate annotations first and afterward compose the resulting code or we compose modules first and afterward evaluate annotations in the result.

Language extensions of C and C++, such as FeatureC++ [Apel et al., 2005] and AspectC++ [Spinczyk et al., 2002], and framework implementations based on C and C++ support a combination of composition and annotation out of the box. For example, Rosenmüller et al. [2009] refactored the C version of Berkeley DB into feature modules with FeatureC++; in their implementation they refactored most, but not all, *#ifdef* directives of the original C code into class refinements. As we observed in [Kästner et al., 2009c], the resulting implementation integrates feature composition and annotations.

Finally, all discussed improvements of annotations can be adopted seamlessly for implementations that integrate composition and annotations. Just as we enforce a mapping from annotations to the feature model, we can enforce a mapping from modules to the same feature model. Regarding views, we handle a module just as a class or package that is entirely annotated; thus, a view on a feature includes all annotated code fragments and all modules associated with this feature and hides all other modules. For consistency, we can even use the same visual representation with background colors on modules. Disciplined annotations are again determined by the grammar of the host language, in this case a language as Jak or AspectJ, and enforce that also additional language constructs as method refinements or pointcuts can only be annotated in a way that cannot introduce syntax errors. A product-line–aware type system for integrated product-line implementations is the biggest technical challenge. In theory, a product-line–aware type system can be build on top of the type system of the host language (e.g., Jak or AspectJ) as described in Section 5.3.5; however, different means to express alternative features and the composition order pose additional challenges. Nevertheless, existing product-line–aware type systems for compositional languages provide a solution how to handle alternative features and ordering [Thaker et al., 2007; Apel et al., 2010], incorporating them is mostly an engineering task.

6.2.2. Benefits

The question of what benefits we gain from such integration remains. We have already shown in Section 6.1 that compositional approaches and virtual separation of concerns have distinct advantages, which we aim to combine. Nevertheless, as soon as we integrate a single annotation in a compositional language, we may loose the benefits of modularity – the distinct advantage of compositional approaches. So, what is there to gain for virtual separation of concerns? Or what is there to gain for compositional approaches?

Benefits for virtual separation of concerns.   As discussed in Section 6.1.1, we can gain some advantages of modularity by partially modularizing code. For example, we can test modularized parts in isolation and we can reuse modularized parts (even in a black-box fashion). By integrating modern compositional languages with annotations, we offer better modularization mechanisms and can presumable modularize a larger portion of the feature's implementation than with a classic host language as C or Java. For some features, we may even switch entirely to a compositional mechanism (pure physical separation), so that for those features we gain all benefits of modularity (including separate compilation, parallel development, black-box reuse etc.). By this integration, we do not necessarily make a big step for virtual separation of concerns, but we provide developers with *more expressiveness to partially modularize features* when they want. We do not force developers to use only compositional mechanisms, but we provide additional implementation mechanisms a developer can select from.

Benefits for compositional approaches.   From the perspective of compositional approaches, we see significant opportunities to lower the adoption barrier. Modularity is a long-term investment for lower maintenance costs and easier extension in later phases of the development cycle. However, it requires a high investment in early phases: developers have to learn new language concepts and tools (for each artifact language), fine-grained extensions are more difficult to implement, and solving the optional feature problem requires significant effort. To lower the adoption barrier of compositional approaches, we envision a *gradual transition from annotations to compositional mechanisms* [Kästner and Apel, 2008a].[2] In early evaluation and adoption stages, developers can implement variability mostly with annotations in an ad-hoc fashion. They can use the lightweight capabilities of annotative approaches without significant changes to their code base. In later stages, when the concept of software product lines is established, developers can gradually make a transition toward compositional approaches. Still, it is not necessary to refactor all annotated code fragments at once, but developers can start with the obvious coarse-grained ones (separate entire classes or method introductions as in Fig. 6.1) and introduce first explicit extension points. Still, they can use annotations inside modules for difficult to express extensions: First, they can implement coarse-grained extensions with compositional mechanisms; but instead of workarounds, they can simply implement fine-grained extensions with annotations. Second, instead of extracting additional modules for the optional feature problem, they can again simply use annotations inside a module. Nevertheless, in the long run, developers can still strive for modularity. They can gradually refactor also remaining annotations into compositional mechanisms and slowly move toward a pure physical separation without any annotations.

As a side effect, with a gradual transition, we delay the decision what and how to modularize artifacts. Sullivan et al. [2001] argue that a delayed modularization is beneficial, because developers gain more insight into the environment and the future of the project during development. Thus, later modularity decisions can respond to changes (new features, different scope, etc.) and even influence changes instead of anticipating them upfront. This delayed modularization makes compositional approaches more effective [Sullivan et al., 2001].

Since a gradual refactoring of existing code is tedious and difficult to achieve in practice, tool support is necessary to ease the transition. In the next section, we propose (and have partially implemented) *automated refactorings* that can automatically replace some or even all annotations by composition mechanism [Kästner et al., 2009a].

With automated refactorings, another benefit of integration for compositional approaches arises: We can use annotations as a means to transform legacy applications into modular product-line implementations with lower effort. It is typically much faster to add an annotation (in CIDE, a developer selects a code fragment and assigns a feature from the Editor's context menu) than to manually restructure the code. For example, our manual refactoring of Berkeley DB required about

---

[2]The idea to adopt product-line technology slowly and in a stepwise manner was originally contributed by Olaf Spinczyk in a discussion at the Dagstuhl seminar "Software Engineering for Tailor-Made Data Management" [Apel et al., 2008a].

one month, annotating Berkeley DB with CIDE took about three days [Kästner et al., 2008a]. We argue that, in many cases, it might be more efficient to annotate a code fragment and afterward perform an automated refactoring. We present some examples, in which we successfully exploited this automation later.

Benefits for theories, models and tools. Integrating both compositional mechanisms and annotations into the same language or environment provides opportunities for theories, models, and tools that use both approaches *uniformly*, in contrast to the current practice of searching for solutions for each representation separately. For example, we can integrate the previously independent research on product-line–aware type systems for composition and annotations.

Given automated refactorings between both representations, we can use tools developed for one representation for the other representation as well. For example, we can refactor a compositional implementation into an annotation-based representation and subsequently use our type checking mechanisms or views on this representation. If we even achieve reversible refactorings in both directions (round-trip engineering), we can always refactor a product-line implementation into the representation that is most suitable for the task at hand. We can eventually *leverage respective strengths of both representations*.

6.2.3. Automated refactoring

For some annotations, refactorings into equivalent compositional implementations are straightforward and can be easily automated. For example, with contemporary compositional languages such as Jak or AspectJ, we can move an annotated method or field into an according class refinement or aspect (as inter-type declaration). However, transformations become more difficult, once we reach limitations of compositional approaches regarding granularity and the optional feature problem and once conceptual differences, such as composition order, become relevant.

Automated refactorings between physical and virtual separation are on the boundary of the scope of this thesis; their main purposes are easing the adoption of compositional approaches and building uniform theories, models and tools for product-line implementation, not primarily improving annotative approaches. Consequently, we give only an *informal outline* by means of examples and illustrate some of the challenges and their solutions. For brevity, we exclude also the details of reverse refactorings from physical separation to virtual separation. Instead, we refer interested readers to [Kästner et al., 2009a], in which we *formally* discussed refactorings between disciplined annotations and Jak-style class refinements (in both directions) for a language that supports both annotations and class refinements. In this work, all refactorings perform small transformations within the spectrum between physical and virtual separation. We subsequently prove that our refactorings – within this language – are complete: Every program with any combination of annotations and refinements (including fine-grained and nested annotations and considering the composition order) can always be refactored into a purely physical separation and a purely virtual separation.

Nevertheless, we still need to introduce some additional terminology for the discussed compositional approach. For describing our refactorings, we use the language Jak. As explained in Section 3.1, Jak can introduce classes and refinements of existing classes; class refinements can introduce new methods and fields and extend existing methods with method refinements. Classes and class refinements are located in a *feature module* – in the simplest case a directory – that is mapped to the feature model with a *feature expression* (propositional formula over the set of features, like annotations). The module is included in the composition process if and only if the feature expression evaluates to true for a given feature selection. Thus, different feature selections lead to different compositions. Feature modules are composed in a specific order. The order is relevant when two method refinements extend the same method. We assume that there is a fixed composition order; a feature selection specifies only which modules are composed, not the composition order. We furthermore assume a feature module BASE that is included in all variants and always composed first.

Refactoring by example

For most coarse-grained annotations, refactorings from annotations to class refinements are straightforward. If an entire class in annotated, a refactoring can drop the annotation and move the class into a feature module associated with the same feature expression (if such feature module does not already exist, the refactoring creates it). If an entire method or field is annotated, a refactoring can move it into an according class refinement. Refactorings can be executed one step at a time or in a batch process. In Figure 6.2, we illustrate refactorings of an annotated method and an annotated class by means of a simple stack example similar to the one in Figure 3.1 (p. 20): Before the refactoring all code is located in feature module BASE and code of the feature LOCKING is annotated; after the refactoring, class *Lock* and method *lock* are moved to a newly created feature module.

Code in nested annotations is included only when all annotations evaluate to *true*. We can move elements in nested annotations into feature modules with a feature expression that conjoins all annotations as shown in the example in Figure 6.3. As shown in the same example, this scales also for more complex annotations: Method *log* is already annotated to be included if feature LOGGING or feature TRACING is included, this is propagated to an according feature module. When many nested annotations occur in a program, the refactoring will produce many modules. Many modules may decrease readability, but, as discussed in Section 3.1.5, this is a problem of compositional approaches in general, not one of our refactorings.

Feature BASE

```
1 class Stack {
2   void push(Object o) { /*...*/ }
3 #ifdef Locking
4   Lock lock(Object o) { /*...*/ }
5 #endif
6 }
7 #ifdef Locking
8 class Lock { /*...*/ }
9 #endif
```

Feature BASE

```
1 class Stack {
2   void push(Object o) { /*...*/ }
3 }
```

Feature LOCKING

```
4 refines class Stack {
5   Lock lock(Object o) { /*...*/ }
6 }
7 class Lock { /*...*/ }
```

(a) Virtual separation. (b) Refactored physical separation.

Figure 6.2.: *Refactoring annotated classes and methods.*

Feature BASE

```
1  #ifdef Stack
2  class Stack {
3    void push(Object o) { /*...*/ }
4  #ifdef Locking
5    Lock lock(Object o) { /*...*/ }
6  #endif
7  #ifdef Logging ∨ Tracing
8    void log(String msg) { /*...*/ }
9  #endif
10 }
11 #endif
```

Feature STACK

```
1 class Stack {
2   void push(Object o) { /*...*/ }
3 }
```

Feature STACK ∧ LOCKING

```
4 refines class Stack {
5   Lock lock(Object o) { /*...*/ }
6 }
```

Feature STACK ∧ (LOGGING ∨ TRACING)

```
7 refines class Stack {
8   void log(String msg) { /*...*/ }
9 }
```

(a) Virtual separation.

(b) Refactored physical separation.

Figure 6.3.: *Refactoring nested annotations.*

Annotations at finer granularity than members can be challenging. It seems that extracting annotated statements inside a method into a method refinement is straightforward, however, there are several conditions [Kästner et al., 2009a]: (1) the annotated statements must occur at the beginning or end of a method (or both), (2) annotated statements at the end of the method must not access variables modified by the inner statements (except the return value), (3) if the target method is already extended by method refinements, the target feature module must be composed before all feature modules that already contain method refinements of the same method. We illustrate these conditions with three examples in Figure 6.4. We start with a version that is already partially implemented with class refinements. First, the annotated statement in method *pop* can be refactored into a method refinement in feature module LOGGING, because it is the first statement in the method. Second, we cannot refactor the first annotated statement in method *push*, because it is not the first statement in the method; we cannot refactor the second annotated statement, because it refers to the local variable *l* defined within the method. Both remain annotated, we refactor them later. Third, we can extract the *lock* and *unlock* statements in method *clear* only if feature module LOCKING is composed *before* LOGGING, because LOGGING already refines that method. If LOCK-ING was composed after LOGGING, we could not apply the refactoring, because it would alter the behavior and execute the *log* statement after the *lock* statement.

Feature BASE

```
1  class Stack {
2    Object pop() {
3  #ifdef Logging
4        log("pop");
5  #endif
6        return elementData[--size];
7    }
8
9    void push(Object o) {
10       if (o == null) return;
11 #ifdef LOCKING
12       Lock l = lock(o);
13 #endif
14       elementData[size++] = o;
15 #ifdef LOCKING
16       l.unlock();
17 #endif
18   }
19
20   void clear() {
21 #ifdef LOCKING
22       Lock l = lock();
23 #endif
24       size = 0;
25 #ifdef LOCKING
26       l.unlock();
27 #endif
28   }
29 }
```

```
30 refines class Stack {
31   void clear() {
32       log("clear");
33       Super.pop();
34   }
35 }
```

(a) Initial version with annotations and re-finement.

Feature BASE

```
1  class Stack {
2    Object pop() {
3        return elementData[--size];
4    }
5    void push(Object o) {
6        if (o == null) return;
7  #ifdef LOCKING
8        Lock l = lock(o);
9  #endif
10       elementData[size++] = o;
11 #ifdef LOCKING
12       l.unlock();
13 #endif
14   }
15   void clear() {
16       size = 0
17   }
18 }
```

Feature LOCKING

```
19 refines class Stack {
20   void clear() {
21       Lock l = lock();
22       Super.clear();
23       l.unlock();
24   }
25 }
```

Feature LOGGING

```
26 refines class Stack {
27   Object pop() {
28       log("pop");
29       return Super.pop();
30   }
31   void clear() {
32       log("clear");
33       Super.pop();
34   }
35 }
```

(b) Refactored version.

Figure 6.4.: *Refactoring annotated statements into method refinements.*

To refactor annotated statements for which method refinements do not provide a solution (as the statements in method *push* of Figure 6.4), we need to apply the workarounds known for fine-grained extensions in compositional approaches (see

Sec. 3.1.4). Typically, this means to prepare the code and extract the annotated statements into one or more hook methods (with a common extract-method refactoring [Fowler, 1999, pp. 110ff.]). After such preparation, which can be automated as well, the annotated statements are the *only* statements in the hook method, so we can extract them with a method refinement (i.e., all three conditions are fulfilled). We show a simple example in Figure 6.5. First, we extract a hook method (Fig. 6.5b). Second, we extract a method refinement as before (Fig. 6.5c). In the presence of local variables as in Figure 6.4, return statements, or wrappers (cf. Sec. 5.2.4), more complex preparations can be necessary. We have already shown a rather complex implementation of *lock* and *unlock* in Figure 6.4 with two nested hook methods in Section 3.1.4 (Fig. 3.3, p. 25). As alternative solution, also with plenty boilerplate code, we can prepare the source code by refactoring a method into a method object [see Fowler, 1999, pp. 135ff.], which, as a useful side effect, replaces local variables by fields.

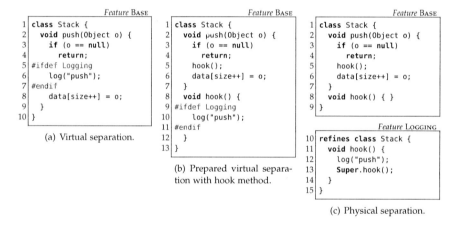

Figure 6.5.: *Refactoring an annotated statement in the middle of a method.*

Similarly, other fine-grained annotations on parameters, expressions, and others can be refactored with a certain effort. We simply have to automate the well-known workarounds. We refrain from further examples. To draw a line, which refactorings to implement, disciplined annotations provide a useful guideline. When we already restrict our tool chain to disciplined annotations, we do not have to deal with all kinds of annotations (for some of which it is already difficult to find a refactoring manually). To ease implementation of automated refactorings, we might even restrict disciplined annotations further (e.g., only classes, members, and statements, but no parameters may be annotated). As a fall-back solution, it is always possible to expand even undisciplined and fine-grained annotations to more coarse-grained disciplined annotations at the price of some code replication [Garrido and Johnson, 2005; Vittek, 2003] (see also Sec. 5.4).

All in all, we can refactor all virtually separated implementations into a pure physical separation. However, nested annotations result in many refactored modules and fine-grained annotations in boilerplate code. We again reach the limitations of compositional approaches. In some cases, the generated code will probably look worse than manually implemented workarounds. It is questionable, whether modular reasoning on modules generated from fine-grained annotations is efficient. We found cases, when it was significantly easier to understand the code in a virtual separation. Thus, we emphasize that automated refactorings do not solve the limitations of compositional approaches. They can decrease the effort to implement necessary workarounds, but developers that plan to refactor annotations later should strive for coarse-grained annotations with little nesting in the first place. This requires more planning and less ad-hoc implementation. Automated refactoring can ease the adoption of compositional approaches and reduce the effort to decompose legacy applications into composable modules, but it is no silver bullet to achieve modularity. We argue that, in many cases, virtual separation of concern with emulated modularity can be a more efficient form of implementation.

Implementation and experience

An implementation of an environment that integrates physical and virtual separation and that supports partial refactorings within the spectrum between both representations is outside the scope of this thesis. Nevertheless, we have exemplarily integrated automated refactorings to a large degree as *export* and *import* functionality in our prototype CIDE [Kästner et al., 2007b, 2009a]. Again, we give only a brief overview of the export functionality.

CIDE can export annotated Java code (with disciplined annotations on classes, members, and statements) in a single step into composable modules implemented with Jak [Batory et al., 2004], FeatureHouse [Apel et al., 2009b], or AspectJ [Kiczales et al., 2001]. During the export, small refactorings (moving methods into class refinements, extracting method refinements, inserting hook methods, etc.) are executed as described above on an internal intermediate representation, which supports both annotations and refinements. Currently, this intermediate representation is not accessible to the developer. The result of an export is a modular implementation without annotations. The export process is very similar for all three compositional languages, because the languages provide similar capabilities. For all languages, we use similar refactorings and have to create similar boilerplate code.

Although our implementation is prototypical (some annotations are not supported yet), we have already used it to export a series of annotation-based product-line implementations. Here, we selected two interesting cases.

- We exported the annotated version of Berkeley DB (see Appendix A.1) to create a large scale case study for feature composition in FeatureHouse [Apel et al., 2009b]. Few annotations were not supported by our refactoring implementation (especially annotated parameters), so we prepared the code slightly (e.g., using overloaded methods instead of annotated parameters). Then, we exported the Java implementation with 2297 annotations mapped to 38 features into feature modules with 338 class refinements and 954 method refinements. In this process, many additional feature modules were created (99 feature modules for 38 features) due to nested annotations. Furthermore, fine-grained annotations caused the generation of 858 hook methods.

  Similar to our experience with AspectJ, we regard the annotated implementation as much more understandable than the decomposed version with lots of boilerplate code. Nevertheless, the refactoring demonstrates that we can reach physically separated implementations even from an annotated code base.

- Kuhlemann et al. [2009a,b] were searching for a case study for a refactoring mechanism of Jak modules. They identified the domain of compression-algorithm libraries as interesting in their context, but, since no such library was developed with Jak, they would have to provide their own feature-oriented implementation. Instead of writing a new library from scratch, they decided to refactor an existing library. They used CIDE to annotate features in three libraries and subsequently export the code into feature modules. Even though they subsequently restructured the result, they valued the automated refactoring as an efficient way to create modules compared to manual refactoring.

Our experience shows that automated refactorings are feasible. We can use the mechanisms of our export also for small-step refactorings within the spectrum between pure physical and pure virtual separation. Our experience confirms that creating modules by refactoring annotations is indeed efficient, but also shows that some planning and restructuring is necessary to generate understandable code.

Related work

Related to our automated refactorings, researchers in the field of aspect-oriented software development have investigated transformations from *#ifdef* statements in legacy C programs into aspects [Adams et al., 2009; Bruntink et al., 2007; Reynolds et al., 2008]. The key concern, so far, is to understand existing preprocessor usage (e.g., classify typical patterns and determine how to extract them) in order to evaluate whether a manual or automated refactoring is feasible [Adams et al., 2009; Bruntink et al., 2007; Reynolds et al., 2008]. The approaches eventually enforce disciplined annotations for this analysis [Reynolds et al., 2008] or parse code partially, while ignoring undisciplined annotations [Adams et al., 2009]. We are not aware of any tool that actually automates refactorings. Also nested annotations and composition order are usually not considered.

Aside from annotations, there is plenty of work on how to refactor legacy applications into a more modular form using aspects or feature models. Examples are refactorings from object-oriented to aspect-oriented implementations [e.g., Hanenberg et al., 2003; Monteiro and Fernandes, 2005; Cole and Borba, 2005; Binkley et al., 2005] and from object-oriented to feature-oriented implementations [e.g., Liu et al., 2006; Kästner et al., 2009d]. Some of these refactorings are automated with tool support. Many of the mechanisms to refactor fine-grained extensions (e.g., code preparation with hook methods) are already described in these refactorings.

In [Kästner et al., 2009a], we even discuss refactorings in the opposite direction from physical separation to a virtual separation. We argue that some features with many fine-grained extensions are easier to understand when annotated in a common implementation instead when implemented modularly with plenty boilerplate code. Reverse refactorings (implemented as *import* in CIDE) can be used to create a virtual view on a physically separated implementation. Additionally, it allows us to apply the discussed improvements (views, visual representation, product-line–aware type checking) also for compositional approaches. With automated refactorings in both directions, we can switch between different representation, and always use the representation best suited for the task at hand. Reverse refactoring become challenging when alternative features are involved, see [Kästner et al., 2009a]. In literature, refactorings from physical to virtual separation are rare, because most researchers regard a physical separation as the more desirable form. The only exception we are aware of is the work of Kim et al. [2008], who discuss differences regarding ordering and type-checking for virtual and physical separation. In their work, they mention that they have mechanically transformed Jak implementations into an annotated code base.

6.3. Summary

In this section, we wrapped up our efforts to improve annotative approaches. We named our concept of an improved annotative approach with tool support *virtual separation of concerns*. In a comparison to compositional approaches and contemporary annotative approaches, we showed how tool support can address almost all problems of traditional preprocessors. Regarding traceability, language integration, and errors, annotations become comparable to compositional approaches.

At the same time, we maintain all benefits of annotative approaches over compositional approaches: Virtual separation of concerns can express fine-grained extensions, provides a straightforward solution to the problem of multiple dimensional decomposition and optional features, is uniform for many artifact languages, and is easy to adopt.

The main obstacles of virtual separation of concerns are rooted in its lack of modularity. Tool support cannot replace modularity but only emulate some of its benefits. Fortunately, modularity is usually not dropped altogether in annotation-based implementations. Instead, parts of a feature's implementation can be modularized using the hierarchical decomposition mechanisms of the host language. This way, we can test, compile, or reuse parts in isolation. Whether missing modularity is a significant limitation in practice depends on the context of the project and on how annotations are used.

Finally, we outlined how we can integrate compositional approaches and improved annotative approaches. An integration allows developers to use both variability mechanisms depending on the task at hand. Automated refactorings between both representations furthermore promise an easier adoption path and lower development effort for compositional approaches. As a typical use case, we expect that developers create modular product-line implementations by annotating feature code and subsequently refactoring these annotations it into composable modules.

7. Conclusion and future work

Software product lines are more difficult to implement than single applications, because they cover the requirements of an entire domain. From a product-line implementation, we can generate an entire family of related variants. Thus, developers need adequate mechanisms to implement variability and generate variants from a common code base. We discussed different approaches to implement software product lines, specifically compositional approaches and annotative approaches.

Research in software engineering and programming languages focuses mostly on compositional approaches, which divide the implementation into modules and generate variants by composing selected modules. Compositional approaches aim at modularity and are a disciplined approach to product-line implementation; they often provide direct language support for encapsulation and composition. Nevertheless, there are several (conceptual) difficulties, such as coarse granularity and feature interactions, which can cause a high effort during implementation and which raise the adoption barrier.

In contrast, annotative approaches provide a simple mechanism to implement variability: Developers annotate code fragments to conditionally exclude them from compilation with preprocessors or similar lightweight tools. Despite well-known problems and strong criticism in literature – for ignoring modularity, being undisciplined and error prone, and obfuscating the source code – annotative approaches are still broadly used in practice.

Contrary to the current research trend, we took sides with annotative approaches. We explored possible improvements of broadly used annotative approaches. We name the improved annotative approach with tool support *virtual separation of concerns*, because – even though we do not *physically* decompose concerns (or features) into modules – we provide some form of *virtual* separation with tool support. Specifically, we contributed five improvements for annotative approaches and implemented and evaluated them in our prototype CIDE:

1. We strictly *integrate a feature model* to avoid scattering of configuration knowledge and to enforce discipline and consistency of annotations. A controlled mapping between the feature model and annotations in the implementation provides a sound base for reasoning about annotations for other improvements. Among others, it prevents inconsistent annotations that refer to undefined features.

2. *Editable views* emulate modularity. A view on a feature shows the feature's implementation, but hides all other code. Switching between views is an easy operation and handling overlapping features (i.e., feature interactions or multi-dimensional decomposition) becomes straightforward this way. Even though a feature's implementation is still scattered in the underlying code base, views allow developers to quickly trace a feature from the feature model to its implementation. Additionally, views on a variant provide even a preview on the resulting variant for a feature selection.

3. Different *visual enhancements* of how annotations are represented are possible. We discussed to use colors instead of textual annotations to reduce obfuscation and implemented a representation based on background colors in CIDE. We demonstrated that colored annotations are quicker to recognize and can speed up program comprehension for some tasks (up to 43 % in our controlled experiment).

4. *Disciplined annotations* restrict annotations such that no syntax errors can occur during generation. Instead of mapping features to sequences of characters or tokens, disciplined annotations map features to elements of an artifact's underlying structure. This way, we prevent (often subtile and hard to find) syntax errors and, as a side effect, provide a useful basis for other mechanisms and tools that reason about annotated code. Although disciplined annotations restrict expressiveness by prohibiting certain kinds of annotations, we demonstrated that they are still expressive enough in practice and applicable uniformly to multiple languages.

5. On top of disciplined annotations, a *product-line–aware type system* detects type errors in the entire product-line implementation in a single step, instead of compiling each variant (of potentially millions) in isolation. Our type system checks the implementation and its annotations against the feature model. Among others, it ensures that a method declaration cannot be annotated and removed if it is still invoked from code fragment that is not removed from the same variants. With our CFJ calculus, we formally proved that all variants generated from a well-typed software product line are well-typed (variant generation preserves typing). With our type system, we enforce consistency of product-line implementations and detect errors early during development.

With such tool support, virtual separation of concerns addresses most problems for which preprocessors are criticized. For example, regarding traceability, language integration, and error detection, we bring annotations to at least the same quality level as compositional approaches. Additionally, annotative approaches provide their own advantages, such as fine granularity, uniformity, and easy adoption. Even though we cannot solve all problems – regarding modularity, we can only emulate modules and advise developers to partially modularize features – we regard virtual separation of concerns as serious alternative to compositional approaches.

Still, we do not intend to give a definite answer on how to implement software product lines. In collaborations, we explore different implementation approaches in parallel and look also at improvements of compositional approaches [e.g., Apel et al., 2008c,e, 2009b, 2010; Kuhlemann et al., 2009b; Steimann et al., 2010]. As shown in this thesis, we have excellent experiences with virtual separation of concerns, and we believe that it can become a respectable approach for product-line implementation. On the other hand, others may still argue against annotative approaches and claim that modular implementation approaches may provide the superior form of product-line implementation in the long term (e.g., with better languages and tools, with variability support in mainstream programming languages, or with better training of developers). So far, beyond isolated case studies, there is only little empirical evidence regarding evolution, maintainability, and program comprehension, which could guide us in an objective decision. To allow a high level of flexibility, we even integrate compositional and annotative approaches and provide a migration path with automated refactorings in case developers eventually decide for a pure compositional approach.

With our work, we have shown that annotation-based implementations are not a lost cause. Researchers have neglected them, but improvements are possible. With adequate tool support, they become a serious alternative to compositional approaches. We want to encourage researchers to overcome their prejudices (usually from experience with *cpp*) and to reconsider research on annotation-based implementations. At the same time, we want to encourage practitioners that are currently using preprocessors to demand improvements from tool builders. Since tool support is necessary for product-line implementation anyway, it is well worth investing also into tool support for new preprocessors and virtual separation of concerns.

Future work. We have suggested many improvements of annotative approaches, but still many remain to explore. Regarding visualization, we barely scratched the surface of possibilities of program visualization approaches. Our approach to background colors is quite naive, and it remains to explore how annotations (or features in general) are best represented to the user. We recently started a collaboration in this direction. Similarly, views should be explored in more detail. It would be interesting to evaluate how developers use views, how much context is necessary, and whether we can further support them in expanding views or switching between views. For example, can we exploit the feature model's structure and provide drill up/down functionality between views on parent and child features? Can we separate features into dimensions and represent software product lines as multi-dimensional cubes with slice and dice operations?

Work on views and visualizations always aims at improving program comprehension. Unfortunately, rather little is known about the program comprehension process, and because it is an internal cognitive process we have to measure it empirically. Even the broadly accepted benefit of modularity is derived mostly from anecdotal evidence and hardly based on empirical result. A major research endeavor (which would require an entire series of experiments) would be to empirically assess the impact of compositional or annotative approaches on program comprehension. For example, can we measure the impact of modularity on program comprehension and can we compare it with the impact of views? More case studies of software product lines that others can analyze as well are needed to this end.

Furthermore, disciplined annotations and a product-line–aware type system open interesting opportunities for future work. A major implementation challenge – that we currently pursue with an industrial partner – is to provide a product-line–aware type system for C that is backward compatible with the C preprocessor and that can be used on the vast amount of existing C implementations. The main challenge is to deal with the peculiarities of *cpp*, so we presumably will have to integrate the automatic expansion techniques of Garrido [2005], symbolic execution techniques as used by Hu et al. [2000] and Latendresse [2004], and attribute feature models and constraint-satisfaction-problem solver as discussed by Czarnecki et al. [2002] and Benavides et al. [2005]. In another line of research, we automatically propose fixes to type errors, for example, we might recommend annotating another method invocation. Taken this idea further, we can use type errors to decide which code fragments belong to a feature, because the type system provides some indication when a feature is consistent or complete. We currently explore this idea as *feature mining* (compared to work on *feature location* [e.g., Eisenbarth et al., 2003; Poshyvanyk et al., 2007], we take the feature model, annotations, and type information into account).

Finally, there are many challenges from integrating compositional approaches and annotative approaches. In future work, we want to develop an environment that supports both representations and small-step refactorings between them. We will evaluate the gradual transition from annotations to compositional mechanisms in an exploratory study. An interesting challenge is to make all refactorings reversible (such that refactoring a code fragment forth and back yields the same source code) to enable true round-trip engineering. We envision using the same technique for an on-demand remodularization of features. Except for the described refactorings, we mostly worked on compositional approaches and annotative approaches in isolation. In the future, we aim at integrating and unifying the developed theories, models, and tools. For example, we intend to develop an integrated product-line–aware type system that supports both annotations and refinements (and can prove that refactorings between them preserve the behavior of all variants).

A. List of case studies

A.1. Case studies developed in CIDE

In the context of this research project, we conducted a series of case studies to explore different concepts. Among others, we explored whether integrating a feature model is feasible (Sec. 4.1), how features and annotations are distributed (Sec. 3.1.7, 4.3.2 and 5.3.6), whether disciplined annotations restrict expressiveness and whether they are applicable uniformly to multiple languages (Sec. 5.2.6), what kind of performance we can expect from type checking a product line (Sec. 5.3.6), and whether automated refactorings are feasible in practice (Sec. 6.2.3). Since our case studies crosscut different topics – we analyzed case studies such as Berkeley DB in different contexts – so far, we provided only a brief description in the corresponding sections. Instead, we give a more detailed description in this appendix. We proceed in alphabetical order. Additionally, we make the source code of all case studies in CIDE (except the industrial product line for Water Boilers) available on CIDE's website `http://fosd.de/cide`.

AHEAD Tool Suite

Version:	February 2008
Developed by:	Don Batory et al. (University of Texas at Austin)
Developed as:	single script/document
Previous decomp. by:	Salvador Trujillo (University of the Basque Country)
URL:	`http://www.cs.utexas.edu/users/schwartz/`
CIDE version:	Annotated artifacts based on prev. decomposition
Annotated by:	Christian Kästner
Language:	ANT (XML), HTML
Size:	17 000 lines of ANT build scripts (54 files)
	28 000 lines of HTML documentation (85 files)
Features:	14 (various tools: xak, guidsl, drc, ...)

The *AHEAD Tool Suite* has been bootstrapped and is implemented in a feature-oriented way [Batory et al., 2004]. Its build scripts and documentation – on which we focused in this case study – were subsequently decomposed into feature modules by Trujillo et al. [2006]. We annotated the original (not decomposed) build scripts and documentation equivalently to Trujillo's decomposition. Our main focus was to evaluate disciplined annotations for noncode artifacts (see Sec. 5.2.6).

Arithmetic Expression Evaluator

Developed by:	Armin Größlinger (University of Passau)
Developed as:	single application

CIDE version:	Identified features and annotated existing artifacts
Annotated by:	Malte Rosenthal (University of Passau)
Language:	Haskell
Size:	460 lines of Haskell code (2 files)
Features:	25 (variables, various operators and lamda abstractions, ...)

With the *Arithmetic Expression Evaluator*, we wanted to explore (1) suitability for Haskell code and (2) how far we can go with fine-grained annotations in CIDE. Armin Größlinger developed an arithmetic-expression evaluation for us, which Malte Rosenthal subsequently annotated at very fine granularity. Within only 460 lines of Haskell code, 25 different features were annotated. We later decomposed some of these features physically as well to compare granularity and expressiveness, for details see [Apel et al., 2009a].

Berkeley DB Java Edition

Version:	2.1.30 (January 25, 2006)
Developed by:	Sleepycat Software, Inc.
Developed as:	single application (with some runtime variability)
URL:	www.oracle.com/database/berkeley-db

CIDE version:	Annotated artifacts based on prev. decomposition
Annotated by:	Christian Kästner
Languages:	Java, HTML
Size:	84 000 lines of Java code (315 files)
	120 000 lines of HTML documentation (390 files)
Features:	38–42 (transactions, statistics, logging, db operations, ...)

Berkeley DB Java Edition is an open source database engine, entirely written in Java. It can be embedded as a library into applications. It provides tables, in which key-value pairs can be stored. Although, it does not support ad-hoc queries (such as SQL), it scales to large amount of data, provides sophisticated multi-threading support, indexes, transactions, and other functionality.

Berkeley DB was originally not developed as a product line, but we have subsequently decomposed it to evaluate product-line implementation mechanisms [Kästner, 2007; Kästner et al., 2007a, 2008a, 2009a,b,c; Apel et al., 2009b; Steimann et al., 2010]. It is our largest and most used case study. There are four decomposed versions of Berkeley DB Java Edition: AspectJ, CIDE, FeatureHouse, and IIIA.

- First, we decomposed Berkeley DB into 38 features using *AspectJ* [Kästner, 2007; Kästner et al., 2007a]. Therefore, we identified the code of each feature and manually refactored it into one or more aspects. The decomposition was performed in about one month. As discussed in Section 3.1, we used the AspectJ decomposition of Berkeley DB to evaluate (1) the shape of features in database systems [Kästner, 2007; Kästner et al., 2007a], (2) the impact of the optional feature problem [Kästner, 2007; Kästner et al., 2009c], (3) the influence of the feature order [Kästner, 2007; Apel et al., 2008b], and (4) the suitability of AspectJ (and compositional approaches in general) as an implementation mechanism [Kästner, 2007; Kästner et al., 2007a, 2008a].

- Based on the previous decomposition with AspectJ, we annotated Berkeley DB in *CIDE*. We added annotations for the same 38 features and 4 additional features. In addition to the source code, we annotated the HTML documentation. Since the code base and features were already known, and since annotating is faster than manual refactoring, this second decomposition was performed in about three days.

  With this case study, we evaluated (1) disciplined annotations (see Section 5.2), (2) the respective advantages and disadvantages of compositional and annotative implementations (see Chapters 3 and 6), (3) the performance of our product-line–aware type system (see Section 5.3), and (4) refactorings between compositional and annotative implementations (see Section 6.2).

- Based on the annotated implementation, we *generated* a feature-oriented decomposition of Berkeley to be composed with *FeatureHouse* by exporting our annotated version with CIDE. The resulting implementation was used to evaluate the FeatureHouse composition tool [Apel et al., 2009b] and the automated refactorings in CIDE [Kästner et al., 2009a] (see Section 6.2).

- In cooperation with Steimann et al. [2010], we rewrote some aspects of the AspectJ-implementation of Berkeley DB with new language mechanisms of the *IIIA* compiler. This implementation strives for strict modularity and introduces join-point interfaces to encapsulate aspect behavior. As an improved compositional approach, it is outside the scope of this thesis.

FAME-DBMS

Developed by: FAME-DBMS team
Developed as: software product line (compositional approach)

CIDE version: Own implementation based on existing compositional impl.
Annotated by: Syed Saif ur Rahman (University of Magdeburg)
Language: C++
Size: 5000 lines of C++ code (15 files)
Features: 14 (inmemory vs. persistent, B-tree, queue, ...)

FAME-DBMS is a prototype of an embedded data management system developed from scratch as software product line. It was originally developed with the compositional language FeatureC++. One of the developers then created an annotation-based implementation with CIDE that demonstrates the feasibility of disciplined annotations for C++. In a different context, we compared both implementations with regard to the optional feature problem in [Kästner et al., 2009c].

Functional Graph Library

Version: June 2006
Developed by: Martin Erwig (Oregon State University)
Developed as: single library
URL: http://web.engr.oregonstate.edu/~erwig/fgl/haskell

CIDE version: Identified features and annotated existing artifacts
Annotated by: Malte Rosenthal (University of Passau)
Language: Haskell
Size: 2600 lines of Haskell code (32 files)
Features: 18 (static vs. dynamic graph, labels, 13 graph algorithms, ...)

The Functional Graph Library is a library of graph data structures and algorithms, but, it contrast to the Graph Product Line, it has not been developed as product line. Malte Rosenthal introduced variability by annotating the legacy code for 18 features. In parallel, the Functional Graph Library was also physically decomposed into feature modules with FeatureHouse [Apel et al., 2009a]. With this case study, we primarily explored suitability and granularity of annotations in Haskell code.

Graph Product Line

Version:	gg4 (last change Feb. 2006)
Developed by:	Roberto Lopez Herrejon (University of Texas at Austin)
Developed as:	software product line (compositional approach)
CIDE version:	Own implementation based on existing compositional impl.
Annotated by:	Christian Kästner
Language:	Jak, HTML
Size:	1350 lines of Java code (16 files)
	200 lines of HTML documentation (1 file)
Features:	18 (directed/undirected, weighted/unweighted, 9 alg., ...)

Lopez-Herrejon and Batory [2001] developed the *Graph Product Line* as a benchmark for product line technology. Similar to the Functional Graph Library, a user can select between weighted and unweighted and between directed and undirected edges, between three different underlying data structures (vertex lists, neighbor lists, edge objects), and several algorithms such as depth first search, cycle detection, or Kruskal's algorithm. The Graph Product Line is interesting as a case study, because it contains many alternative features and nontrivial dependencies (e.g., Kruskal's algorithm requires undirected and weighted edges) and because the domain is well-known.

The Graph Product Line was developed from scratch with the feature-oriented language Jak (27 feature modules). We manually wrote a Java implementation that merges all features in a single code base and annotated that implementation. Additionally, we annotated the HTML documentation, so each variant has a documentation that describes only available features.

Lampiro

Version:	9.6.0 (Subversion revision 30)
Developed by:	Bluendo s.r.l.
Developed as:	software product line (annotative approach)
URL:	http://lampiro.bluendo.com/
CIDE version:	Annotated based on existing textual annotations
Annotated by:	Christian Kästner
Languages:	Java ME
Size:	45 000 lines of Java code (148 files)
Features:	11 (screensaver, compression, encryption, profiling, ...)

Lampiro is an open source project to implement an XMPP instant messenger for mobile phones on the Java ME platform. It was developed with annotations for variability (using the preprocessor *Antenna*) from scratch. Although variability was not explicitly documented, we consider Lampiro as software product line.

We only transformed existing annotations of the textual preprocessor Antenna into disciplined annotations in CIDE. It is the largest of our product lines that were developed with annotations from scratch. We use this case study to evaluate the shape of annotations (Sec. 4.3.2 and 5.2.6) and type correctness (Sec. 5.3.6) in software product lines.

MobileMedia

Version:	July 9th, 2009, releases 5, 6 and 8
Developed by:	Figueiredo et al. (Lancaster University)
Developed as:	software product line (annotative approach)
URL:	`http://mobilemedia.cvs.sf.net`

CIDE version:	Annotated based on existing textual annotations
Annotated by:	Christian Kästner
Languages:	Java ME
Size:	4 000–5 700 lines of Java code (38–50 files)
Features:	6–14 (support for photo, music, video, SMS, ...)

MobileMedia was developed at Lancaster University from scratch as software product line. To implement variability, they used the preprocessor *Antenna*. We directly transferred these textual annotations to disciplined annotations in CIDE. For their research, the authors kept a history of several development steps, with an increasing number of features over time. In different contexts, we use releases 5, release 6, and the latest release 8. We used release 5 with six features and 4000 lines of code in our experiment in Section 4.4, because it is sufficiently complex, but not too large to be understood in a 2-hour experiment. We use the more complex implementations of release 6 and 8 (with 9 and 14 features respectively) to evaluate the shape of annotations (Sec. 4.3.2 and 5.2.6) and type checking (Sec. 5.3.6) in product lines that were developed from scratch with annotations.

Mobile RSS Reader

Version:	Subversion revision 1596 (May 21st, 2009)
Developed by:	Tommi Laukkanen
Developed as:	software product line (annotative approach)
URL:	`http://code.google.com/p/mobile-rss-reader/`

CIDE version:	Annotated based on existing textual annotations
Annotated by:	Christian Kästner
Languages:	Java ME
Size:	20 000 lines of Java code (54 files)
Features:	14 (internationalization, logging, Java ME profiles, ...)

Mobile RSS Reader is an open source project to implement a portable RSS reader for mobile phones on the Java ME platform. It was developed with annotations for variability (using the preprocessor *Antenna*) from scratch. Although variability was not explicitly documented, we consider Mobile RSS Reader as software product line. We only transformed existing annotations of the textual preprocessor Antenna into disciplined annotations in CIDE. As Lampiro and MobileMedia, we use this case study to evaluate the shape of annotations (Sec. 4.3.2 and 5.2.6) and type correctness (Sec. 5.3.6) in software product lines, developed from scratch with annotations.

Prevayler

Version:	2.4
Developed by:	Klaus Wuestefeld et al.
Developed as:	single library
Previous decomp. by:	Irum Godil and others
URL:	`http://www.prevayler.org/`
CIDE version:	Annotated artifacts based on prev. decomposition
Annotated by:	Virgilio Borges de Oliveira (PUC Minas)
Languages:	Java
Size:	8 000 lines of Java code (141 files)
Features:	5 (replication, gzip, censor, monitor, snapshot)

Prevayler is an open-source in-memory database to be embedded in Java applications. It was not developed as software product line, but researchers have identified variability and used it frequently as case study for compositional approaches [e.g., Godil and Jacobsen, 2005; Liu et al., 2006]. The CIDE version of Prevayler was annotated by Virgilio Borges de Oliveira as part of a research project, independent of our work.

Pynche

Version:	1.3
Developed by:	Barry A. Warsaw
Developed as:	single application
URL:	`http://www.python.org/`
CIDE version:	Identified features and annotated existing artifacts
Annotated by:	Alexander Dreiling (University of Magdeburg)
Language:	Python
Size:	2400 lines of Python code (13 files)
Features:	12 (different windows, viewers, and colors)

Pynche (short for "PYthonically Natural Color and Hue Editor") is a color editor written in Python, which is included in the Python distribution. Pynche was not developed as a software product line, but subsequently decomposed by into 12 features to demonstrate the feasibility of developing software product lines written in Python with CIDE (see Section 5.2.6).

SQL Parser

Developed by:	Sagar Sunkle (University of Magdeburg)
Developed as:	software product line (compositional approach)
CIDE version:	Annotated artifacts based on prev. decomposition
Annotated by:	Christian Kästner
Language:	ANTLR
Size:	60 lines of ANTLR grammar (1 file)
Features:	4 (single vs. multi column, set quantifiers, where clause)

As part of a research project on tailor-made data management, Sunkle et al. [2008] developed a decomposed SQL grammar, so that, for different feature selections, they could generate different grammars and parsers. In this case study, we tested feasibility of disciplined annotations for grammar specification languages and annotated four features of an SQL grammar excerpt from this project.

Water Boiler

Developed as:	multiple programs (clone and own)
CIDE version:	Annotated based on existing textual annotations
Annotated by:	Salvador Trujillo (IKERLAN Research Center)
Language:	C
Size:	10 000 lines of C code
Features:	14 (analog, digital, 24 KW, 30 KW, propane, butane, ...)

A customer of IKERLAN developed a control software for a water boiler system. To cope with variability (different hardware), they copied and modified the source code for each system. At IKERLAN, researchers identified features and refactored the existing systems into a single software product line that can generate all previous variants from a common code base. In this project, they originally used the textual preprocessor of Biglever's Gears tool suite [Krueger, 2002]. Subsequently, they transformed this implementation toward disciplined annotations in CIDE. For disciplined annotations, only few minor source code changes were necessary. Our focus of this case study was to apply CIDE to a realistic product line implemented in C. To protect the intellectual properties of our partners, we cannot publish the source code of this product line.

A.2. Forty C programs

We analyzed variability in 40 C programs to determine how many annotations are visible on one page of source code (Sec. 4.3.2) and to determine the percentage of disciplined annotations in practice (Sec. 5.2.6). Liebig et al. [2010] selected the programs for an earlier study on the C preprocessor. They selected well known open source programs from different domains. For completeness, we give some additional information about these programs in Table A.1: domain, web address, analyzed version, lines of code, percentage of annotated lines of code, number of annotations, and number of features (distinct *#ifdef* flags).

Name	Version	Domain	LOC	ALOC	ANN	FE
apache*	2.2.11	web server	214 250	21 %	4 087	1 158
berkeley db*	4.7.25	database system	187 298	15 %	2 907	1 537
cherokee*	0.99.11	web server	51 719	15 %	805	328
clamav*	0.94.2	antivirus program	75 210	14 %	1 361	285
dia*	0.96.1	diagramming softw.	128 850	4 %	614	91
emacs*	22.3	text editor	237 003	32 %	6 072	1 373
freebsd*	7.1	operating system	5 923 123	14 %	85 431	16 167
gcc*	4.3.3	compiler framework	1 615 639	18 %	16 497	5 063
ghostscript*	8.62.0	postscript interpreter	441 411	5 %	3 415	816
gimp*	2.6.4	graphics editor	587 277	3 %	1 836	392
glibc*	2.9	programming library	747 047	12 %	12 981	3 012
gnumeric*	1.9.5	spreadsheed appl.	254 578	5 %	1 548	291
gnuplot*	4.2.5	plotting tool	75 978	27 %	2 054	434
irssi*	0.8.13	IRC client	49 661	3 %	151	55
libxml2*	2.7.3	XML library	210 762	66 %	7 886	2 047
lighttpd*	1.4.22	web server	38 925	22 %	723	167
linux*	2.6.28.7	operating system	5 973 183	11 %	46 757	9 102
lynx*	2.8.6	web server	117 692	37 %	3 765	806
minix*	3.1.1	operating system	64 035	17 %	1 156	356
mplayer*	1.0rc2	media player	605 573	19 %	6 321	1 236
mpsolve[†]	2.2	mathematical softw.	10 170	3 %	30	13
openldap*	2.4.16	LDAP directory	245 907	27 %	2 744	708
opensolaris[‡]	dev[¶]	operating system	8 615 530	19 %	82 728	10 901
openvpn*	2.0.9	security application	38 363	61 %	1 098	276
parrot*	0.9.1	virtual machine	98 227	27 %	1 597	539
php*	5.2.8	program interpreter	573 724	34 %	8 396	2 426
pidgin*	2.4.0	instant messenger	269 178	15 %	2 162	576
postgresql*	dev[‖]	database system	451 259	5 %	2 906	692
privoxy*	3.0.12	proxy server	24 038	37 %	686	153
python*	2.6.1	program interpreter	373 961	27 %	8 726	5 127
sendmail*	8.14.2	mail transfer agent	83 643	38 %	3 116	880
sqlite*	3.6.10	database system	94 419	54 %	1 509	292
subversion*	1.5.1	revision control sys.	509 171	6 %	3 927	409
sylpheed*	2.6.0	e-mail client	101 435	19 %	1 074	271
tcl*	8.5.7	program interpreter	135 078	20 %	3 903	2 481
vim*	7.2	text editor	225 410	59 %	11 001	779
xfig*	3.2.5	vector graphics editor	72 443	7 %	376	107
xine-lib*	1.1.16.2	media library	494 903	34 %	6 163	1 692
xorg-server[§]	1.5.1	X server	527 335	18 %	8 932	1 360
xterm*	2.4.3	terminal emulator	49 589	39 %	2 019	453

LOC: lines of code, after normalization and removal of comments; ALOC: percentage of annotated lines of code; ANN: number of annotations; FE: number of features (distinct *#ifdef* flags); *http://freshmeat. net, [†]http://www.dm.unipi.it/cluster-pages/mpsolve/, [‡]http://opensolaris.org/os/, [§]http://x. org; [¶] version from 2009-11-10, [‖] version from 2009-05-08

Table A.1.: *Additional information on the selected 40 C programs [adapted from Liebig et al., 2010].*

Bibliography

Adams, B., De Meuter, W., Tromp, H., and Hassan, A. E. (2009). Can we refactor conditional compilation into aspects? In *Proc. Int'l Conf. Aspect-Oriented Software Development (AOSD)*, pp. 243–254. New York: ACM Press.

Adams, B., Van Rompaey, B., Gibbs, C., and Coady, Y. (2008). Aspect mining in the presence of the C preprocessor. In *Proc. AOSD Workshop on Linking Aspect Technology and Evolution (LATE)*, pp. 1–6. New York: ACM Press.

Aldrich, J. (2005). Open modules: Modular reasoning about advice. In *Proc. Europ. Conf. Object-Oriented Programming (ECOOP)*, vol. 3586 of *Lecture Notes in Computer Science*, pp. 144–168. Berlin/Heidelberg: Springer-Verlag.

Anastasopoules, M., and Gacek, C. (2001). Implementing product line variabilities. In *Proc. Symposium on Software Reusability (SSR)*, pp. 109–117. New York: ACM Press.

Anderson, T. W., and Finn, J. D. (1996). *The New Statistical Analysis of Data*. New York: Springer-Verlag.

Andrews, J. H. (2001). Process-algebraic foundations of aspect-oriented programming. In *Proc. Int'l Conf. Metalevel Architectures and Separation of Crosscutting Concerns (REFLECTION)*, vol. 2192 of *Lecture Notes in Computer Science*, pp. 187–209. Berlin/Heidelberg: Springer-Verlag.

Apel, S. (2007). *The Role of Features and Aspects in Software Development*. Ph.D. thesis, University of Magdeburg.

Apel, S. (2010). How AspectJ is used: An analysis of eleven AspectJ programs. *Journal of Object Technology (JOT)*, 9(1), 117–142.

Apel, S., and Batory, D. (2006). When to use features and aspects? A case study. In *Proc. Int'l Conf. Generative Programming and Component Engineering (GPCE)*, pp. 59–68. New York: ACM Press.

Apel, S., Batory, D., Graefe, G., Saake, G., and Spinczyk, O. (Eds.) (2008a). *Software Engineering for Tailor-made Data Management*. No. 08281 in Dagstuhl Seminar Proceedings. Wadern: Leibniz-Zentrum für Informatik (LZI).

Apel, S., and Kästner, C. (2009). An overview of feature-oriented software development. *Journal of Object Technology (JOT)*, *8*(5), 49–84.

Apel, S., Kästner, C., and Batory, D. (2008b). Program refactoring using functional aspects. In *Proc. Int'l Conf. Generative Programming and Component Engineering (GPCE)*, pp. 161–170. New York: ACM Press.

Apel, S., Kästner, C., Größlinger, and Lengauer, C. (2010). Type safety for feature-oriented product lines. *Automated Software Engineering – An International Journal*. To appear; submitted August 23, 2009; accepted February 3, 2010.

Apel, S., Kästner, C., Größlinger, A., and Lengauer, C. (2009a). Feature (de)composition in functional programming. In *Proc. Int'l Conf. Software Composition (SC)*, vol. 5634 of *Lecture Notes in Computer Science*, pp. 9–26. Berlin/Heidelberg: Springer-Verlag.

Apel, S., Kästner, C., and Lengauer, C. (2008c). Feature Featherweight Java: A calculus for feature-oriented programming and stepwise refinement. In *Proc. Int'l Conf. Generative Programming and Component Engineering (GPCE)*, pp. 101–112. New York: ACM Press.

Apel, S., Kästner, C., and Lengauer, C. (2009b). FeatureHouse: Language-independent, automated software composition. In *Proc. Int'l Conf. Software Engineering (ICSE)*, pp. 221–231. Washington, DC: IEEE Computer Society.

Apel, S., Leich, T., Rosenmüller, M., and Saake, G. (2005). FeatureC++: On the symbiosis of feature-oriented and aspect-oriented programming. In *Proc. Int'l Conf. Generative Programming and Component Engineering (GPCE)*, vol. 3676 of *Lecture Notes in Computer Science*, pp. 125–140. Berlin/Heidelberg: Springer-Verlag.

Apel, S., Leich, T., and Saake, G. (2008d). Aspectual feature modules. *IEEE Transactions on Software Engineering (TSE)*, *34*(2), 162–180.

Apel, S., Lengauer, C., Möller, B., and Kästner, C. (2008e). An algebra for features and feature composition. In *Proc. Int'l Conf. Algebraic Methodology and Software Technology (AMAST)*, vol. 5140 of *Lecture Notes in Computer Science*, pp. 36–50. Berlin/Heidelberg: Springer-Verlag.

Apel, S., Liebig, J., Kästner, C., Kuhlemann, M., and Leich, T. (2009c). An orthogonal access modifier model for feature-oriented programming. In *Proc. GPCE Workshop on Feature-Oriented Software Development (FOSD)*, pp. 27–34. New York: ACM Press.

Aßmann, U. (2003). *Invasive Software Composition*. New York: Springer-Verlag.

Atkins, D. L. (1998). Version sensitive editing: Change history as a programming tool. In *Proc. ECOOP Symposium on System Configuration Management (SCM)*, vol. 1439 of *Lecture Notes in Computer Science*, pp. 146–157. Berlin/Heidelberg: Springer-Verlag.

Atkins, D. L., Ball, T., Graves, T. L., and Mockus, A. (2002). Using version control data to evaluate the impact of software tools: A case study of the Version Editor. *IEEE Transactions on Software Engineering (TSE)*, 28(7), 625–637.

Aversano, L., Penta, M. D., and Baxter, I. D. (2002). Handling preprocessor-conditioned declarations. In *Proc. Int'l Workshop Source Code Analysis and Manipulation (SCAM)*, pp. 83–92. Los Alamitos, CA: IEEE Computer Society.

Bancilhon, F., and Spyratos, N. (1981). Update semantics of relational views. *ACM Transactions on Database Systems (TODS)*, 6(4), 557–575.

Bass, L., Clements, P., Cohen, S., Northrop, L., and Withey, J. (1997). Product line practice workshop report. Tech. Rep. CMU/SEI-97-TR-003, SEI, Pittsburgh, PA.

Bass, L., Clements, P., and Kazman, R. (1998). *Software Architecture in Practice*. Boston, MA: Addison-Wesley.

Batory, D. (2005). Feature models, grammars, and propositional formulas. In *Proc. Int'l Software Product Line Conference (SPLC)*, vol. 3714 of *Lecture Notes in Computer Science*, pp. 7–20. Berlin/Heidelberg: Springer-Verlag.

Batory, D., Chen, G., Robertson, E., and Wang, T. (2000). Design wizards and visual programming environments for GenVoca generators. *IEEE Transactions on Software Engineering (TSE)*, 26(5), 441–452.

Batory, D., Lopez-Herrejon, R. E., and Martin, J.-P. (2002). Generating product-lines of product-families. In *Proc. Int'l Conf. Automated Software Engineering (ASE)*, pp. 81–92. Washington, DC: IEEE Computer Society.

Batory, D., and O'Malley, S. (1992). The design and implementation of hierarchical software systems with reusable components. *ACM Transactions on Software Engineering and Methodology (TOSEM)*, 1(4), 355–398.

Batory, D., Sarvela, J. N., and Rauschmayer, A. (2004). Scaling step-wise refinement. *IEEE Transactions on Software Engineering (TSE)*, 30(6), 355–371.

Baxter, I., and Mehlich, M. (2001). Preprocessor conditional removal by simple partial evaluation. In *Proc. Working Conf. Reverse Engineering (WCRE)*, pp. 281–290. Washington, DC: IEEE Computer Society.

Baxter, I., Pidgeon, C., and Mehlich, M. (2004). DMS®: Program transformations for practical scalable software evolution. In *Proc. Int'l Conf. Software Engineering (ICSE)*, pp. 625–634. Washington, DC: IEEE Computer Society.

Beck, K. (2003). *Test-Driven Development: By Example.* Amsterdam: Addison-Wesley.

Benavides, D. (2007). *On the Automated Analysis of Software Product Lines using Feature Models: A Framework for Developing Automated Tool Support.* Ph.D. thesis, University of Seville.

Benavides, D., Seguraa, S., and Ruiz-Cortés, A. (2010). Automated analysis of feature models 20 years later: A literature review. *Information Systems, 35*(6), 615–636.

Benavides, D., Trinidad, P., and Ruiz-Cortes, A. (2005). Automated reasoning on feature models. In *Proc. Conf. Advanced Information Systems Engineering (CAiSE)*, vol. 3520 of *Lecture Notes in Computer Science*, pp. 491–503. Berlin/Heidelberg: Springer-Verlag.

Bergel, A., Ducasse, S., and Nierstrasz, O. (2005). Classbox/J: Controlling the scope of change in Java. In *Proc. Int'l Conf. Object-Oriented Programming, Systems, Languages and Applications (OOPSLA)*, pp. 177–189. New York: ACM Press.

Bettini, L., Damiani, F., and Schaefer, I. (2010). Implementing software product lines using traits. In *Proc. Symp. Applied Computing (SAC)*, pp. 2098–2104. New York: ACM Press.

Beuche, D., Guerrouat, A., Papajewski, H., Schröder-Preikschat, W., Spinczyk, O., and Spinczyk, U. (1999). The PURE family of object-oriented operating systems for deeply embedded systems. In *Int'l Symp. Object-Oriented Real-Time Distributed Computing (ISORC)*, pp. 45–53.

Beuche, D., Papajewski, H., and Schröder-Preikschat, W. (2004). Variability management with feature models. *Science of Computer Programming, 53*(3), 333–352.

Biggerstaff, T. (1994). The library scaling problem and the limits of concrete component reuse. In *Proc. Int'l Conf. Software Reuse (ICSR)*, pp. 102–109. Los Alamitos, CA: IEEE Computer Society.

Biggerstaff, T. (1998). A perspective of generative reuse. *Annals of Software Engineering, 5*(1), 169–226.

Binkley, D., Ceccato, M., Harman, M., Ricca, F., and Tonella, P. (2005). Automated refactoring of object-oriented code into aspects. In *Proc. Int'l Conf. Software Maintenance (ICSM)*, pp. 27–36. Los Alamitos, CA: IEEE Computer Society.

Bohannon, A., Pierce, B. C., and Vaughan, J. A. (2006). Relational lenses: A language for updatable views. In *Proc. Symposium Principles of Database Systems (PODS)*, pp. 338–347. New York: ACM Press.

Boxleitner, S., Apel, S., and Kästner, C. (2009). Language-independent quantification and weaving for feature composition. In *Proc. Int'l Conf. Software Composition (SC)*, vol. 5634 of *Lecture Notes in Computer Science*, pp. 45–54. Berlin/Heidelberg: Springer-Verlag.

Bracha, G. (1992). *The Programming Language Jigsaw: Mixins, Modularity and Multiple Inheritance*. Ph.D. thesis, University of Utah.

Bracha, G., and Cook, W. (1990). Mixin-based inheritance. In *Proc. Int'l Conf. Object-Oriented Programming, Systems, Languages and Applications (OOPSLA)*, pp. 303–311. New York: ACM Press.

Bracha, G., and Lindstrom, G. (1992). Modularity meets inheritance. In *Proc. Int'l Conf. Computer Languages (ICCL)*, pp. 282–290. Los Alamitos, CA: IEEE Computer Society.

Bruntink, M., van Deursen, A., D'Hondt, M., and Tourwé, T. (2007). Simple crosscutting concerns are not so simple: Analysing variability in large-scale idioms-based implementations. In *Proc. Int'l Conf. Aspect-Oriented Software Development (AOSD)*, pp. 199–211. New York: ACM Press.

Bryant, A., Catton, A., De Volder, K., and Murphy, G. C. (2002). Explicit programming. In *Proc. Int'l Conf. Aspect-Oriented Software Development (AOSD)*, pp. 10–18. New York: ACM Press.

Calder, M., Kolberg, M., Magill, E. H., and Reiff-Marganiec, S. (2003). Feature interaction: A critical review and considered forecast. *Computer Networks*, 41(1), 115–141.

Cardelli, L. (1997). Program fragments, linking, and modularization. In *Proc. Symp. Principles of Programming Languages (POPL)*, pp. 266–277. New York: ACM Press.

Chapman, M. (2006). Extending JDT to support Java-like languages. Invited Talk at EclipseCon'06.

Chen, L., Babar, M. A., and Ali, N. (2009). Variability management in software product lines: A systematic review. In *Proc. Int'l Software Product Line Conference (SPLC)*, pp. 81–90. Pittsburgh, PA: Carnegie Mellon University.

Chu-Carroll, M., Wright, J., and Ying, A. (2003). Visual separation of concerns through multidimensional program storage. In *Proc. Int'l Conf. Aspect-Oriented Software Development (AOSD)*, pp. 188–197. New York: ACM Press.

Classen, A., Heymans, P., Tuny, T. T., and Nuseibeh, B. (2009). Towards safer composition. In *Comp. Int'l Conf. Software Engineering (ICSE)*, pp. 227–230. Washington, DC: IEEE Computer Society.

Cleland-Huang, J., Chang, C. K., and Christensen, M. (2003). Event-based traceability for managing evolutionary change. *IEEE Transactions on Software Engineering (TSE)*, 29(9), 796–810.

Clement, A., Colyer, A., and Kersten, M. (2003). Aspect-oriented programming with AJDT. In *Proc. ECOOP Workshop on Analysis of Aspect-Oriented Software (AAOS)*. Published online `http://www.comp.lancs.ac.uk/~chitchya/AAOS2003/`.

Clements, P., and Krueger, C. W. (2002). Point/Counterpoint: Being proactive pays off / Eliminating the adoption barrier. *IEEE Software*, 19(4), 28–31.

Clifton, C., Millstein, T., Leavens, G. T., and Chambers, C. (2006). MultiJava: Design rationale, compiler implementation, and applications. *ACM Transactions on Programing Languages and Systems (TOPLAS)*, 28(3), 517–575.

Cole, L., and Borba, P. (2005). Deriving refactorings for AspectJ. In *Proc. Int'l Conf. Aspect-Oriented Software Development (AOSD)*, pp. 123–134. New York: ACM Press.

Conejero, J. M., Figueiredo, E., Garcia, A., Hernández, J., and Jurado, E. (2009). Early crosscutting metrics as predictors of software instability. In *Proc. Int'l Conf. Objects, Models, Components, Patterns (TOOLS EUROPE)*, vol. 33 of *Lecture Notes in Business Information Processing*, pp. 136–156. Berlin/Heidelberg: Springer-Verlag.

Conradi, R., and Westfechtel, B. (1998). Version models for software configuration management. *ACM Computing Surveys (CSUR)*, 30(2), 232–282.

Cook, W. (1991). Object-oriented programming versus abstract data types. In *Proc. REX School/Workshop Foundations of Object-Oriented Languages*, vol. 489 of *Lecture Notes in Computer Science*, pp. 151–178. London: Springer-Verlag.

Coppit, D., and Cox, B. (2004). Software plans for separation of concerns. In *Proc. AOSD Workshop on Aspects, Components, and Patterns for Infrastructure Software (ACP4IS)*. Boston, MA: Northeastern University.

Coppit, D., Painter, R., and Revelle, M. (2007). Spotlight: A prototype tool for software plans. In *Proc. Int'l Conf. Software Engineering (ICSE)*, pp. 754–757. Washington, DC: IEEE Computer Society.

Cordy, J. (2009). Eating our own dog food: DSLs for generative and transformational engineering. In *Proc. Int'l Conf. Generative Programming and Component Engineering (GPCE)*, p. 3. New York: ACM Press. Keynote presentation.

Czarnecki, K., and Antkiewicz, M. (2005). Mapping features to models: A template approach based on superimposed variants. In *Proc. Int'l Conf. Generative Programming and Component Engineering (GPCE)*, vol. 3676 of *Lecture Notes in Computer Science*, pp. 422–437. Berlin/Heidelberg: Springer-Verlag.

Czarnecki, K., Bednasch, T., Unger, P., and Eisenecker, U. (2002). Generative programming for embedded software: An industrial experience report. In *Proc. Int'l Conf. Generative Programming and Component Engineering (GPCE)*, vol. 2487 of *Lecture Notes in Computer Science*, pp. 156–172. Berlin/Heidelberg: Springer-Verlag.

Czarnecki, K., and Eisenecker, U. (2000). *Generative Programming: Methods, Tools, and Applications*. New York: ACM Press/Addison-Wesley.

Czarnecki, K., Helsen, S., and Eisenecker, U. (2005). Formalizing cardinality-based feature models and their specialization. *Software Process: Improvement and Practice*, 10(1), 7–29.

Czarnecki, K., and Pietroszek, K. (2006). Verifying feature-based model templates against well-formedness OCL constraints. In *Proc. Int'l Conf. Generative Programming and Component Engineering (GPCE)*, pp. 211–220. New York: ACM Press.

Czarnecki, K., and Wąsowski, A. (2007). Feature diagrams and logics: There and back again. In *Proc. Int'l Software Product Line Conference (SPLC)*, pp. 23–34. Washington, DC: IEEE Computer Society.

Delaware, B., Cook, W. R., and Batory, D. (2009). Fitting the pieces together: A machine-checked model of safe composition. In *Proc. Europ. Software Engineering Conf./Foundations of Software Engineering (ESEC/FSE)*, pp. 243–252. New York: ACM Press.

Diehl, S. (2007). *Software Visualization: Visualizing the Structure, Behaviour, and Evolution of Software*. Berlin/Heidelberg: Springer-Verlag.

Dijkstra, E. W. (1976). *A Discipline of Programming*. Upper Saddle River, NJ: Prentice-Hall.

Drossopoulou, S., Valkevych, T., and Eisenbach, S. (2000). Java type soundness revisited. Tech. Rep. 09, Department of Computing, Imperial College London, London.

Ducasse, S., Nierstrasz, O., Schärli, N., Wuyts, R., and Black, A. P. (2006). Traits: A mechanism for fine-grained reuse. *ACM Transactions on Programing Languages and Systems (TOPLAS)*, *28*(2), 331–388.

Dunsmore, A., and Roper, M. (2000). A comparative evaluation of program comprehension measures. Tech. Rep. EFoCS 35-2000, Department of Computer Science, University of Strathclyde, Glasgow.

Eaddy, M., Zimmermann, T., Sherwood, K. D., Garg, V., Murphy, G. C., Nagappan, N., and Aho, A. V. (2008). Do crosscutting concerns cause defects? *IEEE Transactions on Software Engineering (TSE)*, *34*(4), 497–515.

Eick, S. G., Steffen, J. L., and Jr., E. E. S. (1992). Seesoft—a tool for visualizing line oriented software statistics. *IEEE Transactions on Software Engineering (TSE)*, *18*(11), 957–968.

Eisenbarth, T., Koschke, R., and Simon, D. (2003). Locating features in source code. *IEEE Transactions on Software Engineering (TSE)*, *29*, 210–224.

Elrad, T., Aksit, M., Kiczales, G., Lieberherr, K., and Ossher, H. (2001). Discussing aspects of AOP. *Communications of the ACM*, *44*(10), 33–38.

Emir, B., Kennedy, A., Russo, C., and Yu, D. (2006). Variance and generalized constraints for $C^{\#}$ generics. In *Proc. Europ. Conf. Object-Oriented Programming (ECOOP)*, vol. 4067 of *Lecture Notes in Computer Science*, pp. 279–303. Berlin/Heidelberg: Springer-Verlag.

Ernst, E., Ostermann, K., and Cook, W. (2006). A virtual class calculus. In *Proc. Symp. Principles of Programming Languages (POPL)*, pp. 270–282. New York: ACM Press.

Ernst, M., Badros, G., and Notkin, D. (2002). An empirical analysis of C preprocessor use. *IEEE Transactions on Software Engineering (TSE)*, *28*(12), 1146–1170.

Favre, J.-M. (1995). The CPP paradox. In *Proc. European Workshop on Software Maintenance*.

Favre, J.-M. (1997). Understanding-in-the-large. In *Proc. Int'l Workshop on Program Comprehension*, p. 29. Los Alamitos, CA: IEEE Computer Society.

Feigenspan, J. (2009). *Empirical Comparison of FOSD Approaches Regarding Program Comprehension – A Feasibility Study*. Master's thesis (Diplomarbeit), University of Magdeburg.

Feigenspan, J., Kästner, C., Apel, S., and Leich, T. (2010). Do colors improve program comprehension in the #ifdef hell? Submitted manuscript.

Figueiredo, E., Cacho, N., Sant'Anna, C., Monteiro, M., Kulesza, U., Garcia, A., Soares, S., Ferrari, F., Khan, S., Castor Filho, F., and Dantas, F. (2008). Evolving software product lines with aspects: An empirical study on design stability. In *Proc. Int'l Conf. Software Engineering (ICSE)*, pp. 261–270. New York: ACM Press.

Fisler, K., and Krishnamurthi, S. (2001). Modular verification of collaboration-based software designs. In *Proc. Europ. Software Engineering Conf./Foundations of Software Engineering (ESEC/FSE)*, pp. 152–163. New York: ACM Press.

Fisler, K., and Roberts, B. (2004). A case study in using ACL2 for feature-oriented verification. In *Proc. Int'l Workshop on the ACL2 Theorem Prover and Its Applications*. Published online http://www.cs.utexas.edu/users/moore/acl2/workshop-2004/.

Flatt, M., Krishnamurthi, S., and Felleisen, M. (1998). Classes and mixins. In *Proc. Symp. Principles of Programming Languages (POPL)*, pp. 171–183. New York: ACM Press.

Foster, J. N., Greenwald, M. B., Moore, J. T., Pierce, B. C., and Schmitt, A. (2007). Combinators for bidirectional tree transformations: A linguistic approach to the view-update problem. *ACM Transactions on Programing Languages and Systems (TOPLAS)*, *29*(3), 17.

Fowler, M. (1999). *Refactoring. Improving the Design of Existing Code*. Boston, MA: Addison-Wesley.

Fuhrer, R. M., Keller, M., and Kieżun, A. (2007). Advanced refactoring in the Eclipse JDT: Past, present, and future. In *Proc. ECOOP Workshop on Refactoring Tools (WRT)*, pp. 30–31. Berlin: TU Berlin.

Gälli, M., Greevy, O., and Nierstrasz, O. (2005). Composing unit tests. In *Proc. SPLC Workshop on Software Product Line Testing (SPLiT)*, pp. 46–49. Ridge, NJ: Avaya Inc.

Gamma, E., Helm, R., Johnson, R., and Vlissides, J. (1995). *Design Patterns: Elements of Reusable Object-Oriented Software*. Boston, MA: Addison-Wesley.

Ganesan, D., Lindvall, M., Ackermann, C., McComas, D., and Bartholomew, M. (2009). Verifying architectural design rules of the flight software product line. In *Proc. Int'l Software Product Line Conference (SPLC)*, pp. 161–170. Pittsburgh, PA: Carnegie Mellon University.

Garrido, A. (2005). *Program Refactoring in the Presence of Preprocessor Directives*. Ph.D. thesis, University of Illinois at Urbana-Champaign.

Garrido, A., and Johnson, R. (2005). Analyzing multiple configurations of a C program. In *Proc. Int'l Conf. Software Maintenance (ICSM)*, pp. 379–388. Washington, DC: IEEE Computer Society.

Giese, H., and Wagner, R. (2009). From model transformation to incremental bidirectional model synchronization. *Software and System Modeling (SoSyM)*, 8(1), 21–43.

Godil, I., and Jacobsen, H.-A. (2005). Horizontal decomposition of Prevayler. In *Proc. IBM Centre for Advanced Studies Conference*, pp. 83–100. Upper Saddle River, NJ: IBM Press.

Goldstein, E. B. (2002). *Sensation and Perception.* Pacific Grove, CA: Wadsworth/Thomson Learning, 6th ed.

Gotel, O. C. Z., and Finkelstein, A. C. W. (1994). An analysis of the requirements traceability problem. In *Proc. Int'l Conf. Requirements Engineering (ICRE)*, pp. 94–101. Los Alamitos, CA: IEEE Computer Society.

Gray, J., and Roychoudhury, S. (2004). A technique for constructing aspect weavers using a program transformation engine. In *Proc. Int'l Conf. Aspect-Oriented Software Development (AOSD)*, pp. 36–45. New York: ACM Press.

Grechanik, M., Batory, D., and Perry, D. (2004). Design of large-scale polylingual systems. In *Proc. Int'l Conf. Software Engineering (ICSE)*, pp. 357–366. Washington, DC: IEEE Computer Society.

Griss, M. L., Favaro, J., and d' Alessandro, M. (1998). Integrating feature modeling with the RSEB. In *Proc. Int'l Conf. Software Reuse (ICSR)*, p. 76. Washington, DC: IEEE Computer Society.

Griswold, W. G., Sullivan, K., Song, Y., Shonle, M., Tewari, N., Cai, Y., and Rajan, H. (2006). Modular software design with crosscutting interfaces. *IEEE Software*, 23(1), 51–60.

Griswold, W. G., Yuan, J., and Kato, Y. (2001). Exploiting the map metaphor in a tool for software evolution. In *Proc. Int'l Conf. Software Engineering (ICSE)*, pp. 265–274. Washington, DC: IEEE Computer Society.

Gruler, A., Leucker, M., and Scheidemann, K. (2008). Modeling and model checking software product lines. In *Proc. Int'l Conf. Formal Methods for Open Object-Based Distributed Systems (FMOODS)*, vol. 5051 of *Lecture Notes in Computer Science*, pp. 113–131. Berlin/Heidelberg: Springer-Verlag.

Günther, S., and Sunkle, S. (2009a). Enabling feature-oriented programming in ruby. Tech. Rep. 16/09, School of Computer Science, University of Magdeburg.

Günther, S., and Sunkle, S. (2009b). Feature-oriented programming with Ruby. In *Proc. GPCE Workshop on Feature-Oriented Software Development (FOSD)*, pp. 11–18. New York: ACM Press.

Habermann, A. N., Flon, L., and Cooprider, L. (1976). Modularization and hierarchy in a family of operating systems. *Communications of the ACM, 19*(5), 266–272.

Hall, R. J. (2005). Fundamental nonmodularity in electronic mail. *Automated Software Engineering, 12*(1), 41–79.

Hanenberg, S., Oberschulte, C., and Unland, R. (2003). Refactoring of aspect-oriented software. In *Proc. Int'l Conf. Object-Oriented and Internet-based Technologies, Concepts, and Applications for a Networked World (Net.ObjectDays)*, pp. 19–35. Ilmenau: tranSIT GmbH.

Harrison, W., and Ossher, H. (1993). Subject-oriented programming: A critique of pure objects. In *Proc. Int'l Conf. Object-Oriented Programming, Systems, Languages and Applications (OOPSLA)*, pp. 411–428. New York: ACM Press.

Harrison, W., Ossher, H., Sutton, S., and Tarr, P. (2005). Concern modeling in the concern manipulation environment. In *Proc. ICSE Workshop on Modeling and Analysis of Concerns in Software (MACS)*, pp. 1–5. New York: ACM Press.

Heidenreich, F., Şavga, I., and Wende, C. (2008a). On controlled visualisations in software product line engineering. In *Proc. SPLC Workshop on Visualization in Software Product Line Engineering (ViSPLE)*, pp. 303–313. Limerick: Lero.

Heidenreich, F., Kopcsek, J., and Wende, C. (2008b). FeatureMapper: Mapping features to models. In *Comp. Int'l Conf. Software Engineering (ICSE)*, pp. 943–944. New York: ACM Press.

Henry, S., Humphrey, M., and Lewis, J. (1990). Evaluation of the maintainability of object-oriented software. In *IEEE Region 10 Conf. Computer and Comm. Systems*, pp. 404–409. Los Alamitos, CA: IEEE Computer Society.

Hettel, T., Lawley, M., and Raymond, K. (2009). Towards model round-trip engineering: An abductive approach. In *Proc. Int'l Conf. Theory and Practice of Model Transformations (ICMT)*, vol. 5563 of *Lecture Notes in Computer Science*, pp. 100–115. Berlin/Heidelberg: Springer-Verlag.

Hu, Y., Merlo, E., Dagenais, M., and Laguë, B. (2000). C/C++ conditional compilation analysis using symbolic execution. In *Proc. Int'l Conf. Software Maintenance (ICSM)*, pp. 196–206. Los Alamitos, CA: IEEE Computer Society.

Huang, S. S., and Smaragdakis, Y. (2008). Expressive and safe static reflection with MorphJ. In *Proc. Conf. Programming Language Design and Implementation (PLDI)*, pp. 79–89. New York: ACM Press.

Huang, S. S., Zook, D., and Smaragdakis, Y. (2005). Statically safe program generation with SafeGen. In *Proc. Int'l Conf. Generative Programming and Component Engineering (GPCE)*, vol. 3676 of *Lecture Notes in Computer Science*, pp. 309–326. Berlin/Heidelberg: Springer-Verlag.

Huang, S. S., Zook, D., and Smaragdakis, Y. (2007). cJ: Enhancing Java with safe type conditions. In *Proc. Int'l Conf. Aspect-Oriented Software Development (AOSD)*, pp. 185–198. New York: ACM Press.

Hunleth, F., and Cytron, R. K. (2002). Footprint and feature management using aspect-oriented programming techniques. In *Proc. Conf. Languages, Compilers and Tools For Embedded Systems (LCTES)*, pp. 38–45. New York: ACM Press.

Hutchins, D. (2009). *Pure Subtype Systems: A Type Theory For Extensible Software.* Ph.D. thesis, University of Edinburgh.

Igarashi, A., Pierce, B., and Wadler, P. (2001). Featherweight Java: A minimal core calculus for Java and GJ. *ACM Transactions on Programing Languages and Systems (TOPLAS)*, 23(3), 396–450.

Igarashi, A., and Pierce, B. C. (2002). On inner classes. *Information and Computation*, 177(1), 56–89.

Jaaksi, A. (2002). Developing mobile browsers in a product line. *IEEE Software*, 19(4), 73–80.

Janzen, D., and De Volder, K. (2003). Navigating and querying code without getting lost. In *Proc. Int'l Conf. Aspect-Oriented Software Development (AOSD)*, pp. 178–187. New York: ACM Press.

Janzen, D., and De Volder, K. (2004). Programming with crosscutting effective views. In *Proc. Europ. Conf. Object-Oriented Programming (ECOOP)*, vol. 3086 of *Lecture Notes in Computer Science*, pp. 195–218. Berlin/Heidelberg: Springer-Verlag.

Jepsen, H. P., and Beuche, D. (2009). Running a software product line – standing still is going backwards. In *Proc. Int'l Software Product Line Conference (SPLC)*, pp. 101–110. Pittsburgh, PA: Carnegie Mellon University.

John, I., and Eisenbarth, M. (2009). A decade of scoping – a survey. In *Proc. Int'l Software Product Line Conference (SPLC)*, pp. 31–40. Pittsburgh, PA: Carnegie Mellon University.

Johnson, R. E., and Foote, B. (1988). Designing reusable classes. *Journal of Object-Oriented Programming (JOOP)*, *1*(2), 22–35.

Jorgensen, B. N., and Truyen, E. (2003). Evolution of collective object behavior in presence of simultaneous client-specific views. In *Proc. Int'l Conf. Object-Oriented Information Systems*, vol. 2817 of *Lecture Notes in Computer Science*, pp. 18–32. Berlin/Heidelberg: Springer-Verlag.

Kang, K., Cohen, S. G., Hess, J. A., Novak, W. E., and Peterson, A. S. (1990). Feature-Oriented Domain Analysis (FODA) Feasibility Study. Tech. Rep. CMU/SEI-90-TR-21, SEI, Pittsburgh, PA.

Kästner, C. (2007). *Aspect-Oriented Refactoring of Berkeley DB*. Master's thesis (Diplomarbeit), University of Magdeburg.

Kästner, C., and Apel, S. (2008a). Integrating compositional and annotative approaches for product line engineering. In *Proc. GPCE Workshop on Modularization, Composition and Generative Techniques for Product Line Engineering*, pp. 35–40. Passau: University of Passau.

Kästner, C., and Apel, S. (2008b). Type-checking software product lines – A formal approach. In *Proc. Int'l Conf. Automated Software Engineering (ASE)*, pp. 258–267. Los Alamitos, CA: IEEE Computer Society.

Kästner, C., Apel, S., and Batory, D. (2007a). A case study implementing features using AspectJ. In *Proc. Int'l Software Product Line Conference (SPLC)*, pp. 223–232. Los Alamitos, CA: IEEE Computer Society.

Kästner, C., Apel, S., and Kuhlemann, M. (2008a). Granularity in software product lines. In *Proc. Int'l Conf. Software Engineering (ICSE)*, pp. 311–320. New York: ACM Press.

Kästner, C., Apel, S., and Kuhlemann, M. (2009a). A model of refactoring physically and virtually separated features. In *Proc. Int'l Conf. Generative Programming and Component Engineering (GPCE)*, pp. 157–166. New York: ACM Press.

Kästner, C., Apel, S., Thüm, T., and Saake, G. (2010). Type checking annotation-based software product lines. Submitted manuscript.

Kästner, C., Apel, S., Trujillo, S., Kuhlemann, M., and Batory, D. (2009b). Guaranteeing syntactic correctness for all product line variants: A language-independent approach. In *Proc. Int'l Conf. Objects, Models, Components, Patterns (TOOLS EUROPE)*, vol. 33 of *Lecture Notes in Business Information Processing*, pp. 175–194. Berlin/Heidelberg: Springer-Verlag.

Kästner, C., Apel, S., ur Rahman, S. S., Rosenmüller, M., Batory, D., and Saake, G. (2009c). On the impact of the optional feature problem: Analysis and case studies. In *Proc. Int'l Software Product Line Conference (SPLC)*, pp. 181–190. Pittsburgh, PA: Carnegie Mellon University.

Kästner, C., Kuhlemann, M., and Batory, D. (2007b). Automating feature-oriented refactoring of legacy applications. In *Proc. ECOOP Workshop on Refactoring Tools (WRT)*, pp. 62–63. Berlin: TU Berlin.

Kästner, C., Thüm, T., Saake, G., Feigenspan, J., Leich, T., Wielgorz, F., and Apel, S. (2009d). FeatureIDE: Tool framework for feature-oriented software development. In *Proc. Int'l Conf. Software Engineering (ICSE)*, pp. 611–614. Washington, DC: IEEE Computer Society.

Kästner, C., Trujillo, S., and Apel, S. (2008b). Visualizing software product line variabilities in source code. In *Proc. SPLC Workshop on Visualization in Software Product Line Engineering (ViSPLE)*, pp. 303–313. Limerick: Lero.

Kersten, M., and Murphy, G. C. (2005). Mylar: A degree-of-interest model for IDEs. In *Proc. Int'l Conf. Aspect-Oriented Software Development (AOSD)*, pp. 159–168. New York: ACM Press.

Kersten, M., and Murphy, G. C. (2006). Using task context to improve programmer productivity. In *Proc. Int'l Symposium Foundations of Software Engineering (FSE)*, pp. 1–11. New York: ACM Press.

Kiczales, G., Hilsdale, E., Hugunin, J., Kersten, M., Palm, J., and Griswold, W. G. (2001). An overview of AspectJ. In *Proc. Europ. Conf. Object-Oriented Programming (ECOOP)*, vol. 2072 of *Lecture Notes in Computer Science*, pp. 327–353. Berlin/Heidelberg: Springer-Verlag.

Kiczales, G., Lamping, J., Menhdhekar, A., Maeda, C., Lopes, C., Loingtier, J.-M., and Irwin, J. (1997). Aspect-oriented programming. In *Proc. Europ. Conf. Object-Oriented Programming (ECOOP)*, vol. 1241 of *Lecture Notes in Computer Science*, pp. 220–242. Berlin/Heidelberg: Springer-Verlag.

Kiczales, G., and Mezini, M. (2005a). Aspect-oriented programming and modular reasoning. In *Proc. Int'l Conf. Software Engineering (ICSE)*, pp. 49–58. New York: ACM Press.

Kiczales, G., and Mezini, M. (2005b). Separation of concerns with procedures, annotations, advice and pointcuts. In *Proc. Europ. Conf. Object-Oriented Programming (ECOOP)*, vol. 3586 of *Lecture Notes in Computer Science*, pp. 195–213. Berlin/Heidelberg: Springer-Verlag.

Kim, C. H. P., Kästner, C., and Batory, D. (2008). On the modularity of feature interactions. In *Proc. Int'l Conf. Generative Programming and Component Engineering (GPCE)*, pp. 23–34. New York: ACM Press.

Koenemann, J., and Robertson, S. P. (1991). Expert problem solving strategies for program comprehension. In *Proc. Conf. Human Factors in Computing Systems (CHI)*, pp. 125–130. New York: ACM Press.

Kohlbecker, E., Friedman, D. P., Felleisen, M., and Duba, B. (1986). Hygienic macro expansion. In *Proc. Conf. LISP and Functional Programming (LFP)*, pp. 151–161. New York: ACM Press.

Krone, M., and Snelting, G. (1994). On the inference of configuration structures from source code. In *Proc. Int'l Conf. Software Engineering (ICSE)*, pp. 49–57. Los Alamitos, CA: IEEE Computer Society.

Krueger, C. W. (1992). Software reuse. *ACM Computing Surveys (CSUR)*, 24(2), 131–183.

Krueger, C. W. (2002). Easing the transition to software mass customization. In *Proc. Int'l Workshop on Software Product-Family Engineering (PFE)*, vol. 2290 of *Lecture Notes in Computer Science*, pp. 282–293. Berlin/Heidelberg: Springer-Verlag.

Kuhlemann, M., Batory, D., and Apel, S. (2009a). Refactoring feature modules. In *Proc. Int'l Conf. Software Reuse (ICSR)*, vol. 5791 of *Lecture Notes in Computer Science*, pp. 106–115. Berlin/Heidelberg: Springer-Verlag.

Kuhlemann, M., Batory, D., and Kästner, C. (2009b). Safe composition of non-monotonic features. In *Proc. Int'l Conf. Generative Programming and Component Engineering (GPCE)*, pp. 177–185. New York: ACM Press.

Laddad, R. (2003). *AspectJ in Action: Practical Aspect-Oriented Programming*. Greenwich, CT: Manning Publications.

Latendresse, M. (2004). Rewrite systems for symbolic evaluation of C-like preprocessing. In *Proc. European Conf. on Software Maintenance and Reengineering (CSMR)*, pp. 165–173. Washington, DC: IEEE Computer Society.

Lauenroth, K., Pohl, K., and Toehning, S. (2009). Model checking of domain artifacts in product line engineering. In *Proc. Int'l Conf. Automated Software Engineering (ASE)*, pp. 269–280. Los Alamitos, CA: IEEE Computer Society.

Leavenworth, B. M. (1966). Syntax macros and extended translation. *Communications of the ACM*, 9(11), 790–793.

Lee, J., Muthig, D., and Naab, M. (2008). An approach for developing service oriented product lines. In *Proc. Int'l Software Product Line Conference (SPLC)*, pp. 275–284. Washington, DC: IEEE Computer Society.

Leich, T., Apel, S., and Marnitz, L. (2005). Tool support for feature-oriented software development: FeatureIDE: An eclipse-based approach. In *Proc. OOPSLA Workshop on Eclipse Technology eXchange (ETX)*, pp. 55–59. New York: ACM Press.

Liebig, J., Apel, S., Lengauer, C., Kästner, C., and Schulze, M. (2010). An analysis of the variability in forty preprocessor-based software product lines. In *Proc. Int'l Conf. Software Engineering (ICSE)*, pp. 105–114. New York: ACM Press.

Linton, M. A. (1984). Implementing relational views of programs. In *Proc. Symp. Practical Software Development Environments (SDE)*, pp. 132–140. New York: ACM Press.

Liskov, B., Atkinson, R., Bloom, T., Moss, E., Schaffert, J. C., Scheifler, R., and Snyder, A. (1981). *CLU Reference Manual*, vol. 114 of *Lecture Notes in Computer Science*. Berlin/Heidelberg: Springer-Verlag.

Litvinov, V. (1998). Contraint-based polymorphism in Cecil: Towards a practical and static type system. In *Proc. Int'l Conf. Object-Oriented Programming, Systems, Languages and Applications (OOPSLA)*, pp. 388–411. New York: ACM Press.

Liu, J., Batory, D., and Lengauer, C. (2006). Feature oriented refactoring of legacy applications. In *Proc. Int'l Conf. Software Engineering (ICSE)*, pp. 112–121. New York: ACM Press.

Lohmann, D., Scheler, F., Tartler, R., Spinczyk, O., and Schröder-Preikschat, W. (2006). A quantitative analysis of aspects in the eCos kernel. *ACM SIGOPS Operating Systems Review*, 40(4), 191–204.

Lopez-Herrejon, R., and Batory, D. (2001). A standard problem for evaluating product-line methodologies. In *Proc. Int'l Conf. Generative and Component-Based Software Engineering (GCSE)*, vol. 2186 of *Lecture Notes in Computer Science*, pp. 10–24. Berlin/Heidelberg: Springer-Verlag.

Lopez-Herrejon, R., Batory, D., and Cook, W. (2005). Evaluating support for features in advanced modularization technologies. In *Proc. Europ. Conf. Object-Oriented Programming (ECOOP)*, vol. 3586 of *Lecture Notes in Computer Science*, pp. 169–194. Berlin/Heidelberg: Springer-Verlag.

Mäder, P., Gotel, O., and Philippow, I. (2008). Enabling automated traceability maintenance by recognizing development activities applied to models. In *Proc. Int'l Conf. Automated Software Engineering (ASE)*, pp. 49–58. Los Alamitos, CA: IEEE Computer Society.

Madsen, O. L., and Moller-Pedersen, B. (1989). Virtual classes: A powerful mechanism in object-oriented programming. In *Proc. Int'l Conf. Object-Oriented Programming, Systems, Languages and Applications (OOPSLA)*, pp. 397–406. New York: ACM Press.

McCloskey, B., and Brewer, E. (2005). ASTEC: A new approach to refactoring C. In *Proc. Europ. Software Engineering Conf./Foundations of Software Engineering (ESEC/FSE)*, pp. 21–30. New York: ACM Press.

McDirmid, S., Flatt, M., and Hsieh, W. (2001). Jiazzi: New-age components for old-fashioned Java. In *Proc. Int'l Conf. Object-Oriented Programming, Systems, Languages and Applications (OOPSLA)*, pp. 211–222. New York: ACM Press.

McDirmid, S., and Odersky, M. (2006). The Scala plugin for Eclipse. In *Proc. ECOOP Workshop on Eclipse Technology eXchange (ETX)*. Published online `http://atlanmod.emn.fr/www/papers/eTX2006/`.

McGregor, J. (2001). Testing a software product line. Tech. Rep. CMU/SEI-2001-TR-022, SEI, Pittsburgh, PA.

McGregor, J., Sodhani, P., and Madhavapeddi, S. (2004). Testing variability in a software product line. In *Proc. SPLC Workshop on Software Product Line Testing (SPLiT)*, pp. 45–50. Ridge, NJ: Avaya Inc.

Mendonça, M., Wąsowski, A., and Czarnecki, K. (2009). SAT-based analysis of feature models is easy. In *Proc. Int'l Software Product Line Conference (SPLC)*, pp. 231–240. Pittsburgh, PA: Carnegie Mellon University.

Mendonça, M., Wąsowski, A., Czarnecki, K., and Cowan, D. D. (2008). Efficient compilation techniques for large scale feature models. In *Proc. Int'l Conf. Generative Programming and Component Engineering (GPCE)*, pp. 13–22. New York: ACM Press.

Metzger, A., Pohl, K., Heymans, P., Schobbens, P.-Y., and Saval, G. (2007). Disambiguating the documentation of variability in software product lines: A separation of concerns, formalization and automated analysis. In *Proc. Int'l Requirements Engineering Conf. (RE)*, pp. 243–253. Los Alamitos, CA: IEEE Computer Society.

Meyer, B. (1997). *Object-Oriented Software Construction*. Upper Saddle River, NJ: Prentice-Hall, 2nd ed.

Mezini, M., and Ostermann, K. (2003). Conquering aspects with Caesar. In *Proc. Int'l Conf. Aspect-Oriented Software Development (AOSD)*, pp. 90–99. New York: ACM Press.

Mezini, M., and Ostermann, K. (2004). Variability management with feature-oriented programming and aspects. In *Proc. Int'l Symposium Foundations of Software Engineering (FSE)*, pp. 127–136. New York: ACM Press.

Mezini, M., and Ostermann, K. (2005). Untangling crosscutting models with CAESAR. In R. E. Filman, T. Elrad, S. Clarke, and M. Aksit (Eds.) *Aspect-Oriented Software Development*, pp. 165–199. Boston, MA: Addison-Wesley.

Monteiro, M. P., and Fernandes, J. M. (2005). Towards a catalog of aspect-oriented refactorings. In *Proc. Int'l Conf. Aspect-Oriented Software Development (AOSD)*, pp. 111–122. New York: ACM Press.

Murphy, G. C., Lai, A., Walker, R., and Robillard, M. (2001). Separating features in source code: An exploratory study. In *Proc. Int'l Conf. Software Engineering (ICSE)*, pp. 275–284. Washington, DC: IEEE Computer Society.

Muthig, D., and Patzke, T. (2002). Generic implementation of product line components. In *Proc. Int'l Conf. Object-Oriented and Internet-based Technologies, Concepts, and Applications for a Networked World (Net.ObjectDays)*, vol. 2591 of *Lecture Notes in Computer Science*, pp. 313–329. Berlin/Heidelberg: Springer-Verlag.

Myers, A. C., Bank, J. A., and Liskov, B. (1997). Parameterized types for Java. In *Proc. Symp. Principles of Programming Languages (POPL)*, pp. 132–145. New York: ACM Press.

Najjar, L. J. (1990). Using colors effectively. Tech. Rep. TR52.0018, IBM Corp., Atlanta, GA.

Nipkow, T., and von Oheimb, D. (1998). Java light is type-safe – definitely. In *Proc. Symp. Principles of Programming Languages (POPL)*, pp. 161–170. New York: ACM Press.

Nystrom, N., Chong, S., and Myers, A. (2004). Scalable extensibility via nested inheritance. In *Proc. Int'l Conf. Object-Oriented Programming, Systems, Languages and Applications (OOPSLA)*, pp. 99–115. New York: ACM Press.

Oberg, B., and Notkin, D. (1992). Error reporting with graduated color. *IEEE Software*, *9*(6), 33–38.

OSGi Alliance (2009). *OSGi Service Platform Core Specification*, release 4, version 4.2 ed. http://www.osgi.org.

Ossher, H., and Tarr, P. (2000a). Hyper/J: Multi-dimensional separation of concerns for Java. In *Proc. Int'l Conf. Software Engineering (ICSE)*, pp. 734–737. New York: ACM Press.

Ossher, H., and Tarr, P. (2000b). On the need for on-demand remodularization. In *ECOOP Workshop on Aspects and Dimensions of Concerns*. Published online.

Ostermann, K. (2008). Reasoning about aspects with common sense. In *Proc. Int'l Conf. Aspect-Oriented Software Development (AOSD)*, pp. 48–59. New York: ACM Press.

Parizi, R. M., and Ghani, A. A. (2007). A survey on aspect-oriented testing approaches. In *Proc. Int'l Conf. Computational Science and its Applications (ICCSA)*, pp. 78–85. Washington, DC: IEEE Computer Society.

Parnas, D. L. (1972). On the criteria to be used in decomposing systems into modules. *Communications of the ACM*, 15(12), 1053–1058.

Parnas, D. L. (1976). On the design and development of program families. *IEEE Transactions on Software Engineering (TSE)*, 2(1), 1–9.

Parnas, D. L. (1979). Designing software for ease of extension and contraction. *IEEE Transactions on Software Engineering (TSE)*, SE-5(2), 128–138.

Pawlak, R. (2006). Spoon: Compile-time annotation processing for middleware. *IEEE Distributed Systems Online*, 7(11), 1.

Pearse, T. T., and Oman, P. W. (1997). Experiences developing and maintaining software in a multi-platform environment. In *Proc. Int'l Conf. Software Maintenance (ICSM)*, pp. 270–277. Los Alamitos, CA: IEEE Computer Society.

Pech, D., Knodel, J., Carbon, R., Schitter, C., and Hein, D. (2009). Variability management in small development organizations – experiences and lessons learned from a case study. In *Proc. Int'l Software Product Line Conference (SPLC)*, pp. 285–294. Pittsburgh, PA: Carnegie Mellon University.

Pierce, B. C. (2002). *Types and Programming Languages*. Cambridge, MA: MIT Press.

Pine II, B. J. (1993). *Mass Customization: The New Frontier in Business Competition*. Boston, MA: Harvard Business School Press.

Pohl, K., Böckle, G., and van der Linden, F. J. (2005). *Software Product Line Engineering: Foundations, Principles and Techniques*. Berlin/Heidelberg: Springer-Verlag.

Pohl, K., and Metzger, A. (2006). Software product line testing. *Communications of the ACM*, 49(12), 78–81.

Poppleton, M. R. (2007). Towards feature-oriented specification and development with Event-B. In *Proc. Int'l Working Conf. Requirements Engineering: Foundation for Software Quality (REFSQ)*, vol. 4542 of *Lecture Notes in Computer Science*, pp. 367–381. Berlin/Heidelberg: Springer-Verlag.

Poshyvanyk, D., Guéhéneuc, Y.-G., Marcus, A., Antoniol, G., and Rajlich, V. (2007). Feature location using probabilistic ranking of methods based on execution scenarios and information retrieval. *IEEE Transactions on Software Engineering (TSE)*, *33*(6), 420–432.

Post, H., and Sinz, C. (2008). Configuration lifting: Verification meets software configuration. In *Proc. Int'l Conf. Automated Software Engineering (ASE)*, pp. 347–350. Los Alamitos, CA: IEEE Computer Society.

Prehofer, C. (1997). Feature-oriented programming: A fresh look at objects. In *Proc. Europ. Conf. Object-Oriented Programming (ECOOP)*, vol. 1241 of *Lecture Notes in Computer Science*, pp. 419–443. Berlin/Heidelberg: Springer-Verlag.

Rabiser, R., Grünbacher, P., and Dhungana, D. (2007). Supporting product derivation by adapting and augmenting variability models. In *Proc. Int'l Software Product Line Conference (SPLC)*, pp. 141–150. Los Alamitos, CA: IEEE Computer Society.

Ramesh, B., and Jarke, M. (2001). Toward reference models for requirements traceability. *IEEE Transactions on Software Engineering (TSE)*, *27*(1), 58–93.

Rashid, A., Sawyer, P., Moreira, A. M. D., and Araújo, J. (2002). Early aspects: A model for aspect-oriented requirements engineerin. In *Proc. Int'l Requirements Engineering Conf. (RE)*, pp. 199–202. Washington, DC: IEEE Computer Society.

Refstrup, J. G. (2009). Adapting to change: Architecture, processes and tools: A closer look at HP's experience in evolving the Owen software product line. In *Proc. Int'l Software Product Line Conference (SPLC)*. Keynote presentation.

Reynolds, A., Fiuczynski, M. E., and Grimm, R. (2008). On the feasibility of an AOSD approach to linux kernel extensions. In *Proc. AOSD Workshop on Aspects, Components, and Patterns for Infrastructure Software (ACP4IS)*, pp. 1–7. New York: ACM Press.

Reynolds, J. C. (1994). User-defined types and procedural data structures as complementary approaches to data abstraction. In C. A. Gunter, and J. C. Mitchell (Eds.) *Theoretical Aspects of Object-Oriented Programming: Types, Semantics, and Language Design*, pp. 13–23. Cambridge, MA: MIT Press.

Rice, J. F. (1991). Display color coding: 10 rules of thumb. *IEEE Software*, *8*(1).

Robillard, M., and Murphy, G. C. (2002). Concern graphs: Finding and describing concerns using structural program dependencies. In *Proc. Int'l Conf. Software Engineering (ICSE)*, pp. 406–416. New York: ACM Press.

Rosenmüller, M., Apel, S., Leich, T., and Saake, G. (2009). Tailor-made data management for embedded systems: A case study on Berkeley DB. *Data and Knowledge Engineering (DKE)*, *68*(12), 1493–1512.

Rosenmüller, M., Kuhlemann, M., Siegmund, N., and Schirmeier, H. (2007). Avoiding variability of method signatures in software product lines: A case study. In *Proc. GPCE Workshop on Aspect-Oriented Product Line Engineering (AOPLE)*, pp. 20–25. Lancaster: Lancaster University.

Rosenthal, M. (2009). *Alternative Features in Colored Featherweight Java*. Master's thesis (Diplomarbeit), University of Passau.

Rosenthal, R., and Jacobson, L. (1966). Teachers' expectancies: Determinants of pupils' IQ gains. *Psychological Reports*, *19*(1), 115–118.

Saleh, M., and Gomaa, H. (2005). Separation of concerns in software product line engineering. In *Proc. ICSE Workshop on Modeling and Analysis of Concerns in Software (MACS)*, pp. 1–5. New York: ACM Press.

Schobbens, P.-Y., Heymans, P., Trigaux, J.-C., and Bontemps, Y. (2007). Generic semantics of feature diagrams. *Computer Networks*, *51*(2), 456–479.

She, S., Lotufo, R., Berger, T., Wąsowski, A., and Czarnecki, K. (2010). The variability model of the Linux kernel. In *Proc. Int'l Workshop on Variability Modelling of Software-intensive Systems (VaMoS)*, pp. 45–51. Essen: University of Duisburg-Essen.

Siegmund, N., Rosenmüller, M., Kuhlemann, M., Kästner, C., and Saake, G. (2008). Measuring non-functional properties in software product lines for product derivation. In *Proc. Asia-Pacific Software Engineering Conf. (APSEC)*, pp. 187Ű–194. Los Alamitos, CA: IEEE Computer Society.

Simonyi, C. (1995). The death of computer languages, the birth of intentional programming. Tech. Rep. MSR-TR-95-52, Microsoft Research.

Simonyi, C., Christerson, M., and Clifford, S. (2006). Intentional software. In *Proc. Int'l Conf. Object-Oriented Programming, Systems, Languages and Applications (OOPSLA)*, pp. 451–464. New York: ACM Press.

Singh, N., Gibbs, C., and Coady, Y. (2007). C-CLR: A tool for navigating highly configurable system software. In *Proc. AOSD Workshop on Aspects, Components, and Patterns for Infrastructure Software (ACP4IS)*, p. 9. New York: ACM Press.

Singh, N., Johnson, G., and Coady, Y. (2006). CViMe: Viewing conditionally compiled C/C++ sources through Java tooling. In *Companion Int'l Conf. Object-Oriented Programming, Systems, Languages and Applications (OOPSLA)*, pp. 730–731. New York: ACM Press.

Smaragdakis, Y., and Batory, D. (2002). Mixin layers: An object-oriented implementation technique for refinements and collaboration-based designs. *ACM Transactions on Software Engineering and Methodology (TOSEM)*, 11(2), 215–255.

Spencer, H., and Collyer, G. (1992). #ifdef considered harmful or portability experience with C news. In *Proc. USENIX Conf.*, pp. 185–198. Berkeley, CA: USENIX Association.

Spinczyk, O., Gal, A., and Schröder-Preikschat, W. (2002). AspectC++: An aspect-oriented extension to the C++ programming language. In *Proc. Int'l Conf. on Tools Pacific*, pp. 53–60. Darlinghurst, Australia: Australian Computer Society, Inc.

Staples, M., and Hill, D. (2004). Experiences adopting software product line development without a product line architecture. In *Proc. Asia-Pacific Software Engineering Conf. (APSEC)*, pp. 176–183. Washington, DC: IEEE Computer Society.

Stata, R., and Guttag, J. (1995). Modular reasoning in the presence of subclassing. In *Proc. Int'l Conf. Object-Oriented Programming, Systems, Languages and Applications (OOPSLA)*, pp. 200–214. New York: ACM Press.

Steger, M., Tischer, C., Boss, B., Müller, A., Pertler, O., Stolz, W., and Ferber, S. (2004). Introducing PLA at Bosch Gasoline Systems: Experiences and practices. In *Proc. Int'l Software Product Line Conference (SPLC)*, vol. 3154 of *Lecture Notes in Computer Science*, pp. 34–50. Berlin/Heidelberg: Springer-Verlag.

Steimann, F. (2006). The paradoxical success of aspect-oriented programming. In *Proc. Int'l Conf. Object-Oriented Programming, Systems, Languages and Applications (OOPSLA)*, pp. 481–497. New York: ACM Press.

Steimann, F., Pawlitzki, T., Apel, S., and Kästner, C. (2010). Types and modularity for implicit invocation with implicit announcement. *ACM Transactions on Software Engineering and Methodology (TOSEM)*, 20(1). To appear; submitted March 15, 2008; accepted March 18, 2009.

Stonebraker, M., Jhingran, A., Goh, J., and Potamianos, S. (1990). On rules, procedure, caching and views in data base systems. In *Proc. Int'l Conf. Management of Data (SIGMOD)*, pp. 281–290. New York: ACM Press.

Streitferdt, D., Riebisch, M., and Philippow, I. (2003). Details of formalized relations in feature models using OCL. In *Proc. Int'l Conf. and Workshop Engineering of Computer-Based Systems (ECBS)*, pp. 297–304. Los Alamitos, CA: IEEE Computer Society.

Strniša, R., Sewell, P., and Parkinson, M. (2007). The Java module system: Core design and semantic definition. In *Proc. Int'l Conf. Object-Oriented Programming,*

Systems, Languages and Applications (OOPSLA), pp. 499–514. New York: ACM Press.

Stroustrup, B. (1994). *The Design and Evolution of C++*. Reading, MA: Addison-Wesley.

Sullivan, K., Griswold, W. G., Cai, Y., and Hallen, B. (2001). The structure and value of modularity in software design. In *Proc. Europ. Software Engineering Conf./Foundations of Software Engineering (ESEC/FSE)*, pp. 99–108. New York: ACM Press.

Sullivan, K., Griswold, W. G., Song, Y., Cai, Y., Shonle, M., Tewari, N., and Rajan, H. (2005). Information hiding interfaces for aspect-oriented design. In *Proc. Europ. Software Engineering Conf./Foundations of Software Engineering (ESEC/FSE)*, pp. 166–175. New York: ACM Press.

Sunkle, S., Günther, S., and Saake, G. (2009). Representing and composing first-class features with FeatureJ. Tech. Rep. 17/09, School of Computer Science, University of Magdeburg.

Sunkle, S., Kuhlemann, M., Siegmund, N., Rosenmüller, M., and Saake, G. (2008). Generating highly customizable SQL parsers. In *Proc. EDBT Workshop on Software Engineering for Tailor-made Data Management*, pp. 29–34. New York: ACM Press.

Sutton, A., and Maletic, J. I. (2007). How we manage portability and configuration with the C preprocessor. In *Proc. Int'l Conf. Software Maintenance (ICSM)*, pp. 275–284. Los Alamitos, CA: IEEE Computer Society.

Svahnberg, M., van Gurp, J., and Bosch, J. (2005). A taxonomy of variability realization techniques. *Software–Practice & Experience*, 35(8), 705–754.

Szyperski, C. (1992). Import is not inheritance – Why we need both: Modules and classes. In *Proc. Europ. Conf. Object-Oriented Programming (ECOOP)*, vol. 615 of *Lecture Notes in Computer Science*, pp. 19–32. Berlin/Heidelberg: Springer-Verlag.

Szyperski, C. (1997). *Component Software: Beyond Object-Oriented Programming*. Boston, MA: Addison-Wesley.

Tarr, P., Ossher, H., Harrison, W., and Sutton, S. M., Jr. (1999). N degrees of separation: Multi-dimensional separation of concerns. In *Proc. Int'l Conf. Software Engineering (ICSE)*, pp. 107–119. Los Alamitos, CA: IEEE Computer Society.

Tartler, R., Sincero, J., Schröder-Preikschat, W., and Lohmann, D. (2009). Dead or alive: Finding zombie features in the Linux kernel. In *Proc. GPCE Workshop on Feature-Oriented Software Development (FOSD)*, pp. 81–86. New York: ACM Press.

Tevanlinna, A., Taina, J., and Kauppinen, R. (2004). Product family testing: A survey. *ACM SIGSOFT Software Engineering Notes, 29*(2), 12–12.

Tešanović, A., Sheng, K., and Hansson, J. (2004). Application-tailored database systems: A case of aspects in an embedded database. In *Proc. Int'l Database Engineering and Applications Symposium*, pp. 291–301. Washington, DC: IEEE Computer Society.

Thaker, S., Batory, D., Kitchin, D., and Cook, W. (2007). Safe composition of product lines. In *Proc. Int'l Conf. Generative Programming and Component Engineering (GPCE)*, pp. 95–104. New York: ACM Press.

Thüm, T. (2008). *Reasoning about Feature Model Edits.* Bachelor's thesis (Studienarbeit), University of Magdeburg.

Thüm, T. (2010). *A Machine-Checked Proof for a Product-Line–Aware Type System.* Master's thesis (Diplomarbeit), University of Magdeburg.

Thüm, T., Batory, D., and Kästner, C. (2009). Reasoning about edits to feature models. In *Proceedings of the 31th International Conference on Software Engineering (ICSE)*, pp. 254–264. Washington, DC: IEEE Computer Society.

Torgersen, M. (2004). The expression problem revisited: Four new solutions using generics. In *Proc. Europ. Conf. Object-Oriented Programming (ECOOP)*, vol. 3086 of *Lecture Notes in Computer Science*, pp. 123–146. New York: Springer-Verlag.

Trujillo, S., Batory, D., and Diaz, O. (2006). Feature refactoring a multi-representation program into a product line. In *Proc. Int'l Conf. Generative Programming and Component Engineering (GPCE)*, pp. 191–200. New York: ACM Press.

Trujillo, S., Batory, D., and Diaz, O. (2007). Feature oriented model driven development: A case study for portlets. In *Proc. Int'l Conf. Software Engineering (ICSE)*, pp. 44–53. Washington, DC: IEEE Computer Society.

Turon, A., and Reppy, J. (2007). Metaprogramming with traits. In *Proc. Europ. Conf. Object-Oriented Programming (ECOOP)*, vol. 4609 of *Lecture Notes in Computer Science*, pp. 373–398. Berlin/Heidelberg: Springer-Verlag.

Vidács, L., and Beszédes, Á. (2003). Opening up the C/C++ preprocessor black box. In *Proc. Symp. Programming Languages and Software Tools (SPLST)*, pp. 45–57. Kuopio: University of Kuopio.

Visser, E. (2004). Program transformation with Stratego/XT: Rules, strategies, tools, and systems in StrategoXT-0.9. In *Domain-Specific Program Generation*, vol. 3016 of *Lecture Notes in Computer Science*, pp. 216–238. Berlin/Heidelberg: Springer-Verlag.

Vittek, M. (2003). Refactoring browser with preprocessor. In *Proc. European Conf. on Software Maintenance and Reengineering (CSMR)*, pp. 101–110. Los Alamitos, CA: IEEE Computer Society.

Voelter, M., and Groher, I. (2007). Product line implementation using aspect-oriented and model-driven software development. In *Proc. Int'l Software Product Line Conference (SPLC)*, pp. 233–242. Los Alamitos, CA: IEEE Computer Society.

Warth, A., Stanojević, M., and Millstein, T. (2006). Statically scoped object adaptation with expanders. In *Proc. Int'l Conf. Object-Oriented Programming, Systems, Languages and Applications (OOPSLA)*, pp. 37–56. New York: ACM Press.

Weise, D., and Crew, R. (1993). Programmable syntax macros. In *Proc. Conf. Programming Language Design and Implementation (PLDI)*, pp. 156–165. New York: ACM Press.

Weiser, M. (1984). Program slicing. *IEEE Transactions on Software Engineering (TSE)*, *10*(4), 352–357.

Wile, D. (1997). Abstract syntax from concrete syntax. In *Proc. Int'l Conf. Software Engineering (ICSE)*, pp. 472–480. New York: ACM Press.

Wirth, N. (1971). Program development by stepwise refinement. *Communications of the ACM*, *14*(4), 221–227.

Wirth, N. (1979). The module: A system structuring facility in high-level programming languages. In *Proc. Symposium on Language Design and Programming Methodology*, vol. 79 of *Lecture Notes in Computer Science*, pp. 1–24. London: Springer-Verlag.

Wright, A. K., and Felleisen, M. (1994). A syntactic approach to type soundness. *Information and computation*, *115*(1), 38–94.

Yang, W. (1994). How to merge program texts. *Journal of Systems and Software*, *27*(2), 129–135.

Zhang, C., and Jacobsen, H.-A. (2003). Quantifying aspects in middleware platforms. In *Proc. Int'l Conf. Aspect-Oriented Software Development (AOSD)*, pp. 130–139. New York: ACM Press.

Zhang, C., and Jacobsen, H.-A. (2004). Resolving feature convolution in middleware systems. In *Proc. Int'l Conf. Object-Oriented Programming, Systems, Languages and Applications (OOPSLA)*, pp. 188–205. New York: ACM Press.

Zhang, H., and Jarzabek, S. (2004). XVCL: A mechanism for handling variants in software product lines. *Science of Computer Programming*, *53*(3), 381–407.